THE INSTITUTE OF
CLASSICAL ARCHITECTURE

FORMERLY
INSTITUTE FOR THE STUDY OF CLASSICAL ARCHITECTURE
FOUNDED IN 1991

"Fabrica et Ratiocinatio"

The Institute teaches the fundamentals of architecture through the exploration and study of the classical tradition. It exists to perpetuate the cultural memory of the past as a resource for architectural issues in the present.

From its center in New York, the Institute serves the needs of students, professionals, and the general public in the following ways:

- Courses of study in the United States and abroad for students and professionals
- Fellowship and research programs
- Publications including an annual journal, a newsletter, and a book series
- Study tours for a general audience
- Public lectures and events
- A membership program for its constituency
- A website resource for both professionals and the public
- A program to recognize and reward outstanding contributions in the practice of classical architecture

FURTHER INQUIRIES ARE WELCOME:

The Institute of Classical Architecture
225 Lafayette Street New York, NY 10012
(917) 237-1208 (telephone) (917) 237-1230 (facsimile)
institute@classicist.org (e-mail)
www.classicist.org

Front Cover: "Constitution Square," by Dino Marcantonio. CG Image, 2000. Logo by S.J. Weine.

Frontispiece: "The Creation of Rome," by Leonard Porter, 1994, oil on linen, 46" x 68".

Back Cover: "The Garden of Palazzo Capponi in Florence," by J. François Gabriel. Watercolor, 8" x 8", fall 1999.

DISTRIBUTED BY:
Transaction Publishers

Rutgers University, New Brunswick, NJ, 08903

DESIGN CONSULTATION & PRODUCTION BY:
Dyad Communications

PRINTED BY:
Meridian Printing
East Greenwich, Rhode Island, 02818

ISBN 0-7658-0757-2
ISSN 1076-2922

THE CLASSICIST

№ 6: 2000-2001

Dear Reader...

The classic spirit is the disinterested search for perfection; it is the love of clearness and reasonableness and self-control; it is, above all the love of permanence and of continuity. It asks of a work of art, not that it shall be novel or effective, but that it shall be fine and noble. It seeks not merely to express individuality or emotion but to express disciplined emotion and individuality restrained by law. It strives for the essential rather than the momentary—loves impersonality more than personality, and feels more power in the orderly succession of the hours and the seasons than in the violence of earthquake or storm. And it loves to steep itself in tradition. It would have each new work connect itself in the mind of him who sees it with all the noble and lovely works of the past, bringing them to his memory and making their beauty and charm a part of the beauty and charm of the work before him. It does not deny originality and individuality—they are as welcome as inevitable. It does not consider tradition as immutable or set rigid bound to invention. But it desires that each new presentation of truth and beauty shall show us the old truth and the old beauty, seen only from a different angle and colored by a different medium. It wishes to add link by link to the chain of tradition, but it does not wish to break the chain. — Kenyon Cox, from *The Classic Point of View,* 1911.

During the last seven years this publication has kept pace with the rapid growth and continued success of The Institute of Classical Architecture. This issue of *The Classicist* marks the first to be published under the Institute's new name and is significant because along with our streamlined name, our mission has been re-evaluated and our goal as an organization redefined and strengthened. With these changes, *The Classicist* remains the Institute's beacon, reaching and informing people all over the world.

The Classicist continues to reexamine what classical architecture and the allied arts are in this age of technology. What does it mean to study and understand how the past can reference the ways we live in this very modern time? As the editors, we want to present a consistent *and* inclusive point of view on current practices of contemporary classicism in professional and academic circles. We hope that our annual publication

contributes to the resurgence of passion for things classical and helps promote a more humanistic approach in architecture as well as in the allied and decorative arts.

Beginning with where *The Classicist, No. 5* left off, we continue to grapple with our collective definitions of what is classical and with the artist's age-old struggle with the burden of a culturally rich past, that is, how can we improve on what has been done before? How does one remain inspired and not stymied? This applies to anyone who has ever created anything and certainly applies to the editors of this publication as we work to bring our readers something fresh and support the Institute's mission of furthering the sensibility of the past for our own time. To help us move forward, we have seriously considered the pertinent criticism that has come from our Board of Directors, our members, Fellows, contributors, and readers alike. We note here some of the issues raised and how we have responded.

To accommodate some of the concern recently expressed regarding the text-heavy *No. 5,* our readers will notice that the new essays section has been somewhat reduced to make room for presenting more professional and academic work. We had more submissions than ever before and wanted to show as many projects as possible. Still, our essays include a challenging, thought-provoking essay excerpted from the lectures of W. Jackson Bate; a photo essay on the ruins of Russian estate architecture; and a new feature that introduces some of the Institute's Advisory Council members.

In part, a plea to put architecture back on the cover prompted the creation of a response to the Canadian Center for Architecture's recent competition in which the invited competitors did not include a single traditional architect or planner. The perspective image on the front of this issue provides an alternative to the winning entry (see Competitions, page 81-85) created by a pair of earnest young classicists. Historically, but not intentionally, our covers generate considerable discussion, even controversy. The renderings for the covers of our first two issues, "The Phoenix of Seventh Avenue" by Richard Cameron and "Come, Let Us Build Ourselves

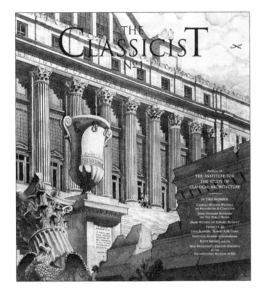  

  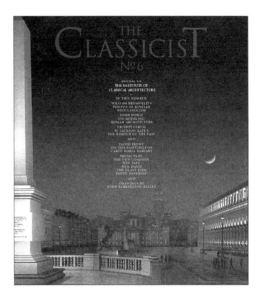

a City" by Jonathon Lee, endured lengthy discussions (what are we saying and how do we show it?) typical of many a new publication. "The School of New York," the computer generated image gracing the cover of *No. 3* was a collaborative effort between John Burge and Richard Cameron that combined then-recent advances in computer technology with architectural rendering. Again, the message we were sending was seriously debated. Was it befitting a publication about traditional architecture to use a computer-generated image or did it confuse our intention?

"Mercury Downloading," the illustration created by Stephen Piersanti for *No. 4,* inspired comments ranging from whether or not a figure should dominate the cover of an architectural publication, to what kind of shoes Mercury should or should not wear! Finally, "The Allegory of Architecture," on the cover of issue *No. 5,* sparked the debate over what exactly *is* classical. The painter John Woodrow Kelley used contemporary figures chosen for the beauty and countenance reminiscent of an ancient time. Many considered this to be naturalism or even realism rather than contemporary classicism.

In the Institute's relatively brief existence, every image for the cover goes through rigorous criticism (the cover of this issue is no exception) that seems initially divisive, but, in the end we find in our differences potential to enlarge our vision. In fact, the covers stand for, even epitomize, the growth of the Institute and this publication, and what we have learned in the process of making it all happen.

We all believe that the work we present encourages us to look closer at our ideals and helps define how narrow or broad the scope of our efforts should be. As practitioners, artists, planners, writers, creators at all levels, we require the push that takes us another step further. Perennial questioning and re-evaluation of our work must not hold us back. As Saint-Exupéry wrote, "It's taking a step that saves a man."

Thank you for your readership these last six issues. We hope that you continue to respond and be as challenged and intrigued as we are with the topics and projects presented in *The Classicist*. As such, you join us in adding links to Kenyon Cox's chain of tradition, or at least in making blips on the timeline of creating history. —H.D.T.

FADED GLORY:

IMAGES OF RUSSIAN CLASSICISM

By William C. Brumfield

In my travels through the Russian country-side I have seen the devastation inflicted upon the treasures of Russia's historic architecture, including many buildings in the neoclassical style. Photographing these master-pieces not only allows me to document and visually interpret their existence but it also confronts me with complex, perhaps universal questions about changing social values and the rise and fall of cultures. Every country has its ruined architectural landmarks, the product of wars, accidents, and the vicissitudes of time. Occasionally, these ruins have been enshrined and poeticized, as in Clarence J. Laughlin's photographs of Louisiana plantation mansions, *The Ghosts Along the Mississippi*. In Europe, as well as in the United States, neoclassical ruins

have long been a staple of romantic genre painting. We do not, however, like to acknowledge that the devastation of history's legacy has often been the product of our own century. In Russia I have found blatant evidence of neglect and cultural vandalism extending to neoclassical secular as well as religious monuments. In some cases the destruction is deliberate, the result of violent social upheavals. In other cases it is less direct, the result of demographic shifts from country to city, which have led inevitably to the abandonment of many country churches, not to mention estate houses. A photographer can only work with what time and fate have left. For the late eighteenth century architect Nikolai Lvov, some of whose work is featured in the follow-

ing photographs, buildings of all designa-tions—temple, house, or pavilion—could be subsumed within a unified aesthetic system based on pure forms and the immu-table prin-ciples of the classical orders. Equally important was the placement of the structure in an open setting appropriate for the picturesque qualities valued in the idealized landscapes of painters such as Hubert Robert. Lvov's extensive work in park design and his estate pavilions reveal not only an understanding of architectural form and interior design, but also an apprecia-tion of the building as noble ruin. It is this quality that makes the work of Lvov so congenial to me. For even in ruined form, great architecture retains its visual power and its hold over our imagination. ❧

This great house (palace might be a more fitting term) was built for Nikita Demidov at the estate of Petrovskoe, near the village of Alabino to the west of Moscow. At the beginning of the eighteenth century the estate, then known as Kniazhishchevo, belonged to P.P. Shafirov, a close associate of Peter the Great and a distinguished diplomat. In the 1740s Shafirov's heirs sold the estate to Akinfii Demidov, one of the most prominent of Russia's eighteenth-century industrialists and holder of a vast fortune in mines, metal-working, and related plants in the Urals. In the late 1770s Nikita Demidov turned his attention to the estate at Petrovskoe, where he apparently commissioned Matvei Kazakov to build a large mansion with detached, flanking wings. The genesis of the design of this palatial edifice, which burned in the 1930s and survives only in the magnificent ruins of its brick walls and limestone columns, has been the cause of much dispute. The discovery at the beginning of this century of a corner stone with an inscription, the date 1776, and Kazakov's name clearly marked seemed to establish the architect's identity; yet the similarity of the design to the centralized structures of Vasilii Bazhenov has led to the supposition that while Kazakov might have built the mansion, its true author was Kazakov's mentor, Bazhenov. It must be admitted that the complex geometry of the plan argues in favor of Bazhenov's participation, yet this is only supposition, as is so much else in the career of that architect.

Whatever the authorship of the mansion at Petrovskoe, the structure's distinctive monumentality is beyond dispute. The original form of each of its four symmetrical facades was dominated—almost overwhelmed—by a loggia of four Tuscan Doric columns of the major order, flanked by pilasters, that support the entablature and cornice. Behind each of the loggias was a large state room. The beveled corner projections, with a less grand Ionic portico of two columns, represent the facades of smaller rectangular rooms, or studies, at the ends of diagonal corridors. The corridors intersected in a circular hall beneath the dome above the center of the structure (this plan was repeated on the second story). The diagonal configuration continued beyond the mansion to four two-story wings—with rusticated facades—that defined the corners of the cour d'honneur and were linked by a brick wall around the square court. The park beyond the central ensemble was landscaped in the natural manner.

FIGURES 3-5, OPPOSITE PAGE, TOP, BOT-TOM LEFT AND BOTTOM RIGHT: Glebov Estate at Znamenskii-Raek. Nikolai Lvov, architect.

This grand design by Lvov was for the estate of General and Senator F. I. Glebov at Znamenskii-Raek (1787-1790s). Located on the small Logovezh River not far from Torzhok, this large estate was intended as a place in which the senator could receive important guests. Its location near the main road between Moscow and St. Petersburg facilitated this function, and Glebov gave Lvov full rein for a grand mansion. Though some of the park buildings were damaged or destroyed during the Second World War, the main house and attached buildings are extant. (Unfortunately, the house, which was formerly used as a tourist park and a children's camp, is in a state of disre-pair, and a restoration effort has been stalled for lack of funds.)

The two-story mansion has an oval vestibule that leads into the main ball room. All flanking rooms are subordinate to this square central space—a clear indication of the house's purpose as a center of reception and entertain-ment. The most distinctive feature of the plan is a grand colonnade that encloses the cour d'honneur in front of the house. It is the largest such design in Russia and is flanked on either side with pavilions and service buildings that are integrated into the colonnade. In some respects this extraordinary entrance court reminds one of Jefferson's design for the colon-naded lawn at the University of Virginia.

At Znamenskii-Raek, Lvov created a dis-tinctive approach for the adaptation of the nat-ural setting to the architectural design of the neoclassical manor and its auxiliary buildings. At this time the concept of landscape gardening centered on the desire to contemplate "unfet-tered" nature, which complemented the belief in the natural logic and meaning of neoclassical forms in architecture. The origins of this intel-lectual, aesthetic, and cultural union of neoclas-sicism and natural principles are many and diverse—including in no small measure English and French literature (e.g. Horace Walpole and above all, Rousseau). Lvov's grand colonnade at Znamenskii-Raek facilitates that union by pro-viding forest vistas through the classical entrance arch and the colonnade itself, a rare achievement through which artifice and nature are both delineated and at the same time fused.

FIGURE 6, RIGHT: Durasov Mansion, Lyublino (southeast Moscow ca. 1801). I. V. Egotov, architect.

Though less refined in its design and detail than the better known Brattsevo villa, the mansion at the Durasov estate of Lyublino (southeast Moscow) ranks not only as a major monument in late neoclassical estate architec-ture, but also can lay claim to possess one of the most idiosyncratic plans of the period, a gen-uine example of symbolic architecture (or architecture parlant) at its most obvious. Attributed to Ivan Egotov, the design consists of four wings that radiate from a round central hall and are connected by a colonnade in the Composite order. The genesis of the configu-ration is plausibly said to have originated with Durasov's desire to memorialize his attainment of the Order of St. Anne, whose encircled cross is reproduced in the form of the house.

Yet the elaborate conceit of the design of the Lyublino mansion serves admirably in one of the most important functions of the estate house—to provide a sheltered yet immediate view of surrounding nature. The brightly illuminated interior, the state rooms, and most especially the central hall, are decorated with grisaille trompe l'oeil wall paintings of archi-tectural motifs and friezes with such attention to detail and illusion as to be distinguished only with difficulty from the plaster medallions that also decorate the upper parts of the walls. The interior walls themselves are a combina-tion of various shades of faux-marbre typical of both urban and country mansions in Moscow at the end of the eighteenth century.

Within Torzhok itself, Lvov created a masterpiece of Russian neoclassicism with the building of the Church of Saints Boris and Gleb at the Monastery of the same name, one of the oldest in Russia. Built in 1785-1796, this monumental church is similar to the Cathedral of St. Joseph in Mogilev, but is more complex in design. The hexastyle Tuscan portico on the west facade is repeated on the east (apsidal) end in a display of the neoclassical aesthetic at its purest. The porticoes provide a visual transition to the central dome, which rests above a polygonal drum with a large thermal window.

For all of its neoclassical rigor, the Church of Saints Boris and Gleb also reflects some of the basic elements of Russo-Byzantine church architecture, not only in the centralized plan but also in the appearance on the exterior corners of arched bays reminiscent of the cathedrals of twelfth century Novgorod. To be sure, the arches contain classically-inspired thermal windows, yet the ability to integrate so unobtrusively traditional features of Russian architecture into the classical tectonic system is a mark of Lvov's genius.

Within this church the massive split-corner piers are faced with Doric columns that support open arches over the arms of the cross. The arches in turn lead upward to the thermal windows and the central coffered dome, which on the interior is hemispherical. Again, the classical rigor of the design is stated with remarkable clarity—referring both to the Pantheon and the thermae—yet the interior space is as appropriate to the needs of the Orthodox liturgy as was the Hagia Sophia and other Byzantine models that laid the basis for Russian church architecture.

Lvov's great neoclassical churches are firmly in the manner of his idol Palladio, whom he studied with great care and whose work he saw in situ in Italy. His efforts bore fruit in 1798 with the first published edition in Russian translation of Palladio's Quattro Libri, in the introduction to which Lvov proclaimed "Long live the Palladian taste in my fatherland. French curls and English subtlety have enough imitators without us."

FIGURE 8: *Church of the Trinity, Viazemskii Estate, Aleksandrovskoe (southeast outskirts of St. Petersburg). Nikolai Lvov, architect.*

One of the most eccentric examples of Lvov's work is the Church of the Trinity at the estate of Prince A. A. Viazemskii at Aleksandrovskoe on the southern outskirts of St. Petersburg. Here he uses the familiar rotunda form, surrounded by sixteen Ionic columns, prefaced on the west by a pyramidal bell tower. Built in 1785-1787, the structure has impeccable classical antecedents (most notably the Temple of Vesta and the reproductions of the pyramids in Rome); yet it also represents the extreme of stylistic and cultural secularization in Russian church design, the culmination of a process well underway in Russia by the end of the seventeenth century.

FIGURE 9: *Valuevo Estate, Hunting House (ca. 1800).*

The estate culture of central Russia produced a remarkable variety of architectural designs for country mansions in the area of Moscow and its surrounding provinces. Some of the manors such as the two-story stuccoed wooden estate house at Valuevo (southwest of Moscow), built in 1810-1811, reveal an unexpected similarity with Greek Revival architecture in the American antebellum South. The Ionic portico with veranda and belvedere speak of influences from grander homes; and yet Valuevo, owned by the distinguished archeologist Alexander Musin-Pushkin (publisher of Russia's great medieval epic, The Igor Tale) is itself of considerable merit for the unity of its ensemble.

In contrast to the neoclassical style of the mansion and its wings—connected to the central structure by extended Doric colonnades—the offices and service buildings flanking the manor have a rough, unstuccoed brick surface with rusticated pillars, and the decorative corner towers of the brick wall enclosing the front of the estate are in a late variant of the Gothic revival (ca. 1830). Thus the design of the ensemble proceeds from the refined mansion in the center to the progressively more "archaic" and eccentric forms. The English-style landscape park beyond the mansion contains a similar contrast of texture between the neoclassical Hunting House, an ethereal structure with light yellow walls, white trim and Tuscan portico, which rests over the heavy rustication of a grotto.

FIGURE 10: Pavilion at the Brattsevo Estate (near Moscow). Attributed to Andrei Voronikhin, architect.

The Stroganovs themselves were not inactive in the Moscow area at the end of the eighteenth century, and though Alexander Stroganov chose not to build on the Demidov scale, he too commissioned one of the most noble of neoclassical houses for his family estate at Brattsevo, to the northwest of Moscow (now within the city limits). The Stroganovs were, of course, preoccupied with their extensive palaces and cultural activities in St. Petersburg; yet the design and placement of the Brattsevo villa are on a level to suggest that the architect was none other than their former serf and one of the great Russian neoclassicists at the turn of the century, Andrei Voronikhin. The structure is centered on a domed rotunda, whose form is reflected in half rotundas projecting from the east and west facades. The main facades—north and south—are marked by Ionic porticos on the background of a rusticated projection of the facade. Above the portico a balustrade frames the thermal window of the upper story.

The economy of this compact, centralized design integrates every carefully considered decorative element into the texture of the structure itself, which is in rare harmony with its landscaped setting—above a green sward on the slope of a hill. Within the natural park of this modest retreat, the single monument is as restrained and elegant as the house itself: a domed pavilion of Ionic columns surrounding a square block in imitation of a classical altar (also attributed to Voronikhin). There could be no clearer expression of the secularization of gentry culture than this noble idealized form, open to the surrounding nature but also entirely self-sufficient and centered beneath the coffered ceiling of the dome.

William Craft Brumfield is Professor of Slavic studies at Tulane University, where he also lectures at the School of Architecture. He is the author and photographer of a number of books on Russian architecture including A History of Russian Architecture *(Cambridge University Press, 1993) and* Lost Russia: Photographing the Ruins of Russian Architecture *(Duke University Press, 1995). His photographs of Russian architecture have been exhibited at galleries in the U.S., Russia, France, and Canada, and are a part of the collection of Photographic Archives at the National Gallery of Art in Washington. He is currently involved in photographing and studying Russian architectural monuments from the Urals to the Pacific as part of the Library of Congress project "Meeting of the Frontiers."*

THE BURDEN
of THE PAST &
THE ENGLISH POET

By W. Jackson Bate

Every so often we come across an essay or book from a field other than architecture or the visual arts that treats certain problems, dilemmas, or central questions facing us in a way that is particularly insightful and we feel would be appropriate for publication in the essay section of The Classicist. So in this issue, we have included some excerpts from the work of W. Jackson Bate, in order to introduce the writer and his work to our readers. Until his death in July 1999, W. Jackson Bate was Porter University Professor emeritus at Harvard, where he taught from 1946 until 1986. Two of his many books, biographies of John Keats and of Samuel Johnson, won the Pulitzer Prize and he was a three-time winner of the Christian Gauss Prize for literary history and criticism.

In 1969, the University of Toronto invited Professor Bate to give the Alexander Lectures, a series of four lectures later published by Harvard University Press under the title, The Burden of the Past and the English Poet. The lectures broadly concern what Mr. Bate identifies as the principal dilemma facing the artist from the Renaissance to the present day, and, more particularly, this dilemma's first major example: The position of the English poet between the English Renaissance—the epoch of Shakespeare and Milton—and the Victorians and near-moderns (1660 to 1830).

The nature of this dilemma can best be expressed by the question: What is there left to do? What new, fresh thing could the poet (or artist) contribute that had not already been anticipated by the great Elizabethans? As Keats told his friend Richard Woodhouse, he often felt that "there was nothing original to be written in poetry; that its riches were already exhausted—and all its beauties forestalled." For many poets this was nothing less than a crisis of self-confidence as they contemplated the monumental heritage of past poetry. "Not only every great poet," wrote T.S. Eliot, "but every genuine, though lesser poet, fulfills once for all some possibility of the language, and so leaves one possibility less for his successors."

The relevance of Mr. Bate's subject to the practice of architecture, especially in the twentieth century, should be obvious. One has only to think of the many self-justifying manifestos of the early high modernists—Adolf Loos, the Futurists, Le Corbusier—manifestos whose central injunction was to "make it new." Indeed, the practice of serious architecture in the twentieth century can in many ways be understood as the attempt by architects to come to terms with an inexhaustibly rich and much admired past.

The following excerpts are taken from three of the four Alexander lectures. They are reprinted by kind permission of the publisher from The Burden of the Past and the English Poet by W. Jackson Bate, Cambridge, Mass: Harvard University Press, copyright ©1970 by the President and Fellows of Harvard College.

—Keith Alexander & Richard Cameron

EXCERPTED FROM LECTURE 1: THE SECOND TEMPLE

Our subject could be expressed by a remark Samuel Johnson quotes from Pliny in one of the Rambler essays (No.86): "The burthen of government is increased upon princes by the virtues of their immediate predecessors." And Johnson goes on to add: "It is, indeed, always *dangerous* to be placed in a state of unavoidable comparison with excellence, and the danger is still greater when that excellence is consecrated by death... He that succeeds a celebrated writer, has the same difficulties to encounter." That word "dangerous" deserves a moment's reflection. In its original, rather ominous sense, it means "having lost one's freedom," having become "dominated" and turned into the position of a household thrall: being placed in jeopardy, subjected to the tyranny outside one's own control as free agent. A cognate is our word "dungeon."

I have often wondered whether we could find any more comprehensive way of taking up the whole of English poetry during the last three centuries—or for that matter the modern history of the arts in general—than by exploring the effects of this accumulating anxiety and the question it so directly presents to the poet or artist: *What is there left to do?* To say that this has always been a problem, and that the arts have still managed to survive, does not undercut the fact that it has become far more pressing in the modern world. Of course the situation is an old one. We need not even start with Rome or Alexandria, those exemplars of what it can mean to the artist to stand in competition with an admired past. We could go back to an almost forgotten Egyptian scribe of 2000 B.C. (Khakheperresenb), who inherited in his literary legacy no Homer,

Sophocles, Dante, Shakespeare, Milton, Goethe, or Dickens—no formidable variety of literary genres available in thousands of libraries—yet who still left the poignant epigram: "Would that I had phrases that are not known, utterances that are strange, in a new language that has not been used, free from repetition, not an utterance which has grown stale, which men of old have spoken." But a problem can become more acute under some conditions than others can. And, whatever other generalizations can be made about the arts since the Renaissance, a fact with which we can hardly quarrel—though we instinctively resist some of the implications—is that the means of preserving and distributing the literature (and more recently the other arts) of the past have immeasurably increased, and to such a point that we now have confronting the artist—or have *in potentia*—a vast array of varied achievement, existing and constantly multiplying in an "eternal present."

We could, in fact, argue that the remorseless deepening of self-consciousness, before the rich and intimidating legacy of the past, has become the greatest single problem that modern art (art, that is to say, since the later seventeenth century) has had to face, and that it will become increasingly so in the future. In comparison, many of the ideas or preoccupations (thematic, social, formal, or psychoanalytic) that we extract as aims, inter-

ests, conflicts, anxieties, influences, or "background," and then picture as so sharply pressing on the mind of the artist, are less directly urgent. In our own response to a constantly expanding subject matter, we forget that what provides opportunity for us, as critics and historians, may be simultaneously foreclosing—or at least appearing to foreclose—opportunity for the artist....

...Goethe rejoiced that he was not born an Englishman and forced to compete with the achievement of Shakespeare. Even if one is writing in another language, said Goethe, "a productive nature ought not to read more than one of Shakespeare's dramas in a year if he would not be wrecked entirely." Direct imitation is obviously not the answer. (Shakespeare, as he says elsewhere, "gives us golden apples in silver dishes." By careful study we may acquire the silver dishes while discovering that we have "only potatoes to put in them.") But attempting—after one knows his works—to proceed differently for the sake of mere difference is even less satisfactory....

...But if we are confronted with the suggestion that one age of achievement in the arts may necessarily—because of its greatness, and because of the incorrigible nature of man's mind—force a search for difference, even though that difference means a retrenchment, we become uneasy. When the change in the arts since the Renaissance is attributed to the loss of religious faith, to the growth of science, to commercialism, or to the development of mass media, we are always at liberty to feel that those circumstances may conceivably change again. But the deepest fear we have is of the mind of man itself, primarily because of its dark unpredictabilities, and with them the possibility that the arts could, over the long range, be considered as by definition suicidal: that, given the massive achievement in the past, they may have no further way to proceed except toward progressive refinement, nuance, indirection, and finally, through the continued pressure for difference, into the various forms of anti-art.

The speculation that this may be so—or that the modern spirit is beginning, rightly or wrongly, to believe that it is so—is a major theme of one of the most disturbing novels of our century, Thomas Mann's *Dr. Faustus.* We find the implications so unsettling, in this modern version of the Faust legend, that we naturally prefer—if we can be brought to linger on the book rather than forget it—to stress other themes, other implications that can be more localized (for instance, the condition of Germany between the two World Wars.) For Mann's twentieth-century Faustus, a German composer of genius, all the most fruitful possibilities in music have already been so brilliantly exploited that nothing is now left for the art except a parody of itself and of its past—a self-mockery, technically accomplished but spiritually dead in hope, in short, an "aristocratic nihilism." It is "anti-art" in the sense of art turning finally against itself. And this modern Dr. Faustus, so cerebral and self-conscious before the variety and richness of what has already been done, sells his soul to the devil—as in the old Faust legend—in order to be able once again to produce great art. The special horror is that this involves the willing, the deliberately chosen, destruction of part of his brain in order to free himself from the crippling inhibitions of self-consciousness—a partial destruction of the brain that is to be followed, after the agreed lapse of years, by what he knows beforehand will be a complete disintegration.

The universality of the problem lies in the fact that the arts, in addition to everything else that can be said of them, are also the sensitive antennae of human life generally; that as with them so, in time, with everything else that we still subsume by the word "culture" (however inadequate the word—but we have no other shorthand term). If what is implied in Mann's fable is or even could be true, or half-true, then what of man's situation in general as he is now beginning to face, and will face increasingly, the potential self-division forced upon him by his growing literacy and sophistication—his knowledge about himself, his past, the immense variety of what has been done and said, all brought with immediate focus and pressure, like a huge inverted pyramid, upon the naked moment, the short flicker, of any one individual life? The self-division arises because, except in the cumulative sciences, where a step-by-step use of deliberately specialized effort can be harnessed, the weight of everything else that has been done, said, or exemplified cannot, in conscience, be wholly denied, though on the other hand there is the natural desire of every human being to assert himself in such time as he has—to contribute in some respect, however small, or, if he cannot contribute, to leave his mark in some other way.

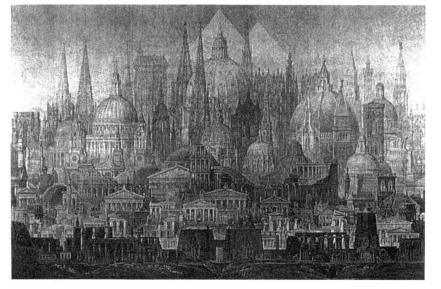

We may feel less naked, less prey to existential Angst and helplessness, if we know that we have not been condemned by history to be the first to face this frightful challenge, unique though it is, in scale, to the modern world. There may be some comfort to our feeling of historical loneliness—and not only comfort but some spur to both our courage and potentialities for good sense—to know we have a predecessor in the eighteenth century, a century that serves as the essential crossroad between all that we imply when we use the word "Renaissance" and much of what we mean when we speak of the "modern." We are only beginning to understand this about the eighteenth century, and to realize how much, in our approach to it and to all that which, in Johnson's phrase, can be "put to use," we have still lingered in the suburbs of its significance—above all, its significance for us now as contrasted with that which it had, or seemed to have, for the nineteenth century. With the nineteenth and the greater part of the twentieth century behind us, the eighteenth has long ceased to be something from which we need to disengage ourselves. We are now free to concentrate less on what differentiates it from ourselves and more on what we share. For us now, looking back on the last four centuries as a whole, the central interest of the eighteenth century is that it is the first period in modern history to face the problem of what it

means to come *immediately* after a great creative achievement. It was the first to face what it means to have already achieved some of the ends to which the modern (that is, the Renaissance) spirit had at the beginning aspired. Simultaneously, we have the start of almost everything else we associate with the modern world—the attempted Europeanization of the globe, with some of its new embarrassments; the American and French Revolutions; the rapid spread of literacy; the beginning of industrialism, urbanization, and the sudden rapid increase of population; and, in its latter half, the creation of most of what we associate with the premises of the modern effort not only in the arts but in philosophy.

What is so reassuring to us, as we look back on this astonishing century now and begin to learn more about it with the kind of perspective just mentioned, is its union of strength (good sense, even shrewdness and worldliness) with openness and generous empathy for all that William James implied when he spoke of literature and the arts as the "tender-minded pursuits." What is so reassuring is that here, if nowhere else, all that we ourselves prize (or should like, if we were bold enough, to say that we prize) in the "tender-minded" is taken for granted as valuable, as indeed supremely valuable, while at the same time we have as "tough-minded" a group of champions for the sympathetic and the humane as, in our most desperate moments, we could ever have hoped for. As we look further into this century, which produced, in David Hume, the greatest skeptic in the history of philosophy but which also produced Mozart and Beethoven and Burke, we feel a growing confidence about what can be "put to use."

This is also true of our special problem here—the whole problem of the "burden of the past" as it applies to the arts (and, by implication, to humanistic interests and pursuits as a whole). My thought, in these lectures, is twofold: to pose for us, in general, this central problem—to express the hope that we can pluck it out into the open and to try to see it for what it is—and, second, to help us reground ourselves, to get a clearer idea of our bearings, by looking back with a fresh eye to the beginning drama of what we ourselves are now living with and feel so deep a need to bring into perspective. In using the word "drama" I am thinking not only of the variety in voice and stance (realistic, sentimental, nostalgic, prejudiced, imaginative, worldly, analytic, sociological, aesthetic, moral) but also of the trauma—and there was one in this massive self-reconsideration—and of its uneasy but brilliantly creative resolutions…

…Our Age was cultivated thus at length;
But what we gained in skill we lost in strength.
Our Builders were, with want of Genius, curst;
The Second Temple was not like the First.
—Dryden

The Second Temple, completed 70 years after the destruction of the First by Nebuchadnezzar, differed in four ways especially from the Temple of Solomon. Though about the same in area, it was not so high. It was also less of a unit, being divided now into an outer and inner court. In equipment and decoration it was barer. Above all, the Holy of Holies was now an empty shrine, as it was also to remain in the magnificent Third Temple built by Herod. The Ark of the Covenant was gone, and no one felt at liberty to try to replace it with a substitute.

EXCERPTED FROM LECTURE 2: THE NEOCLASSIC DILEMMA

...It is necessary to repeat that what we are saying is in no way intended to disparage the result, and there is no reason for the scholar or critic who devotes himself to the study and interpretation of it to become more hotly defensive than were Dryden and Pope themselves in their own conception that what they were building or completing was a "Second Temple," which "was not like the First."

We are speaking of a state of mind—and a state of mind of which the neoclassic experience is only the first major example. The "late-comer"—to use Saint-Beuve's term in "What is Classic?"—may be expected to have the feelings and situation of a "late-comer." And not to recognize this is only to underestimate what was actually done....

From the start a major dilemma confronted the neoclassic effort, and one by no means to its discredit. The essential strength of the movement lay in its firm hold on the classical (or at first a selective conception of the classical) as a prototype of what still remained to be done. But it also faced the risk of being hoist with its own petard. It is one thing to weigh our immediate predecessors against the classical model (a model extracted from the best of eight centuries, with most of the dross removed, and rendered still more compact and formidable through further centuries of study and eulogy) and then to find our predecessors wanting, at least in some respects. But it is another thing to find that the same standard is now to be applied to ourselves, and to our actual performance rather than just our proclaimed aspirations.

The risk was naturally greatest for the poet or the artist, always so much more vulnerable than the theorist; and it is the poet with whom we are principally concerned. But it was shared by the whole movement, and increasingly recognized by it as the classical was reconsidered and as the French neoclassic and its English "Augustan" counterpart began to assume perspective, to take their contours from reality rather than ambition or hope. Before the first third of the eighteenth century was over, it was plain that, by having handed over the conscience so wholeheartedly to the classical ideal, the neoclassic effort was faced with a situation that it could live happily neither with nor without. The gains were enormous in every other aspect of life—intellectual, social, political. Values were quickly incorporated, explicated, developed, popularized, that brought the European world (and the new Europe overseas) into a healthful, badly needed equilibrium, and that then, almost as quickly, began to open up avenues in every direction, which the nineteenth century world was to exploit further. The gain in the arts was obvious too. There would otherwise have been no "Second Temple" at all but only a patchy cleaning of remnants or a rebuilding of cubicles on the site of the First Temple: refinements, for example, on Cowley, and those odes of his that had begun to seem like platters of hors d'oeuvres. But still there was something missing—and did not the major poets themselves admit it indirectly?

The truth is that like Scripture, or like any other comprehensive body of ideals, the classical can always be used for more than one purpose. If we can invoke it to help us in taking a particular stand (especially one in the name of form, order, or sanity—qualities associated almost by definition with the classical, and especially revered as such during the long adolescence of postclassical Europe), there is also much that can be cited against us as soon as we begin to specialize too purely or narrowly within what we think is the classical example. Hence the classical so often proves a Trojan Horse when more restricted movements in the arts try to embrace and incorporate it for authority. More than what is wanted at the start inevitably emerges, and in time the gates of the city are reopened.

Once the effort to reform—to give a "new form" to or simply to cap—the Renaissance achievement was really under way, other qualities of the classical (Greek now rather than Roman) returned by the middle of the eighteenth century to haunt cultivated imagination: the great classical ideal of the moral function of art, and poetry in particular—poetry as an educator of the mind and emotions; the range of appeal in the audience it had touched and should touch; the range of genres—epic, tragedy, and on down through the "lesser" types; the strong, widely shared national involvement in poetry and the other arts; the variety of characters portrayed in epic and dramatic form; the emotional immediacy of language; the imaginative strength of metaphor. Above all there was "originality"—the power of "invention"; and, as Pope said in beginning the preface to his translation of *The Iliad* (1715), it is "invention" that especially "distinguishes all great genius."

This was the dilemma that eighteenth-century neoclassicism inherited, and with which it was to live as it reconsidered its position throughout the remainder of the century. A dilemma, like any other form of challenge, can be fruitful, depending on how we react to it. In fact, if frankly faced, it can be one of the ways by which a movement stays alive, deferring—even avoiding—the senilities of self-congratulation and the irrelevance and thinness of defensive mannerism.

To the eternal credit of the eighteenth century, especially in England, it faced this challenge—as it did so many others in the arts, in philosophy and psychology, in science, and in government—with a union of good sense, honesty, and imaginative resource. In the process it also created the whole modern movement in the arts, of which Romanticism is the first stage. And the great reconsideration of the arts throughout the eighteenth century, especially after 1750, is to a large extent the result of the Jacob-like wrestle of the century with the classical angel, the classical ideal—its attempt to come to terms with that ideal and to secure its blessing....

...He that imitates *The Iliad*, says Young, is not imitating Homer. Of course. And what Young was saying is what Longinus himself said sixteen centuries before in *On the Sublime*.

But even if this was true—and of course it was—how do we proceed? When we are actually confronted with specific answers, we soon complain of being suffocated or inhibited, of being denied the opportunity to contribute "creatively" and "freely" on our own; and we at once begin—usually with some success—to pick holes in what has been presented us. But as soon as we feel we have pushed all this aside, and at last stand free and ready to make our own contribution, the human heart shrinks at its new nakedness and its new gift of what Santayana calls "vacant liberty." We start once again to crave specific direction, and turn reproachfully, notebook in hand, on those who are now exhorting us—in the very spirit we had before demanded—to "go and do likewise."

The later eighteenth century did make an effort to provide helpful answers, as much as any period in the history of critical writing. Boldly and specifically it tried to concentrate, as criticism has rarely done before or since, on both the psychology of genius and the stylistic means of attaining the highest possible reach of art, the "sublime"—and without embarrassment or apology. The particular details may be open to endless quibble. But the concern and effort were to prove healthful in the highest degree. Was not the greatest of classical legacies, after all, the Greek ideal of *arete* or excellence—the "vision of greatness," in Whitehead's phrase—that had proved so fertile in ancient Greece and again in the Renaissance? But the struggle to recapture it, in the eighteenth-century wrestle with itself and with the classical ideal, was far from easy.

EXCERPTED FROM LECTURE 4: THE THIRD TEMPLE

Yes, however seductive the arguments, it was plain that the principal difficulty for the modern poet or artist was not society and "unpoetic" customs and surroundings, not changes in language, not the growing compartmentalization of the mind and experience, competition from analytic philosophy and the sciences, nor the lack of "audience." In the eighteenth-century debate with itself, one after another of these considerations, not to mention others, had been brought forward, been given its due or more

than its due, and been weighted in the balance. True, they were all important (this was taken for granted), and, if an art itself abandoned centrality, they would certainly become more so—particularly competition from other intellectual interests.

But the essential problem—the real anxiety—lay elsewhere, as David Hume had said, and it had to do with the artist's relation to his own art. It had to do with what the artist would least care to dwell on publicly if he were trying either to begin or even to maintain his way, and with what is even now—in the second half of the twentieth century—not openly celebrated but surrounded with a protective fog of other considerations: that is, his nakedness and embarrassment (with the inevitable temptations to paralysis or routine imitation, to retrenchment or mere fitful rebellion) before the amplitude of what two thousand years or more of an art had already been able to achieve. And meanwhile, with every generation, our sense of that amplitude—its variety in subject, in approach, in power or ingenuity of expression—has been further increasing as (justifiably, commendably) we continue to explore that heritage and extend our understanding of it. How could the poet or artist be expected to volunteer the confession that this was his first, his greatest problem?...

...In short, one kept coming back to what Hume had said about emulation in the arts—what promotes, twists, or dampens it. This was the point from which one always seemed to start: perhaps not in one's speculative thinking about art (who really wished to dwell on it, or least of all on its future implications?—for what could one do about it?), but it was the point from which one started in actual feeling if he was even half honest to the pinch of the situation—or even if he was not. For after the merely theoretical issues had been aired for whatever purpose and with whatever gain or loss, this was the situation that confronted the writer as soon as he returned to his closet to face that intimidating object, the blank sheet of paper waiting to be filled.

And in one important way the embarrassment for the poet had sharpened during the fifty years since Hume had written. The whole concept of "originality" had both deepened and spread—deepened as a hold on the conscience and spread horizontally among the literate, and the peripheries of the literate, as something desired per se. Back in the 1730s and 1740s, when the neoclassical had begun to reconsider its own self-limitations, the idea of "originality" had understandably been plucked out into prominence as one way of describing what was felt to be most missing. It had every advantage for that purpose. It was an "open" term, capable of suggesting not only creativity, invention, or mere priority but also essentialism (getting back to the fundamental), vigor, purity, and above all freedom of the spirit. As such it transcended most of the particular qualities that could be latched on to it, qualities that, if taken singly as exclusive ends, could so easily conflict with each other (priority versus essentialism, for instance, or the inevitable confinement of "purity" versus "range," or primitive simplicity versus the creative intelligence of an Isaac Newton). Add to this the social appeal of the concept of "originality": its association with the individual's "identity" (a work that was now increasing in connotative importance) as contrasted with the more repressive and dehumanizing aspects of organized life. What Lionel Trilling rightly describes as one of the principal themes of modern literature—the growing disenchantment of culture with culture itself—had already begun in the second third of the eighteenth century. If for a while the undercut of "originality" seemed like an emotional jag (and it was), even that side of it has more than the interest it used to have for us as merely part of the picturesque folklore of the eighteenth century. We now see it as an anticipation of what the present emerging generation is experiencing, two centuries later, in its own reaction to a half-century of brilliant formalization in sophisticated art and, more important, to what it conceives to be the dehumanizing pressures of an organized and increasingly crowded society.

In any case the spread of the idea of "originality" into the fringes of behavior and into stock value or stock responses was only a symptom of the grip that the ideal was beginning to take on the center of the intellect itself. For the concept of "originality" meshed with so many other things in life aside from the arts (especially the concept of progress in the cumulative sciences, social and historical as well as physical) that the conscience was trapped by it now as it had earlier been trapped by the neoclassic use of the classical example. In short, the conscience had taken another Trojan Horse into the walls, from which the unexpected again appeared. By the 1750s some of the least original minds of the time were beginning to prate constantly of "originality," thus setting a precedent with which the intellectual has since been condemned to live. True, almost every major mind could protest against the new bind that the fetish of originality would create for the arts; could say repeatedly (as had their neoclassical forebears) that this—which they themselves had advocated—could become as much a tyrant to the human spirit as what they themselves had earlier reacted against. But ideas evolved for a special purpose and under special circumstances have a way, as Burke said, of being snatched out of one's hands by others whom have shared little of the experience or imagination of those who first advanced them. The slightest reflection should remind us that "originality" in the arts need not imply vigor, range, or even openness of mind—or power of language or anything else of a qualitative nature. Repeatedly this is said, and with a sadder, more experienced spirit than by the neoclassic critics a century before. But it could always be answered that men like Johnson, Burke, Voltaire, or Goethe could afford to talk this way. Their battle for

insight before the rising multiplicity of experience and achievement was already won, or half won. And, in any case, did not they themselves take for granted the basic psychological fact that, unless the scene is shifted—unless the kaleidoscope is turned, with the pieces tumbling into another pattern—the mind falls asleep, and ceases even to notice? Novelty, said Aristotle long ago, has at least this merit: it reawakens attention. Of course they knew this. (One had only to open Johnson to find this realization implied on every page of his greater writing—though counterbalanced by other considerations.)

In short, the eighteenth century, in its effort to lift the burden of the past or to shift it to one side, had first spun off, then developed as a specific value, and finally elevated to the status of ideal that merely open and elusive (indeed potentially self-contradictory) premise of "originality." True, the period was also beginning to develop antibodies, so to speak, to what a part of itself was preaching. We must return to this later. And it did, after all, train up and give a start to what we think of as the whole romantic and generally nineteenth-century movement in the arts, for which, extending Dryden's imaginative metaphor of "The Second Temple" for the neoclassic, we have suggested "The Third Temple" as shorthand. But in any case the fact remained that the eighteenth-century "Enlightenment" had created, and had foisted upon itself and its immediate child—not to mention its later descendants—an ideal of "originality" sanctioned both officially (theoretically, intellectually) and, *in potentia*, popularly. As a result the vulnerability of the poet, already great enough, was accentuated by having his uneasiness now given a "local habitation and a name." For the first time in history, the ideal of "originality"—aside from the personal pressures the artist might feel to achieve it anyway—was now becoming defined as necessary, indeed taken for granted. At the same time, as an additional embarrassment, the eighteenth-century effort to clear its own mind and to reground itself in the fundamental—to go back to the essentially human, as we ourselves are again trying to do—had evolved for the artist an ancillary ideal: that of *sincerity*.

These two relatively new ideals of "originality" and "sincerity" (new at least for art) were henceforth to lie heavily on the shoulders of almost every English-speaking writer, and very soon almost every Western artist. And like most compensatory ideals that become rigid through anxiety, they only complicated the problem further (and, for that matter, also conflicted with each other). They both quickly became the sort of ideals that you can neither live with nor live without. You cannot openly deny them. You cannot afford to come out and say that you want to be "unoriginal" or "insincere." Yet if you are never to write a line unless you are convinced that you are totally "sincere," then where do you start? You can be sure that something is going to happen both to your fluency and your range. David Perkins, in his *Wordsworth and the Poetry of Sincerity,* has shown the dilemma that Wordsworth inherited and then—through his own individual success—powerfully deepened. Similarly, if you are exhorted to be "original" at all costs, how do you take even the first step—especially if what you have been taught most to admire (and what in fact you really do most admire) is best typified by those very predecessors from whom you must now distinguish yourself, and, even worse, if your "original" departure from those admired models must spring from an "originality" that is itself "sincere"?…

…Was there no way of getting out of this self-created prison? For of course it *was* self-created. How the Oriental artist, during all the centuries that he followed his craft, would have started—or laughed—if told that those past artists by whom, and through whom, he had been taught should suddenly represent territory that was verboten: that he had studied them only in order to be different! Take any of the great past eras we say we most admire: would not the Greek artist, the Renaissance artist, be complimented if told he could be virtually mistaken for his greatest predecessors; and, if he was able to go still further than they, did he not assume that it would be through assimilating the virtues and techniques of his predecessors while perhaps capping them with just a little more? Was it not a sufficient triumph even to recapture a few of the virtues of our greatest predecessors, as Sir Joshua Reynolds said in his last discourse to the students at the Royal Academy?—that last discourse in which he disowned his earlier willingness to abide by "the taste of the times in which I live" and said that, "however unequal I feel myself to that attempt, were I now to begin the world again, I would tread in the steps of that great master (Michelangelo)…To catch the slightest of his perfections would be glory and distinction enough." It requires no heroic effort to be different from the great.…

…If we are forced to try to answer our question in a few sentences, we have only to repeat the clichés about Romanticism—but with a special imaginative sympathy for the particular question we have been discussing here—and we can get a tolerable notion of what at least permitted, if it did not create, this remarkable end-product of the eighteenth century, which provided the creative capital off which the nineteenth century and much of the twentieth (though in the latter case uneasily) has continued to live. For example, one answer is surely to be found in the opening up of new subject matters where the challenge of the past was less oppressive: simple life (of which there were to be twentieth-century urban as well as romantically rural varieties), children, the poor socially slighted; landscape and scenery; such inward experiences as reverie, dream, and mysticism; the whole concept of the "strange" either to awaken attention through difference in mode or phrase, to explore something really new, or to provide setting and focus for familiar nostalgia; the past itself in periods or ways not previously exploited by the traditional genres; the geographically remote or unusual, or conversely its apparent opposite (for example, Wordsworth; or the young Emerson on the central challenge of the age: "I ask not for the great, the remote… I embrace the common, I explore and sit at the feet of the familiar, the low"). Every attempt to "define" Romanticism in the light of subject is doomed to failure except as it applies to a limited part. For the opening of new subject matters, as of approach, proceeds in almost every direction, like spokes pointing outward from the hub of a wheel but with no rim to encase them. The one thing they all have in common is an interest or hope in the hitherto unexploited. And despite the strong attraction of twentieth-century post-romantic formalism to ideals of retrenchment and self-limitation, that still remains with us as a premise with which we are disinclined to quarrel.…

…We cited earlier the belief that there was one possibility for "rescue" of the arts back into centrality— an appeal over the heads of the "sophisticated" to the "popular"—and we also mentioned the theoretical doubts expressed about the likelihood of its happening. But as Imlac in *Rasselas* says about the problem of getting out of the prison of the "happy valley," "Many things difficult to design prove easy to performance." And Hazlitt liked to cite the philosopher who, weary of arguing against Zeno's paradox providing the impossibility of motion, finally rose and walked across the room. To an important extent that "rescue" of the arts through the extension of their public did happen, against all the theoretical probabilities, and was to continue to happen throughout the nineteenth century. Nor was it simply bestowed by social circumstance. It had to be won.[1] Whatever else can be said of Romanticism, it ushered in—indeed involved—the most sustained effort of the last three centuries to secure a popular appeal for the serious arts. If there is no significant aspect of Romanticism on which we have dwelt less, it is partly because of the inferred rebuke to ourselves. For the romantic effort, with its remarkable if emotionally specialized success, was to create an immense problem for the twentieth century in its own traumatic attempt to disengage itself from the nineteenth. Forced to establish and defend a difference, the twentieth century was led into a situation where—as Ortega y Gasset predicted in *The Dehumanization of the Arts*—it often found itself compelled to champion the anti-popular (humanly confusing the "*anti*-popular" with the merely "a-popular" or the "unpopular"), without either wanting to do so or quite knowing why it was doing so. Adding to the psychological conflict was the fact that the twentieth-century artist, with few exceptions, continued to share the humanitarian and social liberalism of the romantic....

...And yet when we put all these things together, we do not get the full answer to our question: why the Romantics—these children of the eighteenth century—were able to do what they did despite the apparent odds against them. Nor do we get closer by merely adding other considerations of the same kind—for our list could be extended.[2] What is still missing is the boldness of spirit that seizes upon opportunity and creates new ones. In that long self-debate during which the eighteenth century seemed to descend theoretically to the belief that so little might still be left for the arts, it also found bedrock. It came to this through its own honesty and essentialism—its ability to cling to essential fact while also keeping hold of essential ideal. The latter—the creative and formative essentialism of ideal—is shown by the fact that throughout the middle and later eighteenth century it rarely occurred to anyone to question the ideal of greatness. The artist as an individual might feel intimidated, even crushed. But the men of that century, and even more the youth of the next generation whom they produced and taught, were haunted by the vision of greatness: "Moral education," said Whitehead—a fundamental education of the whole self into action or being—"is impossible apart from the habitual vision of greatness. If we are not great, it does not matter

what we do or what is the issue. Now the sense of greatness is an immediate intuition and not the conclusion of an argument... The sense of greatness is the groundwork of morals"—of what one really does and is. It is for this reason, more than any other, that the famous work from the first century, Longinus' *On the Sublime,* had, at least since the 1730s, become so central as an authoritative support—at once precept and example (he is "himself the great Sublime he draws," said Pope)—speaking to us from the distant past. This was its primary theme. (The theoretical concept of the "sublime" itself, whether taken simply as "loftiness of spirit," to use Longinus' own phrase, or with all the alternative phrases and nuances this permitted, is not what we are speaking about at the moment—though it is at least as relevant to Romanticism as anything else that we ran through in our list. If the concept of the "sublime" enters directly into what we are now saying, it is in its more literal sense: a release of what is "below the threshold" of consciousness for fulfillment in and through the great.)

The essential message of Longinus is that, in and through the personal rediscovery of the great, we find that we need not be the passive victims of what we deterministically call "circumstances" (social, cultural, or reductively psychological-personal), but that by linking ourselves through what Keats calls an "immortal free-masonry" with the great we can become freer—freer to be ourselves, to be what we most want and value; and that by caring for the kinds of things that they did we are not only "imitating" them, in the best and most fruitful sense of the word, but also "joining them."

ENDNOTES

1. Comments about the growth of literacy, the rising middle class, and so on have a point. But the twentieth century has seen a further extension of these circumstances at a time when much of what we call "serious" art has been frankly, if unwillingly, directed to subcultures and to the academy.

2. E.g., the French Revolution and the challenges of social change—though our own century has had comparable experiences—or, to cite something radically different, the whole modern conception of the evolution and change of genres themselves—so easy to talk about theoretically, so difficult to insinuate into the habitual responses of those whose task is to create or perform rather than to reflect and advise. For the poet, if he is worth his salt, still remembers Lear, and the painter remembers Michelangelo. Our modern sense that genres are not forever stratified as God-given has, seeping into us slowly (against immense inner opposition, including idealistic opposition—with all the possible rigidities as well as advantages of idealism), done something to free the artist. But by itself, unaided by the example of more recent models of another kind from which one can take heart, it can still leave him deeply divided in his sense of what is left him. Perhaps its help has been largely "palliative rather than radical"—what Johnson says is our only hope for most human ills. In any case I do not believe that the liberating influence of the critical theory of the evolution of genres per se had much direct effect on the poet himself (or probably the artist generally) till later in the nineteenth century, and then largely because of the example of romantic models. ❧

Ancient Rome 1.0

By John Burge

The desktop computer revolution has redefined the methodology of the arts as well as the sciences. In architecture, the emergence of 3D CADD (three-dimensional computer aided design and drafting) has effectively merged the former distinct disciplines of architectural rendering and model making. In the digital realm, to make a rendering you have to build a model, and if you build a model it can be easily turned into a rendering. Additionally, multiple views of a given subject can be rendered with only a small additional effort. In the related field of archaeological reconstruction, these advantages are supplemented by the ability to incorporate surviving elements accurately: columns, moldings, etc. As a result, the advent of desktop computer technology has enabled archaeologists and architects alike to take a new and more precise look at the lost monuments of the ancients.

Roman architecture is one of the least appreciated historical styles, the very nature of Roman architectural technique being anathema to modernist ideology. For example, the Pantheon consists of a concrete dome supported on a ring of eight arches, which in turn are supported on eight piers. The entire structure consists almost entirely of bricks and concrete. Yet in its finished form there would not have been a single brick or patch of concrete visible. The dome's exterior was sheathed in gilded bronze plates, the interior encased in elaborately ornamented stucco and gilded bronze ornaments (several of the mounting holes for which survive). The exterior of the rotunda was covered with stucco shaped to look like ashlar stone, the interior completely covered with marble plates, as was the floor. There was no structural honesty in Roman architecture. Like the architects of the American Renaissance, Roman architects drew clear distinctions between structure and ornament, between the practical and the aesthetic.

On the following pages you will see several of the archaeological reconstruction projects that I have worked (and am still working) on since I built my first Pantheon in 1994 (several images of which appeared in *The Classicist No. 3*). The Forum of Trajan, the Pantheon, and the Theater of Pompey are all among the greatest buildings of Rome.

THE WONDERS OF ROME

In the mid-fourth century, Constantius II—son of Constantine the Great—the first true Christian emperor and the first emperor *not* crowned in Rome, made his first official visit to the Eternal City. Accompanying him was the historian Ammianus Marcellinus. His account of the trip records the tremendous impression made upon Constantius by the spectacular architecture of the great old city. He lists a number of important structures by name:

When he surveyed the different regions of the city and its environs, lying along the slopes and on level ground within the circle of the seven hills, it seemed to him that whatever his eye first lit on took the palm. It might be the shrine of Tarpeian Jupiter, beside which all else is like earth compared to heaven, or the buildings of the baths as big as provinces, or the solid mass of stone from Tibur that forms the amphitheatre, with its top almost beyond the reach of human sight, or the Pantheon spread like a self-contained district under its high and lovely dome, or the lofty columns with spiral stairs to platforms which support the statues of former emperors, or the temple of Rome or the Forum of Peace, the Theatre of Pompey or the Odeum or the Stadium, or any of the other sites of the Eternal City.

But when he came to the Forum of Trajan, a creation which in my view has no like under the cope of heaven and which even the gods themselves must agree to admire, he stood transfixed with astonishment, surveying the gigantic fabric around him; its grandeur defies description and can never again be approached by mortal men.

—Ammianus Marcellinus (16.10)

FIGURE 1, ABOVE: *Library/Exedra 'L' of the Baths of Trajan, Rome. Computer model and rendering by John Burge.*

What is interesting about these particular monuments is that all of them were either built or significantly rebuilt during a relatively short period of Roman history:

Tarpeian Jupiter (Capitolium)	Completely rebuilt	Domitian	89 AD
Amphitheatre (Colosseum)	Built	Vespasian	79 AD
Pantheon	Completely rebuilt	Hadrian	118-128 AD
Temple of Rome (Venus & Rome)	Built	Hadrian	121-135 AD
Forum of Peace	Built	Vespasian	75 AD
Theatre of Pompey	Largely rebuilt	Domitian	after 80 AD
Odeum	Built	Domitian	80-96 AD
Stadium	Built	Domitian	80-96 AD
Forum of Trajan	Built	Trajan	106-128 AD

All nine fall within a 60-year period from 75 to135 AD, as do the first of the great baths, the Baths of Trajan, built between104 and109 AD. One of the notable trends of this period, and something that would become characteristic of the High Empire Style, was the development of large-span architecture both using flat ceilings with roof-trusses as well as vaulting. It was in these great interior spaces that Roman architecture is most clearly defined as an architecture of its own and not just a variation of classical Greek and Hellenistic styles.

Large span interiors date from the very beginning of the Empire. The Diribitorium, one of Julius Caesar's pet projects, was commented on by Pliny, who talked of the 100-foot long beams that were used to span it. The Temple of Mars Ultor, in Augustusí Forum, was not far behind with a cella nearly 80 feet wide. But starting with the Flavian emperors there would be a rapid development in large-span interiors culminating in the great dome of the Pantheon.

The Domus Flavia, the new palace built by Domitian circa 90 AD included two enormous halls, the Aula Regia (golden hall, the throne room) and the Triclinium (dining room). Both had spans of 100 feet or more. The Triclinium almost certainly was roofed with trusses and had a flat ceiling. The Aula Regia probably also had a flat ceiling but may have

FIGURE 2, ABOVE: West Apse, Forum of Trajan, Rome. Computer model by John Burge and James Packer. Rendering by John Burge.

FIGURE 3: West Library, Forum of Trajan, Rome. Computer model by John Burge and James Packer. Rendering by John Burge.

been vaulted (the walls were much thicker than those of the Triclinium, but may not have been thick enough for vaulting). The Forum of Trajan had four large (140 feet in diameter) semi-circular halls that were probably truss-roofed. The ultimate truss-roofed structure was the Odeum. There are very few remains, but it was a theater for musical performances that ancient sources say was roofed. Semi-circular in plan, the Odeum had a clear interior diameter of over 250 feet.

The true forerunner of the greatest of all vaulted ceilings—the Pantheon dome—was the vaulting of the great baths. The Baths of Trajan, built just before the Pantheon, featured two domed circular chambers 80 feet in diameter. In addition there were six semi-circular halls (including

two matching libraries illustrated in FIGURE 3) with concrete half-domes, all approximately 100 feet in diameter. Finally there was the Frigidarium, the central hall of the complex. It was a groin-vaulted space 80 feet wide and 180 feet long. It is important to note that ancient sources attribute the Odeum, the Forum of Trajan, and the Baths of Trajan to the same architect: Apollodorus of Damascus. Truly a long-span specialist, he was also responsible for the great bridge across the Danube built during Trajan's Dacian wars. There is a distinct possibility that he was also the architect of the Pantheon. Its 140 foot dome, the largest span until the nineteenth century, would be a fitting climax to the career of one of the all-time great architects and a man at the heart of the High Empire style.

THE FORUM OF TRAJAN

The Forum of Trajan (FIGURE 2) was the last and greatest of the five Imperial Fora, additions to the republican Forum Romanum built during the early Empire. The complex consists of two colonnaded squares on either side of a central basilica. The south complex, the Area Fori (the forum proper), was dedicated in 112 AD. The courtyard is 300 feet wide and over 400 feet long. The nave of the basilica was 300 feet long and 90 feet wide with a 90-foot ceiling. The smaller complex on the north side consisted of two libraries (FIGURE 3) flanking a colonnaded court containing the 140 foot high Column of Trajan, and was dedicated in 113 AD. After the emperor's death in 117 AD, Trajan's remains were placed in the base of the Column. The complex was one of the wonders of Rome until its destruction by earthquake in the early ninth century.

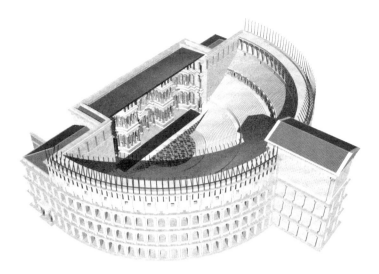

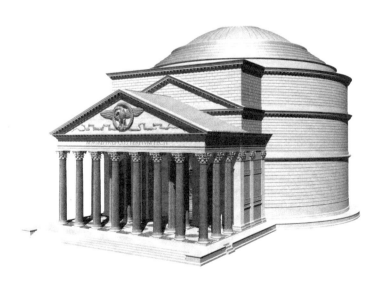

The reconstruction shown here is based on the work of Professor James Packer of Northwestern University, and appears in the revised soft-cover edition of his seminal work on the complex *The Forum of Trajan in Rome: A study of the Monuments in Brief* (University of California Press, 2000). Inspired by his earlier edition of the book, I began this model in late 1997. I have been collaborating directly with Professor Packer since early 1998, and the digital model incorporates many new conclusions and interpretations based on commentary and discussions following the original edition. As of this writing (fall 2000), our work is continuing as new discoveries come to light from the ongoing excavations in the Imperial Fora.

THE PANTHEON

The Pantheon is, with the possible exception of the Colosseum, the best-known building of Imperial Rome. The surviving structure, the third Pantheon to stand here, was built under the emperor Hadrian between 118 and128 AD, and like most of the very large temples in Rome, the Emperor and the Senate commonly used the Pantheon as an audience hall and meeting place. Its dome, with a span of over 140 feet, held the record for the greatest span in the world until the nineteenth century.

These reconstruction models of the existing building (FIGURE 5) and the proposed "original scheme" (FIGURE 4) are based on the work of Mark Wilson-Jones and appear in his book *Principles of Roman Architecture* (Yale University Press, 2000). The original scheme concept was proposed in an attempt to explain the many oddities in the details of the Pantheon's front

FIGURE 4, TOP LEFT: The Pantheon "original scheme", Rome. Computer model and rendering by John Burge.

FIGURE 5, BOTTOM LEFT: The Pantheon, "as built", Rome. Computer model and rendering by John Burge.

FIGURE 6, ABOVE: Aerial View, Theater of Pompey, Rome. Computer model and rendering by John Burge.

FIGURE 7: Scaenae Frons, Theater of Pompey, Rome. Computer model and rendering by John Burge.

porch. The theory is that the Pantheon was intended to have a porch of 60-foot columns, with 50-foot monolithic granite shafts. When an insufficient number of these were available (the temple of the Divine Trajan, which was being built simultaneously, had columns of the same massive dimensions), the design was altered to accommodate smaller 48-foot columns with 40-foot shafts. This would explain the unusually wide spacing of the columns (3 lower diameters, instead of the more typical 2½ diameters) and the lack of alignment between the exterior cornices of the rotunda and the porch.

THE THEATER OF POMPEY

The Theater of Pompey was the premiere theater of Rome. Although there were at least three major theaters in Rome, Pompey's theater was De Theatrum, THE Theater. Originally built by the general Pompey the Great at the end of the Republic in the first century BC, it was one of the first monumental buildings in Rome. It was also one of the first in a nearly continuous building program that lasted from the last decades of the Republic to the early years of the reign of Tiberius over one hundred years later. Renovated several times, it was heavily damaged in the great fire of 80 AD which destroyed much of the Campus Martius. The porticus and stage building were completely rebuilt by Domitian and the handful of reports of fragments and the plan preserved in the Forma Urbis, the great marble map of Rome, confirm its Flavian character.

This reconstruction of Pompey's theater is being done in collaboration with Professor Packer and Professor Richard Beacham of the School of Theater History at Warwick University. This is part of an ongoing project to document the great theaters of Europe. ❧

John Burge is a New York architectural renderer and founder of Paleopolis Inc. (www.paleopolis.com).

THE ROTUNDA~THE ROTUNDA~THE ROTUNDA~THE ROTUNDA~

Inspiration may come in many forms. For an architect or historian, inspiration may come from a childhood memory, or it may be the result of a developed aesthetic sensibility. Perhaps a teacher or mentor provides some initial spark for the student; or an architect may derive inspiration from studying how other architects have solved the same problems that he is facing. In any case, the buildings, places, people, and theories that influence and inspire today's architects and teachers are wide-ranging and provide insight into their careers.

Since 1991 the Institute of Classical Architecture has relied upon the advice and guidance of its Advisory Council in formulating the content and direction of its programs. Diverse in opinion and experience, the Institute's Advisory Council has assisted the Institute in a variety of ways over the years. The editorial staff of *The Classicist* decided to delve into what has inspired some of our Advisory Council members so that our readers might get to know a few of them better. The following ruminations are from four members of the Institute's Advisory Council in response to the request to write about a few of their favorite things, to write about what inspires them, and what has guided the development of their work. — Christine G.H. Franck

ARTHUR MAY: One doesn't often think about those buildings that you go out of your way to see on a regular basis, those that you stare at as you drive by in a cab. But I started to put together a list, and it just grew. First of all, here in New York, there is the building at 917 Park Avenue by Ernest Flagg. It's at 85th Street, on the East Side and is a brick townhouse with a winding stair outside. Then there is Cass Gilbert's Woolworth Building, by far one of the best tall buildings in America. There are a lot of lessons to be learned from the Woolworth Building. As for lessons to learn from Cass Gilbert, I think the United States Court Building in Foley Square is one of the best examples of the Corinthian Order.

For building exteriors, the façade of St. Ignatius Loyola is hard to beat. The granite stonework on Carrere & Hastings' First Church of Christ Scientist at 96th and Central Park West is also extremely beautiful, in a Hawksmoor-like way. Across the Park, of course, the Frick Mansion also shows off Carrere & Hastings' skill. In this neighborhood, I also love the Otto Kahn House at East 91st Street. Then moving downtown there is the fabulous Gorham Building at 19th Street and Broadway; it is a great example of the Queen Anne style. Also in the Ladies Mile historic district is the great example of department store building, the Siegel-Cooper Department Store, on Sixth Avenue between 18th and 19th Streets. The side walls have beautiful textural qualities and the building teaches a lot about the implications for big buildings and classicism. It teaches a good sense of scale and proportion. On a similar note is the Old Singer Building at Prince and Broadway. They are all urban buildings that utilize classicism to deal with urban issues in a variety of ways. In addition to these buildings, there are also all of the major clubs such as the University Club, the Union Club at 38th Street and Park Avenue South, the Metropolitan Club, the Racquet Club and the New York Athletic Club. Then there is the New York Historical Society, showing how to deal with expanses of masonry.

Moving beyond New York to the rest of the United States, John Russell Pope's Jefferson Memorial and National Gallery of Art in Washington, D.C. show how to deal with transitions, corners, and details. The rotunda, halls, and gardens at the National Gallery with those great black granite columns are exceptional. In Nashville, William Strickland's State House is one of my favorites. I visited it as often as I could when I was working on a project in Nashville. Boston has Beacon Hill, one of the loveliest and most urbane places in America. And lastly in Philadelphia, the entry hall at the Museum of Art is a great space.

In Europe I have been inspired by the work of Soane, Hawksmoor, Lutyens, and Mackintosh. For Soane's work the Soane Museum, the Dulwich Picture Gallery, and the old Bank of England are my favorites. Hawksmoor's Christ Church Spitalfields also ranks high on my list of favorite things as well as Lutyen's Liverpool Cathedral, Midland Bank, and Theosophical Society. In Glasgow, Mackintosh's Glasgow School of Art and "Greek" Thompson's neoclassical churches are inspiring to me. In addition to public and religious buildings, Europe also boasts one of my favorite bridges, the Pont du Gard, while the other is in New York, the

FIGURE 1, TOP: Federal Courthouse competition design, 1991, White Plains, New York. Arthur May, Architect.

FIGURE 2, BOTTOM: Sketch of S. Giovanni dei Fiorentini from across the Tiber. Elizabeth Plater-Zyberk.

Hell's Gate Bridge. I have also always liked Schinkel's Altes Museum, as well as the French Romanesque style.

Some of my favorite buildings are by Robert Smythson, such as Hardwick Hall and Longleat, Wilts, where the classicism is suppressed to what is an almost curtain wall-like construction. Buildings such as these are, by far, my favorite buildings. They are the ones where the architects have been inventive in their willingness to take the classical language further than the Palladian example and are particularly successful in using classicism to deal with a large scale while maintaining the essence of the classical language.

ELIZABETH PLATER-ZYBERK: My childhood years were spent in Southeastern Pennsylvania surrounded by spacious, beautifully proportioned farmhouses and fieldstone houses of memorable simplicity. This experience still plays a role in my visual resources, as I strive for that essential simplicity in my work. Childhood trips to Dover and Old Newcastle in Delaware and Williamsburg, Virginia had a tremendous impact and I have warm memories of visiting these places. My father was an architect, and he admired these towns. I remember how sensual his pencil drawings of historic buildings appeared to me as they lay on his desk. It seemed like such a luscious medium. I remember vividly the drawings of those small-scale urban and rural buildings.

In my formal education there were numerous people who influenced my development. In no particular order: Kenneth Frampton's urban history course opened up a world of positing form for our cities as a worthwhile endeavor; Vincent Scully and Allan Greenberg's courses at Yale; and Robert A.M. Stern was a role model for many of my generation; Stern was excited about design, loved to teach, and loved to write, and loved to speak, and thus he presented an ideal way to be an architect. At Princeton we received a formal Corbusian education, which was then balanced by a historically deeper approach at Yale. Robert Venturi's intelligent and kind approach to the profession was an important influence too.

Andres (Duany) and I came to Florida in the recession of the seventies and we ended up cutting our teeth in the world of speculative development. At that time schools were object-building oriented, with little regard for urbanism, as there was in Europe with Leo and Rob Krier, Rem Koolhas, Aldo Rossi, and Massimo Scolari. We were aware of the Europeans, but it was not until the Architectural Club in Miami hosted these people that we had any real exposure to them. Our early buildings in Miami were urban in spirit, but not in actuality. Then Bob Stern got us involved in the Anglo-American Suburb exhibit at the Cooper-Hewitt, and in very short order, we got around to see all of the garden suburbs, which introduced us to the town planning work of John Nolen and his contemporaries. As important for us was Pat Pinell's discovery of *The American Vitruvius: An Architects' Handbook of Civic Art*. When he ran across Hegemann and Peet's book at the University of Maryland library in 1978, it had not been checked out since 1922! He told us to go and look it up in our library, we did, and I used it in my studio at Miami. This book influenced our design at Charleston Place.

In our work at Seaside with Robert Davis, we learned the importance of using precedent to illustrate and inform design ideas. We also learned, from CIAM [the International Congress of Modern Architecture], the importance of a good drawing. Because, of course if you read CIAM's manifestos the neighborhood and the community figure prominently, but it was the drawings of CIAM architects, the drawings of Le Corbusier above all that had the truly long-term influence.

At the CNU [Congress for the New Urbanism], we always have to remember the importance of design. Design is generally seen as irrelevant or having to do with personal taste. People who have participated in a public *charrette* can tell you how powerfully design can unite and resolve various points of view. Drawings have lasting political power. Thus, designers wield a tool of transformation that others cannot. Our early projects at Charleston Place and Seaside had an essentially aesthetic initiative, but we have discovered that design can have environmental, social and economic impact while creating something beautiful.

CARROLL WILLIAM WESTFALL: Raised and trained in a world that was becoming increasingly committed to modernism, I swam with that stream as I pursued my career as an academic architectural historian. In 1972 fate took me to teach architectural history at the University of Illinois in Chicago, a city that knew and loved Louis Sullivan and Frank Lloyd Wright and knew and cared for little else.

I had earned the degrees authorizing me to be assertive in using the reigning opinions in my field. I knew that the Zeitgeist had made obsolete the old books, buildings, and cities I had studied. But that left me in a quandary: What useful role could an historian play in a school of architecture? With what authority could I judge the quality of what my students had learned from me? For what reasons might I require them to accept my criticism of their designs? Moreover, my academic training had ill prepared me for participating in the preservation battles that soon drew my energies. On what basis can we compel a person to save a building or require people to pay taxes to build a public building, or to pay me to teach, for that matter?

What, then, was I to make of my early work with Leon Battista Alberti and his friends Pope Nicholas V and the others involved in the tumultuous events of the fifteenth century? Were they mere cultural

FIGURE 3: *Frost and Granger, Chicago and Northwestern Station, Chicago, 1908. A privately financed public building built to form an enduring connection between modern Chicago and a long civil tradition, destroyed in 1983 in the interest of economic expediency and replaced by a modernist office tower.*

artifacts producing what Erwin Panofsky called cultural symptoms capable of telling us how things were in their time with the certain conviction that they therefore are not like that in our own? Or were those people right then, which would mean that they are right now? Being right means being connected to a realm of truth outside time or place and not merely congruent with current preference and opinion. But being right changes with circumstances that allow what is right to emerge, and that dialectic between right and circumstance, between truth and contingencies, was what I had to learn and teach. The insight that we must seek the best possible versions of truth available within the circumstances in which we live allowed me to form a kinship with my old friends. It also enlarged the dialogue to include their teachers, for example, Plato, Aristotle, Christ, Paul, Augustine, Aquinas, and the rest, as well as with their successors, Palladio and Geoffrey Scott, Thomas Jefferson and Martin Luther King, Jr., Machiavelli and Leo Strauss. Here were models for all people of good will who engage in the public discourse essential to a people who aspire to embody goodness in their actions, truth in their knowledge, beauty in their artifacts, and moral perfection in their character.

As an historian I had been taught to place each of these people in his own niche or period in the past and thereby insulate him from the present. Now I had to learn how each of them contributed to knowledge in the present.[1] My reeducation required purging my language of words like style, period, and influence. That trilogy formed the essential components of the Zeitgeist theory, a modernist, determinist position that deprives people of their individuality and character, relieves them of responsibility for their actions, and gives them a mechanical means of answering complicated questions about what actually happened in the past. After all, the modernists justify their designs by saying the Zeitgeist demands that style. Their historian colleagues tabulate the influences that explain why an old building looks as it does. And preservationists plead for the salvation of this or that fine representative of some past "period" or "style."

This insight freed me to work with people who, like myself, are endowed with differing talents, are variously equipped with knowledge, who are responsible for their actions, and who seek to perfect their natures through activities in the civil and religious realms. Together we could work to embody goodness in our civil actions, truth in what we know, beauty in what we make, and moral perfection in our character.[2]

People seeking these ends draw from and contribute to natural law and natural right traditions. The political life is one form these traditions take, architecture and urbanism is another. The congruence between these traditions and the constitutional regime of the United States and the traditional, classical architecture and urbanism serving the American democracy is a particularly happy one.[3] The republic and its architecture flourish when its citizens realize this, and we all benefit when we hold in common several convictions that flow from this realization. One is that the traditions of the several fields of citizens' endeavors provide the knowledge used in confronting the contingencies of the present. Another is that within traditional knowledge and the current practice extending from it, the term classical refers to the best resolutions of the most important problems people have confronted as they have sought to live nobly and well. And a final conviction is that the public life is valuable to the extent that it contributes to the private life of every person and that the private life is improved and ennobled only through the public life.

With rights come responsibilities, with freedoms come duties. The one finds its complement in the other. The public life and the private life are in dynamic reciprocity with one another, just as are the past and the present, the architectural and the urban, and the civil and the religious. Understanding how that is so and trimming one's actions in accordance with that knowledge is surely more important than charting the wayward movements of the Zeitgeist or adhering to its "influence."

ENDNOTES

1. See for example "Adam and Eden in Post Modern Chicago," *Threshold: Journal of the School of Architecture,* University of Illinois at Chicago, I (1982), 102-119; and "Towards a New (Old) Architecture," *Modulus 16 (The University of Virginia Architectural Review)* (1983), 78-97.

2. See for example "The True American City," in *The New City: The American City,* University of Miami School of Architecture, II (1993-94), pp. 8-25.

3. See "Architecture and Democracy, Democracy and Architecture," *Democracy and the Arts,* ed. A. Melzer, J. Weinberger, M. Zinman, Symposium on Science, Reason, and Modern Democracy, Michigan State University, 1994-95, Ithaca and London (Cornell University Press: 1999), 73-91.

THOMAS GORDON SMITH: One of the most delightful remains from Hellenistic antiquity is the Choregic Monument of Lysicrates. It stands in an archaeological clearing at the center of the Plaka in Athens. The structure was built as a monumental base to support a now-lost bronze tripod won by a young man as the trophy for a theatrical competition in 334 BC. His proud and wealthy parents exalted this victory by constructing a marble structure to not only raise the bronze on a pedestal, but to create an elaborate and, as it turned out, lasting architectural paean to poetic triumph.

Athough the diminutive structure is insignificant compared to the size or civic importance of the Parthenon, or the Temple of Zeus Olympus, the architectural refinement of its planning and detail have attracted historical attention and architectural emulation since 1750. The square base supports a cylindrical tower surrounded by six engaged columns with unique Corinthian capitals. The number of columns is divided in half to culminate in a three-pronged finial covered with intertwining acanthus leaves and stalks which provided the rests for the tripod.

The capitals are particularly beautiful variations on the Corinthian theme. This type had been invented less than one hundred years earlier, when Kallimachus was inspired to fabricate a new capital type on his way past the cemetery of Corinth. The stately Lysicrates capitals have a first range of small tongue-like leaves below florid acanthus leaves pinned-in by rosettes. Bouncy cauliculi, or tendril stalks, do the job of supporting the diagonal horns of the abacus above. The columns support an Ionic entablature.

James Stuart and Nicholas Revett worked in Athens in the early 1750s, measuring and drawing Greek monuments. They focused on the Lysicrates monument to make detailed presentations of a classical architecture whose proportions and refinements challenged many conceptions of the Vitruvian-Palladian legacy. Their first volume of 1762 did not present the Parthenon or the Erectheum. Instead, a series of minor structures were featured, such as the Tower of the Winds, the Propylon to the Roman Agora (both of Roman date), and the now-lost Ionic temple on the Illusis River (possibly burnt for lime). In addition, the gem of the Choregic Monument of Lysicrates was published in minute detail. Thus, for the first

serious European presentation of Greek architectural models, a group of small and idiosyncratic buildings were proposed as new norms. Subsequent volumes of *The Antiquities of Athens* would present the Parthenon and its sculpture in great detail, but the first neo-Greek structures in England were garden pavilions in the form of the Tower of the Winds and the Lysicrates Monument. Consistent with the paradigmatic approach developed since the Renaissance, these buildings and their individual elements were used to formulate a new canon of classical architecture.

The first generation of American-born architects included William Strickland and Robert Mills. They created the first articulate Grecian buildings in the United States around 1820. They preferred the medium of the Doric type, based on the Temple of Hephestos located above the Agora in Athens. Around this time, several examples of the Lysicrates Corinthian were also made. It was not until 1830, however, that the severe, often abstracted, Doric was used in contrast to the ebullient Lysicrates Corinthian. One could almost say that there was a twenty-year fad in the United States for the Lysicrates type of Corinthian, from 1830-1850. In 1832 Strickland used the Lysicrates type as freestanding columns around the apse of the Merchant's Exchange in Philadelphia. He adapted the whole Choregic monument to become a lantern set atop the radial structure. A decade later, Strickland created a stone, eight-columned version of this beacon instead of a dome atop the Tennessee State Capitol on the acropolis of Nashville. The structure was completed on the eve of the Civil War.

New York was another city where enthusiasm for the Lysicrates column was pronounced. Extant structures like the disheveled La Grange Terrace of 1832, near the Astor Place station, retains four of its original nine townhouses which have continuous porticos of Lysicrates columns cut from Westchester marble.

From this period onward the Lysicrates capital was used as an expression of Corinthian elegance in exterior and interior applications throughout the United States. Though Schinkel in Germany, Briullov in Russia, and Inwood in London had used the type, it achieved its most pervasive use in the United States in public buildings, hotels, and houses until about 1850. Thus, an exquisite but obscure monument in Athens was rediscovered and promoted to represent the refined side of American Republicanism during the first half of the nineteenth century.

FIGURE 4: The Choregic Monument of Lysicrates, Athens, 334 B.C..

FROM THE OFFICES

When selecting the featured architects for this year's Professional Portfolio section, it was clear, based on the quantity and quality of the work submitted, that classical architecture has not just been re-born in America, it is taking its place among respected twenty-first century architecture. In a "modern" culture where society's values revolve around technology, service, and convenience; the new, the fast, and the never-been-seen attracts the most attention. Notwithstanding the entertainment value of movies, personalities, the Internet, and sometimes even buildings, we must ask ourselves if it is enough to simply be entertained. What in life presents a challenge to us? In regard to architecture and design, the editors of the Professional Portfolio section were heartened to find inventive solutions in the following projects. All are noteworthy for their bold existence in spite of the style of the times, or even because of it.

Success is not measured by the same standards in every situation, as the problems to resolve are often greatly varied. Challenges faced by architects are two-fold: those relating to design, and others dealing with practicalities, such as cost or the particular demands of a client. In this portfolio, the architects have addressed their work with a conscious, rigorous referral to traditional and vernacular architecture. Solutions of this nature significantly differ from the self-referencing buildings and products typical of signature architects; or conversely, the generic cookie-cutter architecture that gives the onlooker little clue to where they might be. Naturally, every architect struggles with the issues intrinsic to building—architectural language, sensitivity to context, choice of materials—but all represented here share a common attitude about the value of beauty, propriety, and sustainability. These are the end results of good design, whether it is a pedestal, a church, or an entire community.

Modern classicism does embody the spirit of the times. It embraces and promotes many of the ideals valued in our society. Invention, originality, and individualism characterize the architects presented here. Not only have they incorporated modern technology into their designs and responded successfully to higher demands of service and convenience, but they have also created objects, buildings, and communities that will remain respected and cherished long after any "entertainment value" has vanished. The challenge in architecture and design today is not about being the newest, most technologically advanced product or structure available to the public. Nor should design be about creating something so different that most people find it unrecognizable and impossible to understand. Instead, the challenge is to build and design with a purpose and cause greater than its own end. —M.P., C.G., P.G., M.D.S.

FOLLOWING PAGE: American Society of Landscape Architects Centennial Celebration Poster. Rendering by Craig Farnsworth.

This image was created to commemorate the selection of 20 medallion sites by the Illinois ASLA Fellows and broaden public awareness of the ASLA centennial year. From the beginning of the project, the artist/landscape architect was committed to a design that would be restrained and elegant. The transparent medium of watercolor subtlety conveys historical information as well as the nuances of Midwestern regionalism and the native landscape.

The medallion sites are represented in the grid design recalling the settling and patterning of the Midwest, as are the Illinois state flower, tree, nickname, and motto for Chicago. The layering of messages extend beyond commemoration to education.

The medallion itself is designed in a classical motif and rendered with a weathered bronze patina to suggest that the sites will remain important hallmarks of the profession long into the future. The sites shown on the left are from the Chicago suburbs and downstate regions and are arranged in a north-to-south pattern. The City of Chicago and Cook County sites are represented on the right. All the parks selected from the Chicago Park district are shown collectively to emphasize their interrelationship as well as to provide a break in the grid of the overall design.

The poster has been well received by both the professional and general public in Illinois and the upper Midwest. It has played a key role in publicizing the medallion program and other initiatives related to the centennial. Lastly, the image has successfully recognized the medallion sites in a manner that is deferential to their status and inferential to their place in the larger regional landscape.

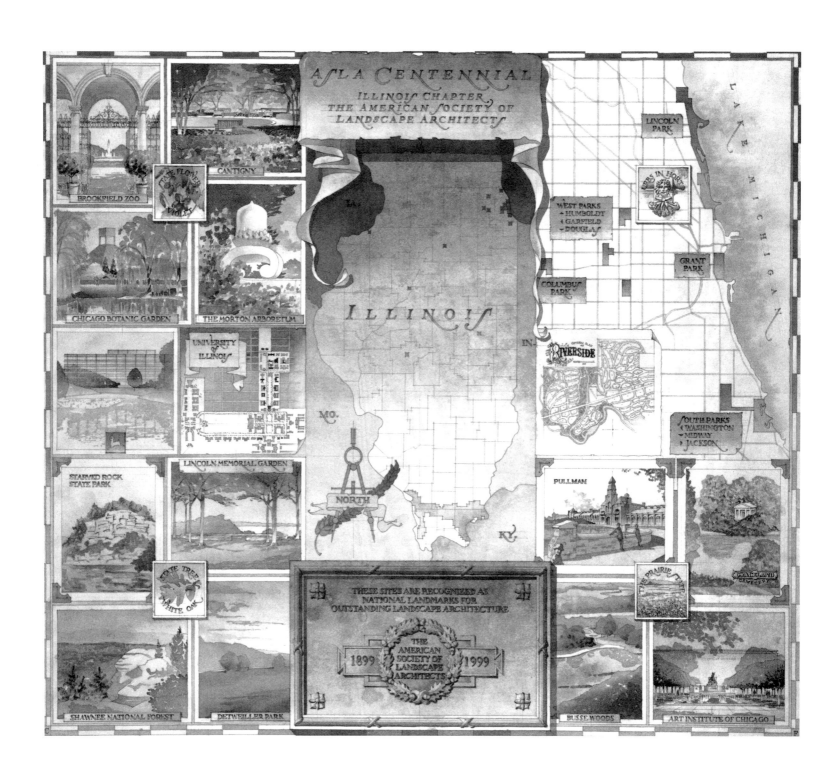

THE I'ON COMPANY
CHARLESTON, SOUTH CAROLINA

I'On, located five miles north of Charleston, South Carolina, is a planned neighborhood reminiscent of early Atlantic coastal towns such as Savannah and Beaufort. Filled with tree-lined streets, gardens, and finely crafted homes, I'On is perfectly sited in a natural landscape characterized by marshes, oaks, green vistas, and lakes. Nationally recognized in the field of traditional neighborhood development, I'On was recently granted a Best Community Award in the Nation by the National Association of Home Builders.

In a period of American suburban development, often equated with the destruction of nature and the loss of identity, I'On adheres to a growth management strategy that is strengthened by careful planning and building practices. Fundamental to this philosophy is the goal of establishing balanced relationships, between nature and the built environment, or between architects, builders, and residents. As a result, new growth in the shape of homes and civic spaces become beneficial, not overwhelming. Unlike conventional subdivision developments, the I'On Company subscribes to a small set of simple guidelines, more suggestive than restrictive, that focus on proportion, materials, building placement, and craftsmanship. Called the I'On Code, it is intended to help create beautiful and picturesque streetscapes, and consequently ensure home marketability. The code assists with future development by placing emphasis on skilled architects, builders, craftsmen, and subcontractors working together to build a high quality traditional neighborhood.

The architects of I'On, in an effort to create a community rooted in character, beauty, and sustainability, rely primarily on traditional American urban planning models, and the classical and vernacular architecture of the Lowcountry region of the South. The proportion and order of individual buildings and their relationship with the community as a whole are carefully considered. Fundamentally, I'On is a group of neighborhoods composed of an interconnected network of streets and blocks that encourage a variety of housing types, a commercial center, and preserved civic spaces.

Details of traditional Lowcountry architectural elements, such as porches and balconies, windows and shutters, entry and door design, fences, walls, and gates are all mindfully designed and constructed. Well-planned civic spaces, beautifully crafted architecture, and preservation of the natural environment all facilitate this community's bright future.

ABOVE LEFT: Typical streetscape at the I'On community.

ABOVE RIGHT: Front view of a typical house. Here, the porch serves as a semi-public room, mediating between the house and the street.

BOTTOM: Partial view of the I'On masterplan.

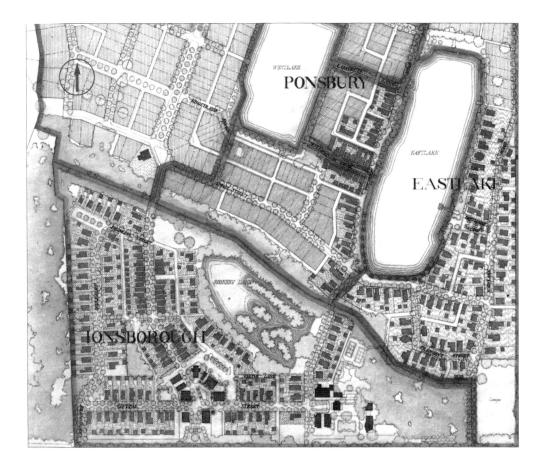

DAVID THOMAS MAYERNIK,
ARCHITECT & PAINTER IN
ASSOCIATION WITH STUDIO CONZA

PROJECT TEAM:
DAVID THOMAS MAYERNIK
STUDIO CONZA: MARCO CONZA,
PIER ANGELO REALINI, DAVIDE LOCATI

Based upon premises found in the traditional European village model, the new master plan for TASIS responds to the current planning needs of the school with an architectural philosophy rooted in history and cultural continuity. Oftentimes, the planning of new academic buildings in existing historical contexts results in poor spatial relationships between buildings, usually at the expense of successful open, green spaces. The challenge at TASIS is one of preserving character and of harmonizing old and new forms of architecture in a manner that adds beauty to the campus and to the way of life found there.

Referencing the architectural plans of university towns such as Bologna, Oxford, or Eton, one can clearly see that schools and towns have had a long and intertwined history. The new master plan for TASIS and its first realized building, The New Gymnasium, considers the synergy between the academic institution and the larger community beyond.

The new gym building, situated between a dormitory and the library, is pivotal on the campus both functionally and architecturally. It accommodates the requirements for various types of athletic, performance, and educational facilities that includes an international standard basketball court with seating for 400, dance performance spaces, music practice rooms, a commons room, and a computer server room. Exteriorly it preserves the memory of the original gymnasium in type and spirit and provides a spacious piazza.

Overall, the new master plan for TASIS strives architecturally to provide an environment for it students and places equal importance on the spaces between buildings as on the buildings themselves. Architect David Mayernik has provided TASIS with a holistic perspective of a nurturing community on a multitude of levels.

BELOW: Watercolor perspective view of the TASIS master plan, D.T. Mayernik.

VIEW OF THE TASIS MASTER PLAN

ABOVE: Watercolor analytic of the TASIS master plan, D.T. Mayernik.

TOP RIGHT: Interior view of the New Gymnasium.

MIDDLE RIGHT: View from the upper loggia and piazza.

BOTTOM RIGHT: Entry detail from a public stair.

KEN TATE, ARCHITECT
MADISONVILLE, LOUISIANA

PROJECT TEAM: KEN TATE, JOHN GAUDET,
M.J. IRANTALAB, KEITH PITRE, RALPH MAISEL

Set in the uptown district of New Orleans between Audubon Park and the edge of the Tulane University campus, Audubon Place is one of New Orleans' last remaining private, gated boulevards. Dating back to the late nineteenth century, the boulevard was conceived as a park-like street that would be solely for the use of private residences. The original site developer in 1893 was George Blackwelder and Company who envisioned an urban plan that would encompass about twenty-eight private residences built along a landscaped avenue. The avenue had a prominent terminus of two stone lodges connected by large iron gates. Determined in the early stages of planning, the building lot sizes were roughly one hundred feet by two hundred feet, which are still the respective sizes used there today. The architectural character of the Audubon Place streetscape is resonant of the various classical traditions found in New Orleans, particularly that of the opulent French tradition, the Ecole des Beaux-Arts, and of a regional eclecticism influenced mainly by French Creole architecture. Covered porches, second story arcades and galleries, deep projecting eaves, columns, arches, and pediments are typically found on the grand homes throughout the street, all of which attest to the very classical origins of Audubon Place's building tradition.

The first twenty-eight houses of Audubon Place were completed before 1910; there have been however, several building campaigns throughout the century. Designed by Louisiana architect Ken Tate, #25 Audubon Place is currently under construction and will complete the last vacant lot on the boulevard, as the former house on the lot was demolished. Keeping true to the predominantly classical architectural tradition, Ken Tate looked to the purity of the Venetian villa as a suitable and unpretentious architectural paradigm. Drawing from various Palladian villas of the Veneto region, Tate composed plans and elevations which are harmoniously proportioned and of simple and clear geometry. Also characteristic of Venetian villas, the larger public rooms, such as the family room, and the living and dining rooms, are situated on the ground floor and open out onto a loggia or terrace with views of the garden beyond. The secondary and ancillary spaces, such as the kitchen, library, and laundry are also located on the ground floor. The three main bedrooms, not including the guest bedroom and the master suite, are all accessed through the family room—the central core of the second floor. The master bedroom suite and the guest suite are privately accessed off the main stair or the back stair. Each bedroom looks onto either a private garden or a terrace.

The circulation through the house is tightly planned so that one might travel through rooms rather than through undefined corridors. Tate's depiction of the classical villa type is also expressed through the simplicity of the interior architecture. Planer walls with shallow moldings, heavy wooden ceiling beams, and stone lintels and floors create an expression of understated elegance throughout the house.

The exterior elevations are a well-balanced composition of architectural elements that express a logical and unified whole. There is particular attention to the expression of openings and classical detailing that is highly regarded by the community of Audubon Place. Remarkably, Tate's house is a fine example of contemporary residential urbanism combined with a classical thematic architectural tradition that is all but lost today.

BELOW: Front Elevation as seen from the boulevard.

OPPOSITE PAGE, TOP: Interior perspective sketch of family room looking towards the loggia.

OPPOSITE PAGE, BOTTOM LEFT: First floor plan showing garden pavillion and garage.

OPPOSITE PAGE, BOTTOM RIGHT: Second floor plan.

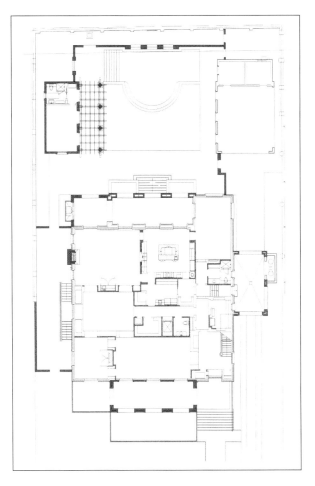

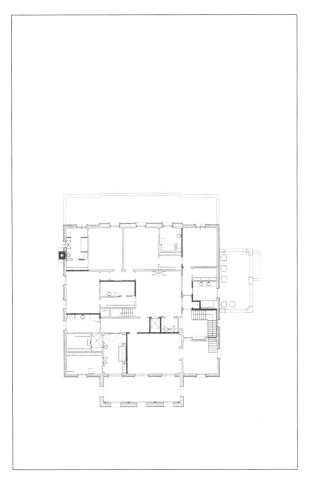

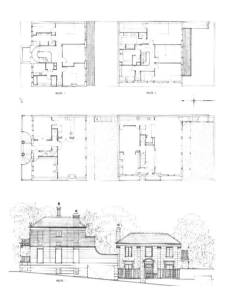

LEFT: View of front porch of house numbered one.

ABOVE: Plans and elevations of houses numbered one and two.

BELOW: Elevation of house numbered one.

CHRISTOPHER DOYLE ARCHITECTS
MELBOURNE, AUSTRALIA

PROJECT TEAM: CHRISTOPHER DOYLE, PAUL JONES, NEIL WILSON, DENIS JOACHIM

These two houses, completed in 1998 in the historic inner suburb of South Yarra, echo the smaller simple houses of the colonial period that previously characterized the area. The attempt was to recapture much of the detail that has given the area its personality and distinction, and to redeem the tenuous historic links with this young city's stirring past.

The building tendency in historic Australian districts is usually a replication of the prevailing architectural language/style, or for object buildings with little sensitivity to the context. The problem of replica solutions of previous Australian architectural styles is in the lack of architectural invention, which produces anemic likenesses of Victorian, Italianate, Boom Style, and Queen Anne Buildings. These types of houses were largely decorative, eclectic, and stylistically connected to a specific historic period. This is understandable when one considers that Melbourne was predominantly developed in the late nineteenth century.

An alternate view is to rediscover the simplicity of earlier unpretentious domestic structures. These houses by Christopher Doyle Architects show clearly that their own integrity was based upon purpose and proportion. This outlook reflects an ideology that seeks to avoid unnecessary complexity, and that discovers creative solutions firmly based on a simple traditional outlook. The gentle austerity of early Melbourne, prior to the extravagant expansion that followed the economic boom of the gold rush greatly influenced the feel of these houses.

The sloping corner site has been divided into two allotments, with the house entrances separated on to different streets. Living spaces and bedrooms are focused onto the north facing open terraces, and vehicles are conveniently housed under the terraces. Urban gestures such as covered porches and visually permeable fences connect to the street while still maintaining a certain amount of privacy. It is encouraging to discover projects such as these houses, particularly in Australia where there is limited interest in traditional architecture.

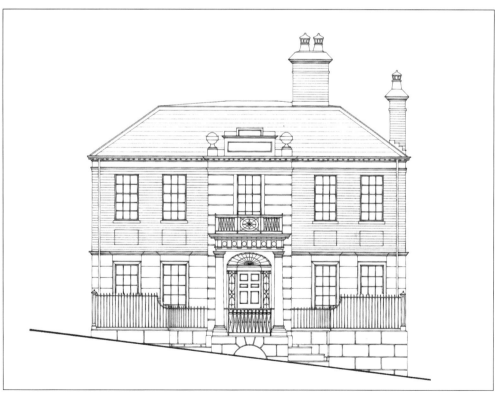

GEOFFREY GRAHAM, DESIGNER
MICHAEL DALY, DALY & SAWYER
CONSTRUCTION; BUILDER,
TAMARA CALABRIA; SCOTT MELROSE
& ASSOCIATES, LANDSCAPE DESIGNER

AS-BUILTS PREPARED BY:
NED COLLINS HOME DESIGN
PERMIT SET PREPARED BY:
CARL MCCANTS, MC3 DESIGN
PRELIMINARY CONCEPTUAL WORK PERFORMED
BY VICTORIA PARTRIDGE AND GRETCHEN STRAUSS

75 Sowell Street rests on the smallest lot in I'On, a new and celebrated neighborhood in Mount Pleasant, South Carolina. This exemplar of urban design maintains simple and universal tenets of planning and building character. The owner of this house, a member of I'On's development team, chose this lot in order to demonstrate how a comfortable home and garden can be built on a small and constrictive lot.

The house faces directly south, taking advantage of the region's prevailing breezes and optimum orientation toward the winter and summer sun. The zero setbacks of I'On help to define the street edge despite the relatively small size of a home like 75 Sowell Street. A deep porch and high ceilings allow for sunshine in the winter and shade in the summer.

To reinforce a sense of grandeur within a small house, the design emphasis was placed on simple progressions of hierarchy from the public to the private areas. From the pavement, one proceeds into a raised and modest courtyard; climbs to a commodious porch, then crosses to the recessed alcove, and finally arrives into the foyer and stair hall. The experience continues on the interior with careful attention to material and details throughout. The success of such a building strengthens arguments for the availability of traditional architecture in suburban developments.

TOP: Photograph of 75 Sowell Street as realized.

BOTTOM LEFT: Detail of shutter.

BOTTOM RIGHT: Porch detail at N. elevation.

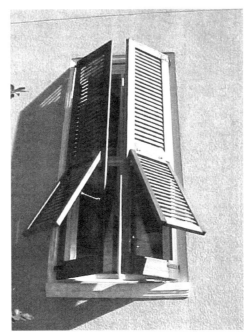

DAVIS ARCHITECTS,
BIRMINGHAM, ALABAMA

PROJECT TEAM:
T. PAUL BATES, LARRY BURDETTE,
NEIL E. DAVIS, LAURIE HEWELL,
ADRIENNE RETIEF, MELVIN SMITH,
DAVID STURGIS, BRIAN YOUNG

When Samford University approached Davis Architects with plans to renovate an abandoned dormitory into classrooms and offices for its divinity school, they envisioned a new and updated facility that would be architecturally as aspiring and inspiring as the institution's mission and program. Additionally, the Beeson School of Divinity wanted a chapel that would be an instructive space for students, employing symbolism, artistic expression, and liturgical architecture rooted in the reformed Christian tradition.

Samford University's campus was originally designed and built in the 1950's, with an architectural language reminiscent of traditional Georgian American architecture. The main quadrangle features two prominent buildings that terminate the north and east axis. At the north, opposite the gated main entrance to the campus, is a three story brick and stone library, complete with a bell tower. To the east is Reid Chapel, a traditional protestant "hall church" flanked by two brick arcades and crowned with a wooden steeple. With the site of the new divinity school terminating the west axis of the main quadrangle, the most difficult challenge rested in creating a new building of distinction that would complement rather than compete with the existing structures. The new design, inspired by Palladio's Il Redentore in Venice, resulted in a domed chapel with a nave, featuring a copper clad exterior shell surmounted by a golden cross.

Creating a cohesive marriage between the existing U-shaped dormitory and the new chapel however, presented many problems. The building's understated relationship with the main quadrangle prompted two dramatic alterations which impacted the specific location of the chapel. The U-shaped plan of the building was reversed by first removing the center connector on the east facade, and secondly, by

CLOCKWISE: Detail of entablature; Interior view of nave looking towards the dome; Exterior view of the chapel main entrance.

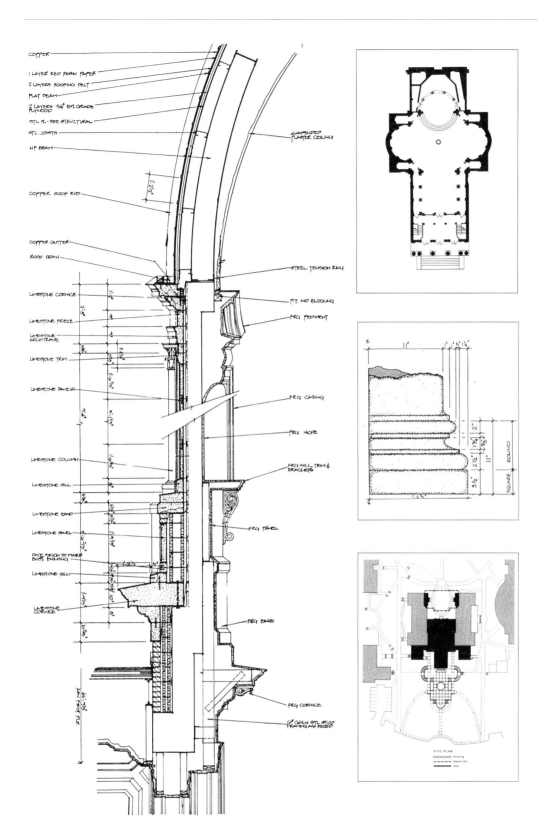

replacing it with the new chapel on the west facade. This preserved the two side wings with their elegant Doric porticos, provided a formal entrance to the building from the street, and created a more intimate courtyard with views overlooking the quadrangle.

The interior design of the chapel focuses primarily on issues of character, ornament, and symbolism as a declaration of faith and as a means of learning. The clients, realizing that institutions of distinction are often housed in buildings of distinction, saw the new chapel as an opportunity to establish a presence not only on the physical campus of Samford University, but also throughout the theological circles they traveled. Ecumenical in nature, the Beeson School of Divinity felt it important to consider the traditions of various Christian denominations during development of the iconographic program. The chapel is filled with literal and symbolic artistic representations of the Christian faith, crafted and painted by Christians from different denominations across the world. Imagery such as the four gospels in the pendentives, the "Cloud of Witnesses" fresco on the dome, and scenes from the life of Christ in the side apses, all enrich the worshiper's complete experience of the space. Classical detailing such as hand-carved pews, elaborate marble paving, and ornamented Corinthian columns and entablature add beauty and elegance to the space. Though used primarily for private instruction to seminary students and open to the public only for Sunday church services, the chapel has quickly become one of the most popular spiritual and architectural destinations on campus.

FAR LEFT: Wall section through dome.

NEAR LEFT, TOP: First floor plan of chapel.

NEAR LEFT, MIDDLE: Detail of corinthian column base.

NEAR LEFT, BOTTOM: Site plan showing phases of demolition and new construction.

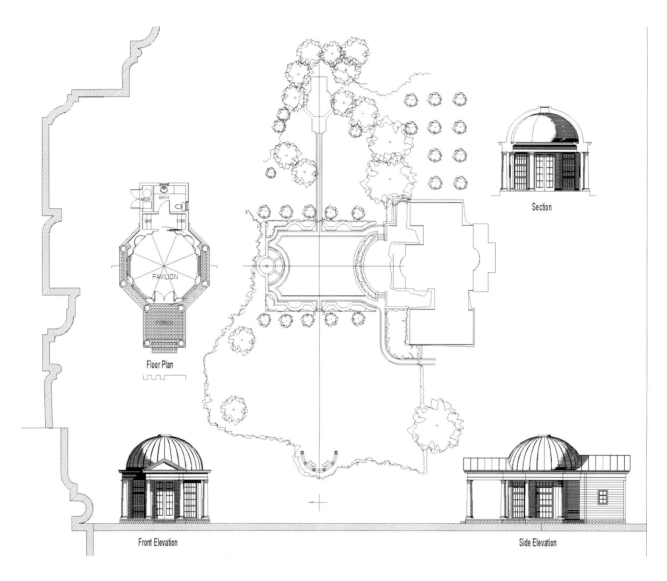

Section

Floor Plan

Front Elevation

Side Elevation

APPLETON & ASSOCIATES, INC.,
SANTA MONICA, CALIFORNIA

PROJECT TEAM: MARC APPLETON,
STEFANIE BECKER, ERIK EVENS,
CYNTHIA GRANT, KIM KARCHER-NELSON,
PATRICIA SKERMONT-POHRTE

Built as a freestanding structure located in the formal gardens surrounding a Georgian revival residence, the Writer's Pavilion draws upon several influences to create the "romantic vision" often associated with traditional garden architecture and design. Responding to a program that calls for one room to serve as a library and study for a retired professional turned writer, the design takes advantage of its garden setting and creates an architectural event within the natural landscape.

Thematically, the pavilion references the Pantheon in Rome. With a centralized plan, front portico with classical orders, and a domed ceiling with an oculus, the pavilion takes these elements and transforms them from the grandiose into the intimate. Taking inspiration from Jeffersonian America and Monticello, the circular plan becomes an octagon, and niches are translated into triple hung windows, providing views out into the garden and blurring the distinctions between indoor and outdoor spaces. English pavilions and follies of the eighteenth and nineteenth centuries also influence the character of the building. The esoteric and playful nature of the Writer's Pavilion is best seen inside, where the domed ceiling is customized with a painted mural and the interior entablature is carved with a quote selected by the writer. Furthermore, the diminutive scale, delicacy, and playfulness of its forms all work together with the surrounding gardens to create an idealized place of contemplation seemingly far away from the pressures of the modern world.

HABLINSKI ARCHITECTURE,
BEVERLY HILLS, CALIFORNIA

PROJECT TEAM:
WILLIAM HABLINSKI, PARTNER IN CHARGE
RICHARD MANION, PARTNER
DAVID HOGAN, PROJECT MANAGER
NASER ELAYYAN, PROJECT ASSISTANT

The Italianate residence of some 16,000 square feet incorporates imagery drawn from fifteenth and sixteenth century villas in Northern and Central Italy. The program, for a movie studio executive and vinophile, called for a formal layout of public and private family spaces elevated with a grand and prominent facade to establish a presence on the street front. The extensive use of loggias was an integral part of the design; planned both as outdoor entertainment spaces and for future enclosed family functions.

The front facade is punctuated with a central two-story Palladian portico that provides shelter from the California sun to arriving guests. A pair of arcaded loggias and galleries span apart from the central portico to opposing corner towers, reminiscent of Italian Castelli with large, irregular quoining. The garage elevation, taking its cues from the Late Renaissance and Counter-Reformation Italian churches, is composed of a central pediment flanked by large scrolls and obelisks. This elevation's subdued prominence lends an air of dignity to the garage court, which functions as the main family entrance in this suburban locale. The rear facade takes full advantage of the expansive views of the adjacent canyon and the city of Los Angeles with a double height portico. The rear garden, overlooking the canyon beyond, has a central lawn flanked by the balanced masses of the sunken swimming pool and tennis court.

The main construction materials include plaster walls and run plaster pediments, mahogany doors and windows, cast stone columns and mouldings, and Roman roof tiles. Construction began in early 1996 and was completed in 1998. The house is currently being furnished.

TOP: Aerial view of front façade.

MIDDLE: Perspective view of Back Court.

BOTTOM: Perspective view of Entry Court.

ROBERT A.M. STERN ARCHITECTS, NEW YORK, NY

PROJECT TEAM: MELISSA DELVECCHIO, THU DO, MARK GAGE, KELLY GREESON, ALEX LAMIS, JEFFERY POVERO, ROBERT A.M. STERN, MEI WU, SUSI YU, PAUL ZEMBSCH

Winning the commission for the New Public Library of Nashville and Davidson County presented Robert A.M. Stern Architects with two challenging opportunities: first, to provide Nashville with a technologically state-of-the-art library worthy of its architectural history; and secondly, to help revitalize the city's diminished downtown civic center. Naturally, the design process incorporated both concerns and resulted in a classically proportioned building that enhances the downtown cityscape and generously serves as an extension of the civic realm.

With an unapologetic departure from popular post–World War II library design, with its endless open stacks of books, low ceilings, and nondescript office building aesthetics, the new Nashville library centers around a complex sequence of public spaces that guide patrons to clearly defined destinations. These spaces include the Main Entry Lobby, the skylit Grand Stair, the Great Reading Room, and the Garden Courtyard. Also, careful attention has been given to the siting of the library, with its important axial relationship to William Strickland's Tennessee State Capital. The formal and grand spaces of the library are all located on this axis, and one's progression through these spaces culminates with its spectacular views back to the State Capital.

TOP: Rendered perspective view of the Garden Courtyard.

BOTTOM: North-South section showing the sequence of the library's major public spaces.

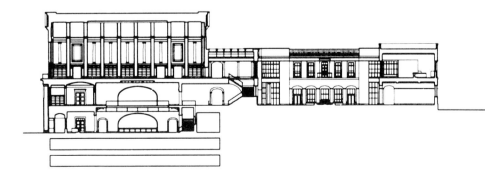

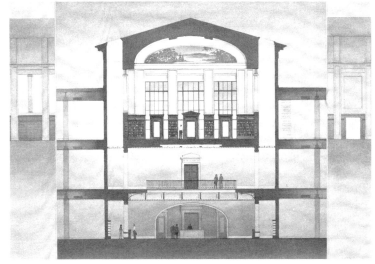

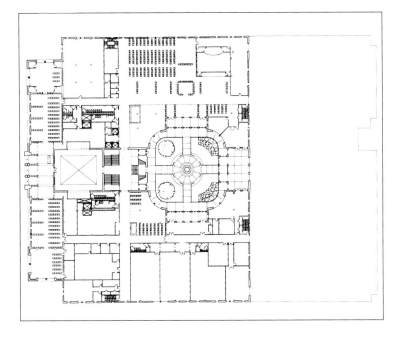

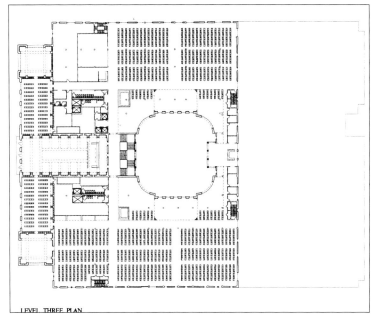

LEVEL THREE PLAN

Conceptually, the new library is rooted in traditional attitudes that view the process of learning as both an individual's private pursuit of knowledge as well as the experience gained from social interaction. Though clearly influenced in spirit by the great public libraries of New York and Boston, and without omitting the need for uplifting spaces for community and repose, Stern's new library design successfully incorporates these principles along with those that encourage easy and direct public access to research materials. For example, open stack areas are located around the formal public spaces and in contrast, also provide quiet eddies of informal seating. The sensitivity given to both concerns has resulted in a library that provides the necessary functional qualities that today's society demands, without sacrificing the aesthetic qualities that are instrumental in registering the experience of learning in the minds of library patrons. Acknowledging that library buildings are repositories of both knowledge and culture, the new Nashville Public Library is distinct in its unique contribution to the city of Nashville. The library is a center for learning as well as a link to the classical tradition of a city known as the "Athens of the South."

TOP LEFT: Rendered elevation detail of the Library entrance.

TOP RIGHT: Rendered section detail showing the Main Entry Lobby and the Great Reading Room.

MIDDLE LEFT: Third level plan cut through the skylit Grand Stair and the Great Reading Room.

MIDDLE RIGHT: Second level plan cut through the Main Entry Lobby and the Garden Courtyard.

HILTON-VANDERHORN ARCHITECTS,
GREENWICH, CONNECTICUT

PROJECT TEAM:
DOUGLAS VANDERHORN, PARTNER IN CHARGE
DANIEL J. PARDY, PROJECT ARCHITECT
DAVID DUNN

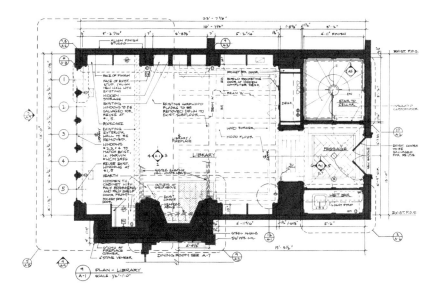

Originally constructed in the 1920s as a Tudor Style home, this private residence underwent a series of additions and renovations including a remarkable oak library and a quaint sub-terrain wine cellar. Intended to retain the feel of a traditional Manor House, the library was paneled with quarter-sawn oak that was used to enrich the space and bring unity to the entire scheme. The newly designed fireplace is punctuated with a limestone surround that, in turn, receives an intricate hand carved frieze of Gothic Quatrefoil detailing. In order to resolve the issue of transition from the main entry hall to the library, a passage was proposed. This passage allows for the integration of a hidden wet bar and a circularly winding stone stair.

The stair graciously takes one to the next highlight of this residence, the wine cellar. The wine cellar features a spectacular tasting room in a space that is vertically culminated with a plaster groin vault. This vaulting results in a series of arches that house the oak cabinetwork. The cabinetry rests on a fieldstone wainscot and a stone tiled floor. The intricate metal strap hardware and chandelier were also custom designed to bring the entire space together.

TOP: *Plan of Library.*

MIDDLE: *View of Library towards wet bar and winding stiar. Note mantle and surround details.*

BOTTOM NEAR RIGHT: *View of Wine Cellar.*

BOTTOM FAR RIGHT: *Fireplace Elevation.*

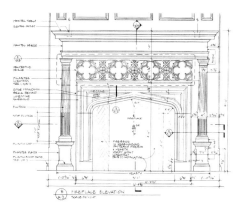

CHARLES WARREN ARCHITECT,
NEW YORK, NY

PROJECT TEAM:
CHARLES WARREN, ANDREW BALLARD

Charles Warren's Wilder House is the final building that completes a residential block on Tupelo Street in the town of Seaside, Florida. Drawing from regional antecedents from Florida and the Caribbean, which are very much a part of the local color of Seaside, the Wilder House's architectural language is of the classical tradition. This is best demonstrated by the architect's use of the Doric order, expressing a monumental and civic tie to the public realm on the exterior. Additionally, the tectonic arrangement of heavy brackets, deep eaves and large roof overhangs reference the regional origins of the existing vernacular tradition.

The Wilder House's typology, based on the classical villa, is clearly described in the elevations that are comprised of a series of visually distinct masses; the main pavilion of the house, the kitchen pavilion, the observation tower, and the cylindrical screened porch. As a result of the variation in height and scale, Warren composes a harmoniously balanced asymmetrical composition on the exterior elevations that distinguish the Wilder House from its surrounding context.

The footprint of the Wilder House is based on specific site requirements determined by Seaside's codes and a very restricted building lot size. Warren's response to the limited lot size was to utilize vertical circulation by creating two main axes both initiating from a double height entry hall. The principal axis found on the ground floor unites the entry hall to the cylindrical porch towards the back of the house and leads to the sea. The second is a vertical axis also from the entry hall that spirals up and out to the top of the observation tower. It is these two axes that bind the plan to the elevations, and allow for a well-conceived and interlocking play of forms. Taking note of Wilder House's plans and elevations, one will find rigorous geometric ratios throughout, which is very much a part of Warren's idea for creating a villa by the sea.

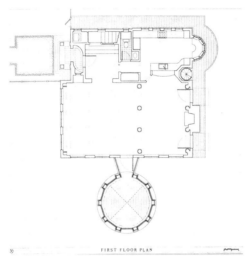

FIRST FLOOR PLAN

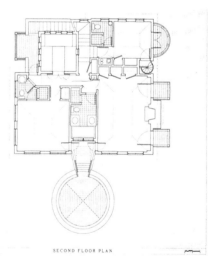

SECOND FLOOR PLAN

TOP: *Elevation of the house from the sea. Photo by Peter Aaron/Esto.*

MIDDLE LEFT: *First Floor Plan.*

MIDDLE RIGHT: *Second Floor Plan.*

BOTTOM: *Interior view of the living room looking towards the dining area. Photo by Peter Aaron/Esto.*

FAIRFAX & SAMMONS ARCHITECTS,
NEW YORK, NY

PROJECT TEAM: RICHARD SAMMONS, PROJECT
ARCHITECT, PHILLIP DODD, CHRISTIANE FASHEK,
NINA STRACHIMIROVA, SETH WEINE

This recently built house is sited on 50 acres and stands on an isolated hilltop in northwestern Connecticut. The ruggedness of the site led the architect to look at Scottish precedent for the character of the design. Much of the detail and proportions follow the work of Scottish-Palladian architect William Adam, author of the *Vitruvious Scoticus* and father of the more famous brothers Robert and James Adam.

The residence, with its simple geometry and latent baroque flourishes, provides a strong presence from a lofty prospect that overlooks Litchfield County. Over-sized handmade brick with broad, buttered joints are paired with stone quoins, stone columns, and a heavily detailed cornice. The roof is laid with thick green slates, purposefully diminishing in size as they near the ridge. Though the house is relatively small, less than 3,500 square feet, it has the stature of a county manor house that has forever been a part of the landscape.

TOP: Entry Façade with formal garden court in foreground.

RIGHT: Orangerie, sited on the garden court opposite the Entry Façade.

BELOW: Entry Façade rendered by Christiane Fashek, watercolor, 1997.

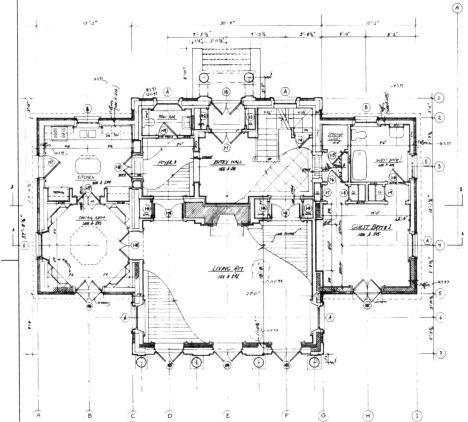

TOP LEFT: *Entablature and Finial detail of Entry Façade.*

TOP CENTER: *Column detail from West Façade. Also note the Flemish bond and brick diapering.*

TOP RIGHT: *Detail of Living Room woodwork, and ornamental frieze.*

BOTTOM LEFT: *Floor plan.*

BOTTOM RIGHT: *Interior overdoor with paneling.*

CAMERON CAMERON & TAYLOR,
DESIGN ASSOCIATES,
BROOKLYN HEIGHTS, NEW YORK

DESIGN TEAM: RICHARD CAMERON,
VICKY CAMERON, ANDY TAYLOR,
DINO MARCANTONIO (COMPUTER MODELING
AND RENDERING)

The University of Toronto's Convocation Hall was built with funds donated by alumni in 1910 to hold graduation ceremonies and for large lectures and concerts. It is the principal ceremonial building at the University, and every graduating student receives his or her degree from the Chancellor here. It is located on the diagonal axis of the central formal space, King's College Circle, of the St. George Campus of the University. It is the only neoclassical building in the central ensemble. The modernist medical sciences building stands nearby and the other college buildings around the circle are gothic and Romanesque-revival in nature.

Cameron Cameron & Taylor was asked to create a setting for honoring donors to the University in the annular entry foyer, immediately inside the front doors of the hall. This space had not been completed in the original building campaign and over time has deteriorated into a mean hallway filled with wastebaskets and covered in notice boards. This project proposed a new interior to fit into the existing space that would bring architectural order to it, create an appropriate entry to the building, and establish a framework for the names of the donors.

The space is articulated with a series of anta-pilasters that carry elliptical arches and that frame the bronze name-plaques of the donors. At each end of the curving hall, two rotundas were introduced to terminate the hall, and to create formal entries to the stage area for University dignitaries during convocation ceremonies. Here the orders change from pilaster and engaged half columns to full Greek Doric columns embedded in the wall in Michelangelesque fashion. Each of the rotundas has a shallow dome and artificial oculus carried on a compressed entablature. Bronze pendant chandeliers ring the space, and a series of niches was created for busts of major figures in the history of the University.

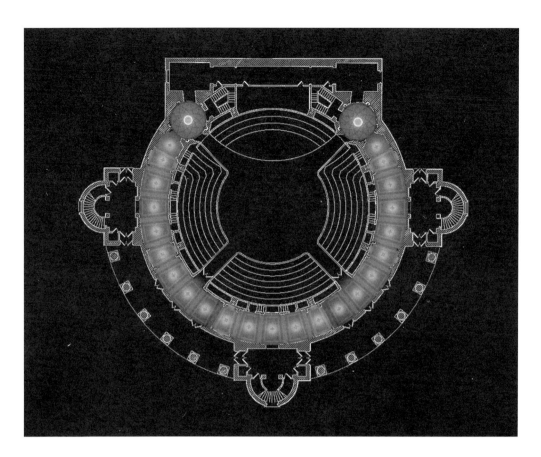

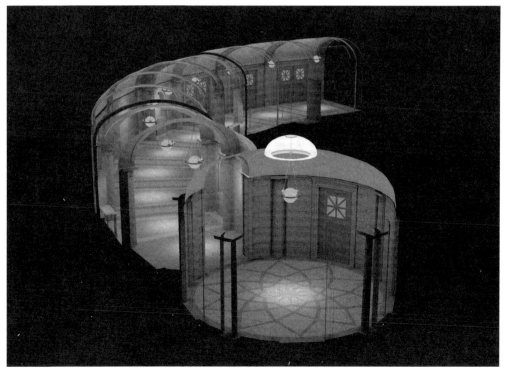

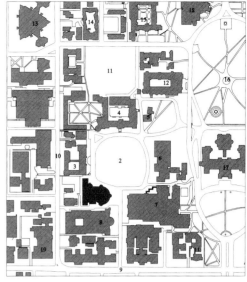

UNIVERSITY OF TORONTO PLAN

LEGEND

1 CONVOCATION HALL
2 KING'S COLLEGE CIRCLE
3 KNOX COLLEGE
4 UNIVERSITY COLLEGE
5 OBSERVATORY

7 MEDICAL SCIENCES
8 SANFORD FLEMING
9 COLLEGE STREET
10 ST GEORGE STREET
11 PLAYING FIELDS

12 HART HOUSE
13 ROBARTS LIBRARY
14 MASSEY COLLEGE
15 TRINITY COLLEGE
16 QUEEN'S PARK

17 |
18 |
19 |

OPPOSITE PAGE, TOP: Plan showing proposed lobby.

OPPOSITE PAGE, BOTTOM: Ariel view of the computer model of the proposed lobby.

TOP LEFT: View of the computer model of the Chancellor's rotunda.

LEFT: View of entry showing bronze name-plaques.

BOTTOM LEFT: View of Convocation Hall from King's College Circle.

BOTTOM RIGHT: View of the existing lobby.

ABOVE: Plan of the St. George Campus, University of Toronto.

The proposal was designed and modeled in AutoCAD 14 and rendered in Lightscape.

THE GLAVE FIRM, RICHMOND, VIRGINIA

PROJECT TEAM: JAMES M. GLAVE, MORGAN PIERCE, DAVID RAU, WILLIAM TALLEY, MEGAN MCIRVIN

Completed in 1895, The Jefferson Hotel in Richmond, Virginia epitomizes the classical grandeur of the Gilded Age. Designed by Carrere and Hastings—by then already renowned for their design of the Ponce de Leon in St. Augustine, Florida—The Jefferson captured the regal character desired by affluent travelers of the period and continues to provide an elegant atmosphere today. In the century since its completion, the hotel has undergone a series of modifications, most notably those resulting from a devastating fire around 1902.

As this structure entered its second century of use, the owners sponsored a competition to reconfigure the motor court and to add an indoor swimming facility. After detailed research and numerous concepts, The Glave Firm arrived at a design solution that returned the sense of grandeur to the arrival sequence, taking cues from the urban context as well as from other Carrere and Hastings landmarks, in particular the Plaza Hotel in New York City. Dominated by a new urban plaza, which marries the building to the streetscape, the design incorporates a striking entrance pavilion and fountain that augments a much needed importance to the arrival areas. Additionally, the reintroduction of an axial relationship into the entry sequence adds a degree of finish commensurate with that of the original structure and reinforces the architectural significance of this building.

TOP: *Plan of motor court and hotel at the entry level.*

MIDDLE LEFT: *Elevation of The Jefferson Hotel with The Glave Firm addition.*

MIDDLE RIGHT: *Plan at the second level.*

BOTTOM: *Section of The Jefferson Hotel with The Glave Firm addition.*

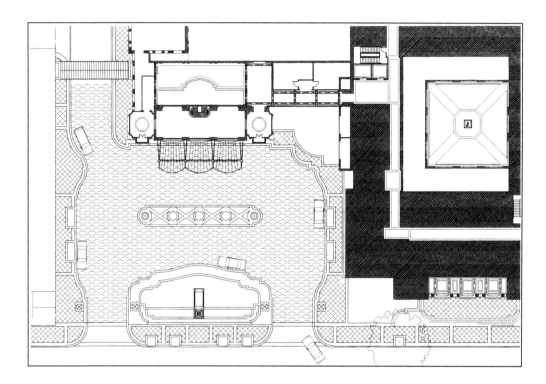

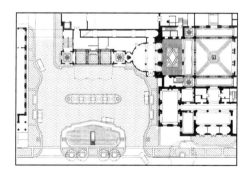

THE FRANCK PARTNERSHIP
NEW YORK, NEW YORK

PROJECT TEAM: MICHAEL FRANCK, CHRISTINE
FRANCK

In comparison to the preceding projects, the magnitude of this commission is of a more moderate nature yet the attention to detail is the same. The program called for the design of a pedestal on which would rest a previously purchased bronze sculpture. The sculpture itself is a gracious piece by Cordelia Hepburn that incorporates three blissful muses raising a shallow basin to the sky. In keeping with the tri-partite nature of the sculpture, the pedestal was designed with three slender accentuated facets that relate to each of the muses. Transition from facet to facet was gracefully achieved through the use of larger concave paneled faces. The pedestal is of hand carved limestone by Chris Pellettieri. Together, the bronze statue and the limestone pedestal create a charming focus for this garden setting.

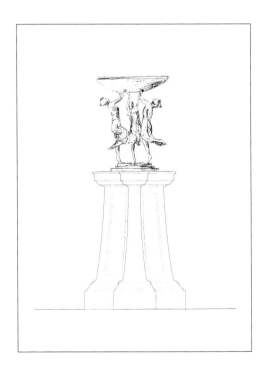

ABOVE: Elevation of pedestal and sculpture.

RIGHT: View of pedestal and sculpture.

KOENIG DISTILLERY & WINERY

THE NEW IDAHO VERNACULAR

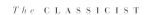

Deep in the heart of fruit country in the Snake River Valley of southwest Idaho, surrounded by blue mountains and countless rows of orchards, sits a modest distillery and winery that redefines the existing building tradition of rural agricultural architecture in the American northwest. With his design, architect Greg Koenig demonstrates his desire to convey a sense of permanence to future generations. His broad vision coupled with the inclination towards the expression of traditional architecture unites the themes of industry, craft, technology, and agriculture to create this family-run enterprise. In Koenig's opinion, there was not a suitable prototype in his region for wineries and agrarian buildings that satisfied his criteria. His goal was to develop a "true working building," as Koenig calls it, totally unlike the average side of the highway office-park with short lifespans and limited functionality. Instead he set out to create a building type that utilizes the best that modernity and technology has to offer while also embracing traditional methods of building construction. Koenig believes that his building is a vast improvement on the rural agricultural buildings that are being built throughout the Northwest; that it challenges what he has termed the "Idaho vernacular"—buildings that look like temporary shed-like industrial building facilities constructed of wood or metal.

The original idea for the Koenig distillery and winery was developed during Koenig's fifth year thesis project while studying architecture at the University of Notre Dame. Initially, the project was simply conceived as a distillery with ancillary buildings but later evolved into an elaborate planning project that incorporated multiple building types for both public and private use, all of which were associated with the distillation process and other communal functions. The 1994 thesis project laid the ideological foundations and formal footprint that would eventually be realized as the Koenig Distillery and Winery. One of Koenig's main themes, consistent throughout his thesis, was the idea of creating flexible building types that would ideally prove functionally adaptable over time. This strategy was best demonstrated in the plans of each building—and though much of the original design went through a number of changes, the building adaptability concept remained.

Greatly influenced by Tuscan and Austrian farmsteads and the rural hill towns throughout Italy, Koenig modeled his masterplan on the typical arrangement of rural farm buildings that share a common centralized courtyard. In Koenig's thesis plan, the courtyard of the complex is surrounded by five auxiliary buildings to be used for commerce and public functions. Clearly resembling a small rural village, the buildings that distinguish the formal aspects of the private realm from those of the public, include a small inn for housing the employees and visitors, a residence for the groundskeepers, and a private residence for the owners of the distillery.

Koenig's cultural heritage and his education abroad further influenced the sensibility of his early vision. Koenig, who is Austrian-American, had the opportunity to live in Austria where he observed traditional distillation processes used by his family there. The thesis design allowed for utilization of these "Old World techniques" and knowledge of traditional metal and woodworking lent him greater understanding of character and detailing in vernacular architecture; crafts that Koenig feels are nearly obsolete today. This early interest in construction and craftsmanship contributed to Koenig's decision to study architecture.

Additional research for the project occurred while traveling with his family to Italy and Austria where Koenig studied and documented regional models of farmstead buildings and wineries. He observed that most rural architecture in Europe, unlike many traditional American barns in the Northwest, were constructed of heavy load bearing masonry, which led to a more permanent life span. Koenig therefore chose a limited palette of building materials that would formulate the character of his thesis architecture, and also become the precedent for the realized winery and distillery building today. Stone, heavy timber, stucco, and terracotta tiles were specified as the basic vocabulary. Koenig felt strongly about expressing exactly how buildings were going to be crafted—idealistic and bold, Koenig's thesis won a design award from the school of architecture.

After Koenig graduated from Notre Dame, he returned to Idaho, where he and his family decided to make his thesis vision a reality. Koenig believed that by combining "new world" farming techniques, that is, American style farming, with the traditional practice of distillation, he and his family could create a world class product. Within one year, after the purchase of a 70-acre, nearly abandoned farm, the Koenigs planted new fruit orchards and vineyards. An irrigation system was constructed on the site, thus completing the initial phase of

programming and planning the Koenig Winery and Distillery. From 1995 to 1999, Koenig, his family members, and close friends have worked together to create a sustainable working agrarian complex that is meaningful today and will have an impact on future generations.

From the beginning, the thesis masterplan served as a guide enabling Koenig to map out several building campaigns that would occur over time. The first building to be developed had to be selected from the original five and was designated to become the main fermentation and distillation hall. Koenig chose what he calls the tower building and by the fall of 1996, Koenig completed a full set of construction documents in preparation for construction the following May. Ultimately, deemed too large and costly for the first building phase, Koenig

found himself once again reworking his original design ideas and postponed the anticipated construction date.

Starting again, Koenig selected a smaller rectangular building to develop—a more modest building that flanked the tower building in plan to the Northeast. The building was to incorporate both of the fermentation and distillation functions, bottling and equipment storage, and include a visitor's area with a tasting room open to the public. All these

---

TOP LEFT: Phase I, Completion of masonry construction of distillery and winery building, South Elevation.

TOP CENTER: Phase I, Completion of all roof framing and interior truss work.

TOP RIGHT: Phase I, Completion of exterior finish work and detailing.

BOTTOM LEFT: Phase I, View of Completed North Elevation.

BOTTOM CENTER: Phase I, Interior view of the Fermentation Hall looking East.

BOTTOM RIGHT: Phase I, Interior view of the truss work in the fermentation hall looking West.

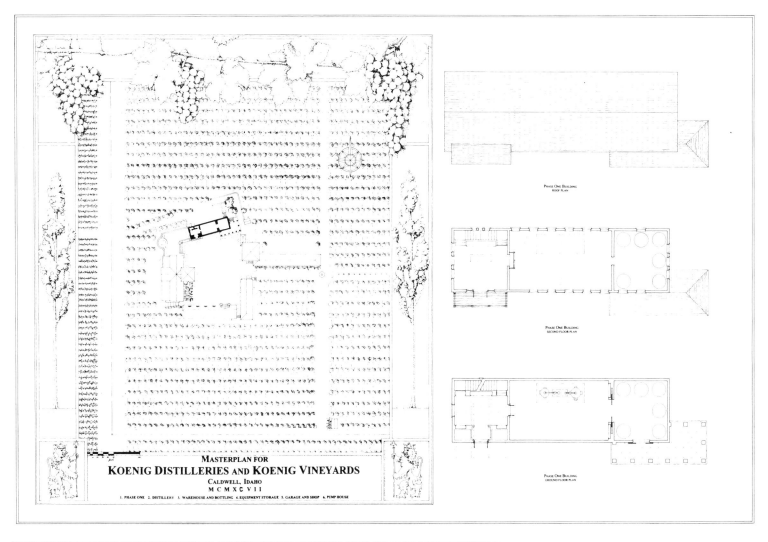

MASTERPLAN FOR
KOENIG DISTILLERIES AND KOENIG VINEYARDS
CALDWELL, IDAHO
M C M X C V I I

1. PHASE ONE 2. DISTILLERY 3. WAREHOUSE AND BOTTLING 4. EQUIPMENT STORAGE 5. GARAGE AND SHOP 6. PUMP HOUSE

PHASE ONE BUILDING
ROOF PLAN

PHASE ONE BUILDING
SECOND FLOOR PLAN

PHASE ONE BUILDING
GROUND FLOOR PLAN

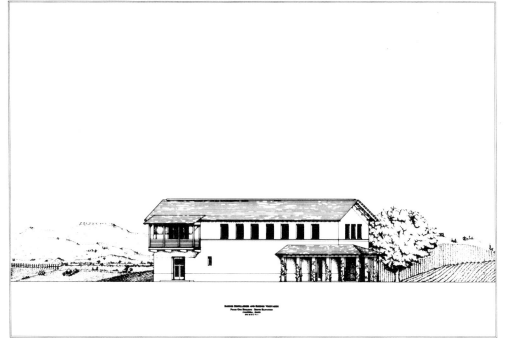

ABOVE: Master plan for Koenig Distilleries and Vineyards with Phase I building plans of ground floor, second floor, and roof plan.

LEFT: South Elevation of Distillery and Winery building.

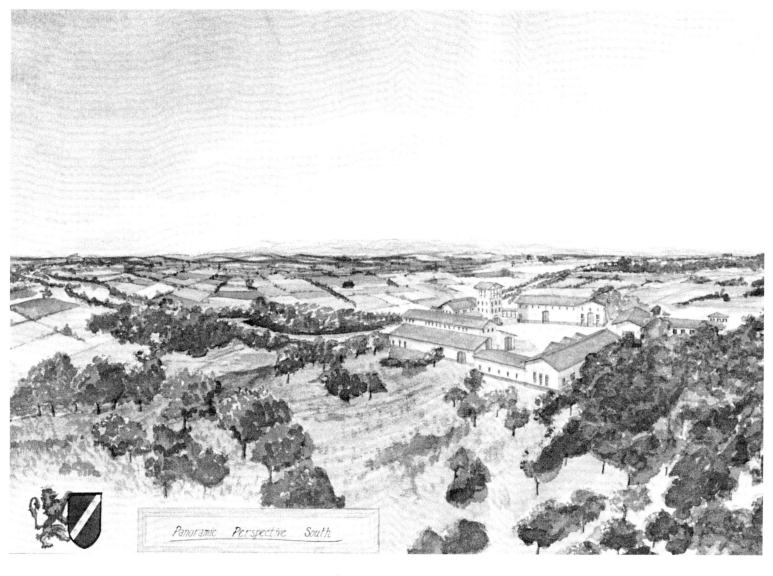

Panoramic Perspective South

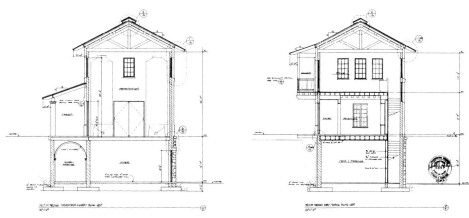

TOP: Panoramic Perspective of Koenig's thesis project, the distillery complex.

ABOVE: Working drawings for the Distillery and Winery building for Phase I: Sections through the fermentation hall and entry & tasting room to the West.

functions housed under one streamlined roof naturally were accommodated by Koenig's initial willingness to have a more flexible building type. He did not want the building to be functionally compartmentalized.

In redesigning the building, its footprint retained the original plan, measuring 22 feet by 80 feet in length, as well as the building's overall proportions. However, because of "real factors" such as climate, material changes, and budget that critically influence a building's design, the character of the building changed from the original thesis scheme. Not surprisingly, the final outcome of the built work is distinguished by the compromises that still allowed Koenig to achieve a well-crafted and uncommonly beautiful debut.

Koenig felt the most conservative approach for minimizing the budget was to diversify the type of building materials used. Originally, the buildings were to be erected of stone with timber detailing, tiled roofs, and deeply overhung eaves. These evolved into buildings assembled with concrete block and cast stone detailing, stucco finish work, and wrought iron, which proved to be significantly less expensive. Koenig did, however, keep a series of nine exposed trusses that span the lofty double-height space in the fermentation hall and are constructed of heavy beams to support the weight of the roof structure. As for the interiors, Koenig relied heavily on his knowledge of metal and wood working from his education in Austria, which is carefully showcased by his choice of limited building materials such as stucco, wrought iron, and pre-cast stone floors. All the attention to detail and craftsmanship, though minimal, is refined and consistent throughout the entire structure, keeping true to Koenig's vernacular model.

Before Koenig finalized the design of the distillery and winery, a friend and colleague from Notre Dame was intrigued by Koenig's building vision and decided in July of 1997 to join him as a designer and builder. David Colgan, a licensed architect with previous construction experience, aided Koenig with clarification of the architectural detailing and overall proportions of the building. By September 1997, they had prepared a full set of construction documents and obtained a building permit. During the fall of that year, Koenig, Colgan, and Koenig's brother Andy commenced building construction. They were fully aware of the tremendous task and huge learning experience for everyone involved but Koenig knew that if he had hired a full construction crew to build his building, the outcome would not achieve the specific attention to detail that he so desired. Looking critically at current methods of building construction and technology, Koenig observed that how one builds and intends to craft a building is the essence of what separates good architecture from the ordinary and lifeless.

So, over a period of nearly two years the building task of Phase One was accomplished. By November 1997 the main excavation and site work was completed along with all the masonry work at the cellar level (which was to contain the winery storage and mechanical area). By April, Koenig began construction on all of the masonry for the upper level of the

building, as well as all of the precast floor slabs, which were finished in July. The nine roof trusses, constructed of heavy timber with metal plate detailing were completed in September. From November 1998 to June of 1999, all of the exterior detailing, cast stone flooring, plasterwork, mechanical and electrical was completed. In July of 1999 the winery and distillery officially opened to the public for business, for tasting and touring.

The Koenig Winery and Distillery, producing about a thousand cases of wine a year, is run by Koenig and his wife. Additionally, the building and vineyards are used as the setting for formal affairs and special occasions for members of their community. It is evident that Koenig's vision does not stop here. Already, future plans have been made to completely build the masterplan that Koenig conceived as a student. He has determined that the next building phase will separate the dual functions of wine making and distillation into two buildings. The tower building he set out to originally build would become the main body of the winery, which in plan flanks the already built distillery. Between the future winery building and the current distillery building, Koenig intends to design an exedra on an elevated terrace that would be used for outdoor public concerts and events. Koenig also hopes to build two more buildings that would be used as a warehouse and bottling area to keep up with their anticipated production increases. A building for equipment storage, a building for a public shop, and a parking garage are also being planned.

Koenig says that in the process of their unique experience, he and his family feel a bit like the pioneers who settled the west. They have made a place in Idaho that is truly theirs; it is a place that was firmly cultivated by the hands and strength of family and friends. Unlike many other industrial agrarian sites and buildings today, the Koenig Winery and Distillery has achieved tremendous success by virtue of its level of design and pure craftsmanship. It is much more than just a working building in rural America. It is a unified and thematic expression working in the broader context of a family tradition and community. Koenig has successfully married together the themes of agriculture and technology, "Old World and New World," into a dignified building in an uncomplicated landscape that would have been impossible without a clear vision grounded in beauty, conviction, and reality. —C.G.

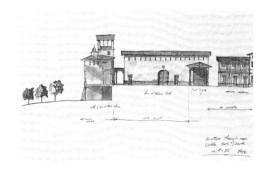

TOP: "Duck's Eye" Perspective of preliminary thesis idea. Image from Koenig's sketchbook.

MIDDLE: Site Perspective of the proposed thesis site view taken from the South. Image from Koenig's sketchbook.

BOTTOM: Site section taken through the main courtyard looking North for thesis idea development. Image from Koenig's sketchbook.

DRAWINGS BY
JOHN BARRINGTON BAYLEY

Initial sketch of a proposal for New York's Columbus Circle. Pencil on tracing paper.

As a student of the Harvard Graduate School of Design in the early 1940s, John Barrington Bayley and his fellow classmates believed they were at the epicenter of the modern movement. While the United States was fighting fascism across the Atlantic in the Second World War, young designers attempted to defeat a perceived fascism in architecture with new building forms and details. Turning a blind eye to the past, students at the GSD charged ahead.

Ironically it was the Second World War that sent Bayley to Europe. While stationed in Paris, Bayley made pilgrimages to the buildings of Le Corbusier around which he had based his studies at Harvard. Initially enamored with his idol's work, Bayley soon grew disenchanted. The buildings he studied and admired for hours in books seemed demure and grim in reality and Bayley began to question the wave of modernism that had carried him that far.

Our barracks were high in Montmartre. Early in the morning we would get on our bicycles and coast down the slopes of the mount to the Opéra, on through the Rue de la Paix, Place Vendôme, Rue Castiglione, Rue de Rivoli, Place de la Concorde and up the Champs Élysées to the Étoile, to arrive at last at our office on Avenue Wagram. There, standing at a French window and staring out at the city over the clipped trees of the Avenue, we deemed the modern movement curious indeed. —John Bayley, "A Personal Account," Classical America, 1971.

Upon his return to the States at the end of the war, Bayley was determined to design more classical buildings like the ones he had seen in Paris. The architectural landscape in the United States, however, was distinctly modern. There was no place for a young classical architect. Eventually, Bayley sought refuge in the interior design firm of McMillen, Inc. There, he thought, he could practice the tenets of classi-

cal design within a room and hope that clients would recognize the beauty of the room and desire houses in the same vein; then clubs and other public buildings. This hope unfortunately did not come to fruition, so Bayley returned to Europe to continue his studies. At the American Academy in Rome from 1947 to 1950 he slowly fell in love with the Eternal City in the same way he had with Paris years earlier. While modernists studied in Scandinavian countries for their sleek housing projects, Bayley was discovering gardens, courtyards, buildings, marble sculptures; all the beauties of Rome. He stayed in Italy for a number of years, collecting and cataloging images of architectural forms that he could reference in the course of his future designs.

Bayley returned to the States in the late 1950s and worked for a modernist architectural firm in New York City. He would stay late, after business hours, and redesign the firm's

Interior elevation of a proposal for New York's Columbus Circle. Pen and ink on tracing paper.

projects for his own sake, using the language of classical architecture but maintaining the modern program. He wanted to express the fact that classicism could be used to compliment the demands of modern life.

Always striving for ways to encourage acceptance of classical art and architecture, Bailey became the founder and first president of Classical America, an organization of classically minded artists and architects that survives to this day. From 1963 to 1972 Bayley also worked with the Landmark's Preservation Commission of New York. And in 1977, he completed his best known work—the masterful addition to the Frick Museum in New York City. His *magnum opus,* the Frick addition demonstrates Bailey's exquisite command of classical architecture and a zeal for the art that is also expressed in his writings, including *Letarouilly's on Renaissance Rome* published by Classical America in 1984.

During the 1960s and 70s the architectural establishment was still under the influence of

Developed sketch of a proposal for Columbus Circle. Pen and ink on film.

Perspective view of a waterfront proposal for Long Island City. Colored pencil on tracing paper.

A design for a corner church on Park Avenue. Pencil on tracing paper.

Two perspective views of a waterfront proposal for Long Island City.

TOP: Colored pencil on tracing paper.

BOTTOM: Pencil on tracing paper.

modernism. John Barrington Bayley practiced at a time when classicism was much more unpopular than it is today. He was in that sense, the precursor of today's classical revival among practicing architects, especially those in New York City. For him, there was no better place to advocate classicism than New York. In his own words:

Classicism belongs in New York, the nation's definitive seat of power. An escape into the past is always in cities in Europe. Here there is no surcease: we face the facts of our time head on. The problems of art and the city will be solved here, and when they are New York will revive as a great and complete metropolis.

As one can see in his sketches, Bayley's proposals for New York City echo his vision. The scale is beyond monumental—almost colossal—befitting Bayley's belief in New York's prominence as a New World capital. The style of Bayley's sketches from this period (1957) is simple, almost cartoonish. It is not aimed at giving an accurate impression of the materials or textures nor is it a study of light, shadow, and mass. Rather, his drawings convey an architectural idea with almost single minded purpose—a circular place at the intersection of several important streets and a park; a hemicycle and a promenade at the water's edge; a window with a view. The idea is always grand and detail yields to the idea that aims at giving man and the city their noblest and most beautiful form.

…Classicism instills a desire for glory because it loves man and nature. And loving them, it attempts to give them their greatest beauty.… For Classicism, the style of glory, the paradigm of art is the human form. —J.B.B.

John Barrington Bayley died in Newport in 1981 at the age of 67. He knew that the defense of classicism would be an uphill battle, but was aware of the invincible ally of time. "The modern movement can't last forever," he said. —M.M., T.M.

A heartfelt thank you to Mr. Henry Hope Reed, Mr. Clark McLain, and our other friends at Classical America for sketches and inspiration for this article. Thanks also to National Reprographics and Jubilee Gallery for their assistance.

VIEW OF WASHINGTON SQUARE FROM AN ENTRESOL APARTMENT   J.B.BAYLEY '57

ABOVE: An apartment on Washington Square Park, NYC. Pen and ink on film.

FROM THE ACADEMIES

Within academic arenas, forums for and debates on traditional and classical architecture are continuously on the rise. Today, many Institutions, historically not known for their classical sympathies, are beginning to offer courses and surveys in classical architecture.

Elizabeth Dowling, professor of Architectural History at Georgia Tech, is one of those trying to expand the ideologies of both her students as well as her institution. In 1998, Professor Dowling introduced the school's first studio on classical architecture at the urging of her students. In the brief essay below, Professor Dowling describes her experience and the development of the course.

In the Spring of 1998, Mark Taylor, a second year graduate student in architecture, expressed his interest in taking a classical design studio. I discussed the issue with our program director and he concluded that classical design was not an appropriate topic for studio length projects for graduate students. Undeterred, Mark enlisted additional graduate and undergraduate students and requested that I organize a special topics elective class to enable students to acquire the knowledge they desired. The course I organized placed great time demands upon the students because I felt they needed not only an introduction to academic information, but also direct application through design. Because of this, the students took on a studio assignment in addition to their regular studio.

I am very familiar with the thorough classical design education available from the University of Notre Dame and the years of study they spend learning and digesting the material. In comparison I felt that a single term offered hardly more than a brush with classical design, but I felt it could serve as an introduction to a discipline with which the students were unfamiliar. Our architecture program at Georgia Tech provides a thorough grounding in architectural history and several of the students had participated in a summer program in Italy that I organize, so I believed that they would have the foundation upon which to build. The students who enrolled were each quite determined to seek out alternatives to the traditional modernist design approach offered at Georgia Tech.

The course teamed lectures with visits to both offices and job sites of local classical designers. The course texts included Tzonis and Lefaivre, *Classical Architecture: the Poetics of Order;* Robert Adam, *Classical Architecture;* and Nathaniel Curtis, *Architectural Composition* (1926). Additional readings on a variety of subjects ranged from architects such as Lutyens, Palladio, and Serlio, to design issues such as symmetrical versus asymmetrical composition.

Many Atlanta architects supported the concept of the class and generously opened their offices to my students, or explained their design approach during site visits. The architects that contributed were Norman Askins, Gene Surber, Clay Ulmer, Bill Harrison, and Keith Summerour and all are involved in both new construction and historic preservation.

To apply the knowledge gained through lectures, readings, and site visits, the students were required to draw at full scale an order of their choice and to design their personal villa. The building type of villa was selected to allow the greatest freedom of personal expression. Because this second studio work was essentially doubling the design demand of each of these students, the presentation requirements were left up to the individual. The designs were developed through the term and were reviewed each week by the entire class. The resulting work was of an extremely high quality and most students reported their only difficulty lay in their desire to work on these projects rather than their regular studio projects. The work produced by Jonathan Lacrosse and Greg Harrell are displayed in this section.

ABOVE: Jonathan Lacrosse, Detail. Pencil on paper, Georgia Institute of Technology. Spring, 1998.

ELECTIVE STUDIO PROJECT: "Villa LaCrosse." Elizabeth Meredith Dowling, studio instructor. Spring, 1998.

ABOVE: Jonathan Lacrosse, Elevation. Pencil on paper.

ELECTIVE STUDIO PROJECT: "Greek Ionic." Elizabeth Meredith Dowling, Studio Instructor. Spring, 1998.

LEFT: Greg Harrell, Elevation Detail. Pencil on paper.

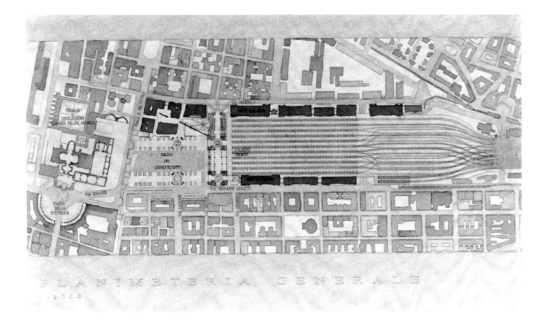

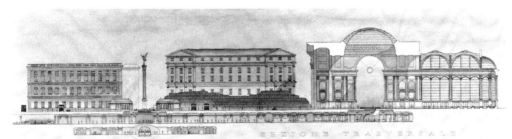

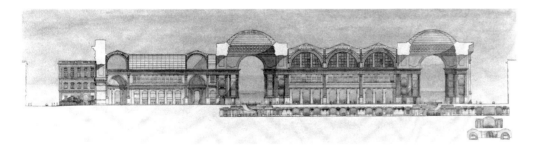

THESIS PROJECT: "Il Stazione Termini Terzo." John Blatteau, thesis advisor. Spring, 1998.

John Blatteau, known for his commitment to classical architecture in both the academic and professional fields, took the role of thesis advisor for this project that develops a replacement scheme for the Termini train station in Rome, Italy. The current Termini station, near the historic center of Rome, is the transportation core for the entire city. The city's bus and taxi systems, as well as two metro lines, all converge at this location. Master's student Marco DiDominico proposes that the current station be replaced with a classical scheme to create an appropriate balance between contemporary technology and the ancient setting of its surrounding. The Third Terminal Station, or La Stazione Termini Terzo, incorporates the typology of the ancient Roman baths as precedent for the design. The new station would create a new gateway to Rome, one that is representative of the spirit of the "eternal city."

TOP TO BOTTOM:

Site plan. Water color on paper.

Section. Water color on paper.

Section. Water color on paper.

Front elevation. Water color on paper.

Artwork by Marco DiDomenico.

THESIS PROJECT: "A Counter Proposal to the Millennium Master Plan and Design for the Manchester Victoria Opera House" by Phillip Dodd. Robert Amico, thesis advisor. Spring, 1999.

In June 1996 the Irish Republican Army detonated a 3,300 pound bomb in the center of Manchester—the largest explosion in Britain since World War II. The devastation inflicted upon the infrastructure of the city provided a unique opportunity for the enhancement of the city's architectural and cultural heritage. By modeling itself on the ideals of the traditional city, this counterproposal aims to create an improved environment in which Mancunians can fully participate in city life. The design by Phillip Dodd for a new Opera House is intended to act as an urban catalyst that reflects the aspirations of the city's urban renaissance, while fitting seamlessly within the existing eclectic dialogue of Manchester.

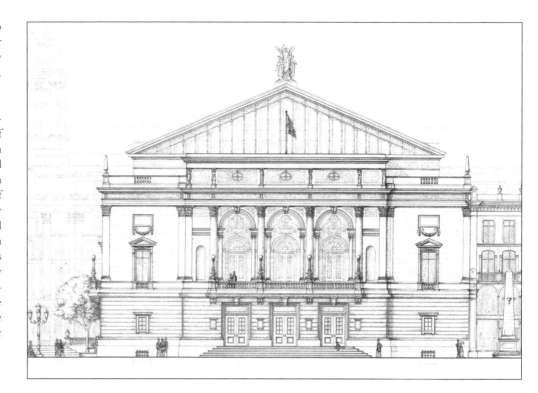

TOP: Phillip Dodd, Front elevation. Ink on paper.

RIGHT: Phillip Dodd, Master plan. Ink on paper.

FIFTH YEAR PROJECT: "A Bridge on the Ohio River" by Erin Christensen. Michael Lykoudis, critic. Fall, 1999.

This bridge was designed to connect historic Madison, Indiana and Milton, Kentucky. The bridge allows vehicular, pedestrian, and light rail traffic to enter Madison at its commercial spine. The mixed use of materials creates a dialog between both craft and technology and mediates the scale differences between the two towns.

TOP: Erin Christensen, Plate. Watercolor on paper.

FIFTH YEAR PROJECT: "Secretary and Chair" by Ayako Kawashima. Robert Brandt, critic. Fall & Spring, 1999.

ABOVE: Ayako Kawashima, Furniture. Mahogany.

THESIS PROJECT: "The Buffal-O-Asis: truckstop and visitor center" by John Carlo Blanchet-Ruth. Michael Lykoudis, thesis advisor. Spring, 1999.

RIGHT: John Carlo Blanchet-Ruth, Perspective. Color pencil and chalk on paper.

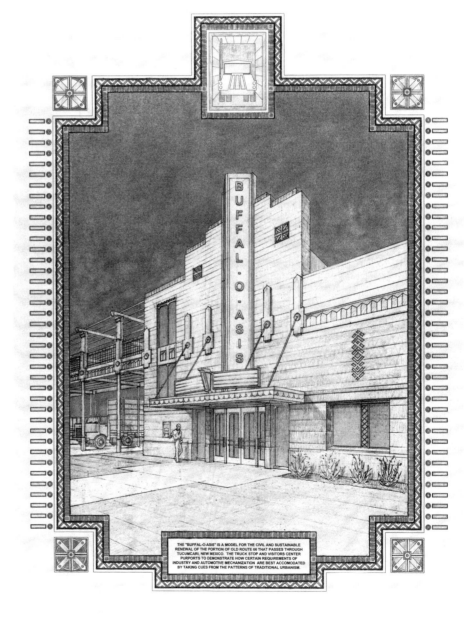

FIGURES 1 and 2: Dana K. Gulling, Notre Dame, Front and Back elevations. Watercolor on paper.

FIFTH YEAR PROJECT: "Meig's Field Airport." Michael Lykoudis, University of Notre Dame, and Robert Pilla, University of Miami, critics. Fall, 1998.

Two schools of architecture, The University of Miami and the University of Notre Dame, have had long-standing shared attitudes towards traditional architecture and urbanism. Students from both institutions were given an identical architectural problem that was the vehicle for the exploration of several themes. The studio program was organized by Michael Lykoudis, who spent alternate weeks at Notre Dame and Miami. In Miami, during the opposite weeks, Robert Pilla reviewed the student's progress.

The project was the design of a new small airport terminal building for Meigs Field in downtown Chicago. It raised interesting questions: Can industrial use such as that of an airport be compatible with civic life? Does this use prescribe that the building's character be derived solely from an industrial vocabulary? How can principles of urbanism tie an object building into the landscape?

These students were pressed upon by these seemingly opposing concerns and established criteria. First, that the typological principals of traditional urbanism and architecture could play a mediating role in resolving the opposing and mutually exclusive positions of civic art and industrial infrastructure. Second,

modern materials and methods, as well as scales of economy, could reveal new ways of understanding traditional forms. Two paradigms were given as possible precedents: The Villa Gamberaia in Settignano and Isola Bella on the Lago Maggiore. Villa Gamberaia offered an organizational solution for a system of buildings and garden around an axial area such as a runway. Isola Bella demonstrated how the natural, rustic, vernacular, and classical (and by extension the industrial) forms of architecture might be connected.

The process that each school's students employed had both common and divergent approaches. Both Miami and Notre Dame's students are well versed in typology, historical precedent, and drawing skills. Both schools' students began with organizing the site along the principles of the Italian villa. The site, for both studios, was approached with clear figural qualities through clearly defined streets, blocks, and squares (interpreted as gardens, groupings of buildings, or series of interconnected spaces). The common site planning approaches diverged somewhat as the project developed into the architectural realm. Both groups used traditional interpretations of building typology, though some of the Miami students integrated principles of the free plan while relying on finite platonic geometric volumes for spatial clarity and character. For structural typologies, both groups engaged a full range from the traditional load-bearing to contemporary tensile tectonic elements.

Of the Miami students, Diosdada Perrera's building (FIGURE 4) employed free plan organization within geometric masses; a substitute for traditional typology that facilitated the change to the industrial. The use of a glass and steel curtain wall contained the figural space of the main hall, and the dialogue of the massive bearing walls retained typological clarity and ensured durable construction. Alain's Bartroli's proposal (FIGURES 5 AND 6) stretched the limits of the quantity of openings in a load-bearing wall, maximizing the horizontal rhythms. His scheme borrowed much from Louis Kahn's tectonic explorations and offered some insights towards a reconciliation of some of Kahn's reductivist forms with more traditional applications.

Of the Notre Dame Students, Damian Samora's project (FIGURE 3) replaced vernacular structural elements with contemporary materials—steel, glass, and masonry—in a tempered and picturesque composition. The scheme took the limited free plan approach of McKim Mead and White's Casino at Narragansett Pier where each part of the principle mass of the building was an identifiable building type with an open interior plan. Dana Gulling's design (FIGURES 1 AND 2) engaged a dialogue between the proportions and rhythms of the masonry walls and openings, and their steel and glass counterparts to maximize the transparency of the upper floor and engaging the site visually. The shallow pitch of the roof and the deep overhangs retained the typological durability of traditional construction while using contemporary materials to their maximum advantage.

FIGURE 3: Manuel Damian Samora, Notre Dame, Elevations. Watercolor on paper.

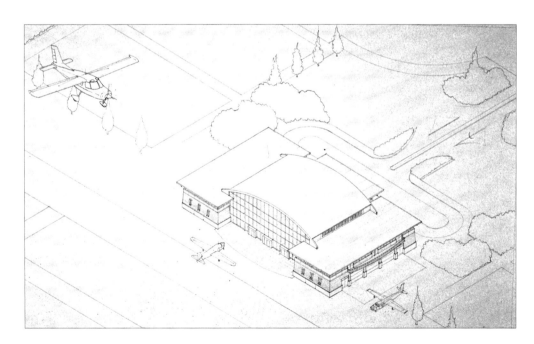

FIGURE 4: Diosdada Perrera, Miami, Axonometric. Pencil on paper.

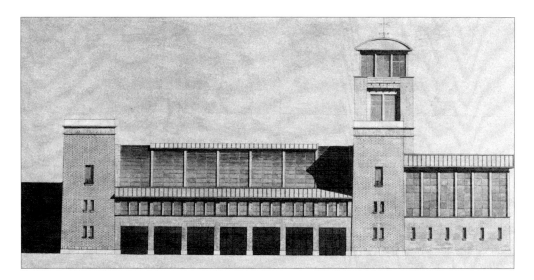

FIGURE 5: *Alain Bartroli, Miami, Front Elevation. Coffee on paper.*

In the end, both studios realized there is much middle ground between the contributions of modernism and traditionalism. If one can draw any conclusions about the pedagogy of Miami and Notre Dame it is that the Miami students were more comfortable integrating notions of free plan and planometric organizations. The Notre Dame students were more interested in transforming the structural typologies that affected the character of the building, than the hierarchical relationship between the parts. Both studios were firmly rooted in traditional urban typologies. Both succeeded in offering convincing proposals of how can we mediate between industrial and civic use. Both groups successfully explored how principles of urbanism can tie an object building to the city. The commonalties and differences of two schools were very welcome, as it is in the dialectic between the two approaches where the discoveries about new ways of looking at architecture are to be found. —M.L.

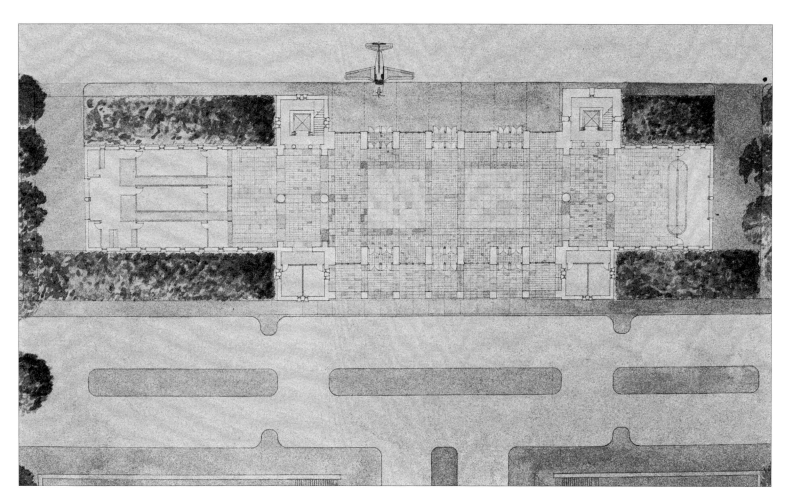

FIGURE 6: *Alain Bartroli, Miami, Plan. Coffee on paper.*

SUMMER PROGRAM IN CLASSICAL ARCHITECTURE: "Classical Architectural Rendering: The Traditional Methods." Andy Taylor, instructor. Summer 1998, 1999.

This summer school class introduces students to the traditional architectural rendering media of India ink, and the various ways in which it can be used to create wash drawings and studies of architectural subjects. Among the topics covered are India Ink wash, understanding shades and shadows, simulating texture, sheet composition, materials, and the production of an analytique.

As part of a team, students are required to measure a building and produce a set of measured drawings from which they then create an analytique. This is then rendered throughout the six-week program. In each example, the measured drawing and analytique project was related to the subsequent design project, thus enabling the student to learn about the design project site before beginning the design project.

LEFT: Orestes del Castillo, Analytique of Merchant's House Museum. Ink wash on paper. Summer, 1999.

ABOVE: Nadine Dacanay, Analytique of Prospect Park Entrance Pavilion. Ink wash on paper. Summer, 1998.

ABOVE: Todd Furgason, Perspective of Flat Iron Building. Charcoal on paper. Summer, 1999.

RIGHT: Norimasa Aoyagi, Sketch of statue. Charcoal on paper. Summer, 1999.

SUMMER PROGRAM IN CLASSICAL ARCHITECTURE: " Drawing and perspective sketching." Leonard Porter, instructor. Summer, 1999.

This course is an introduction to the drawing of objects leading to sketching of architectural subjects in perspective. Observation of architectural subjects and proficiency in hand drawing are important goals of this course, allowing the student to achieve better work during the design studio of the summer school. The class covers simple shapes, complex shapes, shade and shadow, one- and two-point perspective, leading up to exterior perspective sketching.

SUMMER SCHOOL DESIGN STUDIO:
"The Design of a Market Structure for Grand
Army Plaza, Brooklyn." Steve Bass and
Christine Franck, instructors. Summer, 1998.

On Wednesday and Saturday of every week, a
small group of produce trucks pulls into the
wedge of pavement between Grand Army Plaza
and Prospect Park in Brooklyn. While the
occurrence of this market is positive for the
civic and commercial life of Brooklyn, the current physical reality of this market is neither
pleasant nor dignified. The general exposure to
the elements, including the traffic in the circle,
prohibits this market from being the public
experience that it could be. This design studio
explored the building of a structure to house
the market which would shelter it from the elements and provide an appropriate setting.

_TOP RIGHT: Nadine Dacanay, Bay details for the
Grand Army Plaza market design. Ink on
vellum. Summer, 1998._

_BOTTOM RIGHT: Nadine Dacanay, Site plan
and front elevation for the Grand Army Plaza market
design. Ink on vellum. Summer, 1998._

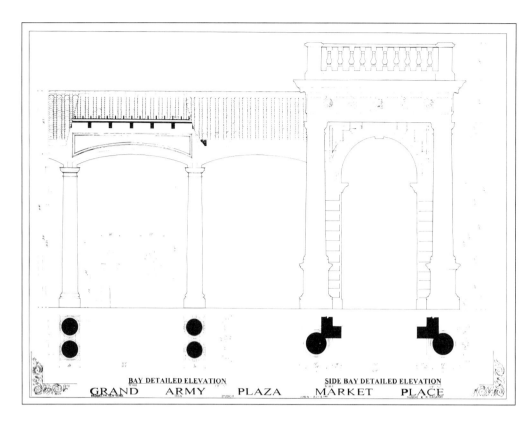

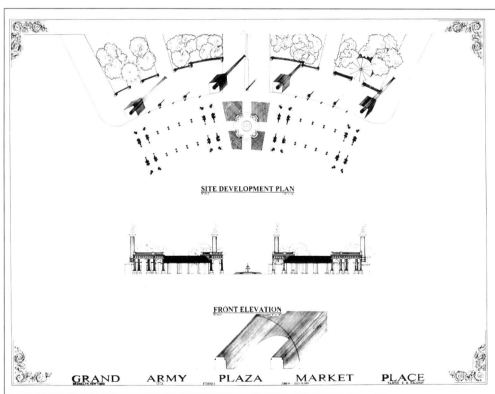

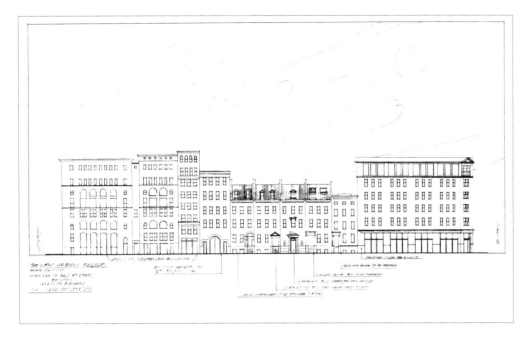

SUMMER SCHOOL DESIGN STUDIO: "Merchant's House Museum Project." Melissa del Vecchio and Jim Tinson, instructors. Summer, 1999.

This project considered the possible expansion of the Merchant's House Museum. Student designs addressed the reconstruction of the block with the focus being the infill of row-houses within the three vacant lots between the Old Merchant's House and the Skidmore House on East 4th Street. Students first worked as a team to develop master plan guidelines and a cohesive solution, then worked individually to develop one townhouse that would fill one of the three available sites.

This portion of the summer school curriculum included walking tours, sketching exercises, and precedent research, as part of a broader study of the rowhouse and townhouse and its development in New York City, as well as the role of this building type in the structure of traditional streets and neighborhoods.

ARCHITECTURAL DRAWING TOUR IN ROME, ITALY. Richard Wilson Cameron, Christine G.H. Frank, instructors. Leonard Porter, Fellow in Residence. Summer, 1998.

The Institute's drawing tour provides direction and instruction for participants in the observation and assimilation of classical Roman forms of architecture. Observation, analysis, and drawing are used as a means of gaining familiarity with Roman architecture. The emphasis of these tours is on direct drawing experience rather than classroom instruction. These images are from the Institute's inaugural Architectural Drawing Tour in Rome.

ABOVE LEFT: Leonard Porter, Fellow in Residence, View at Ostia Antica. Watercolor on paper. Summer, 1998.

ABOVE RIGHT: Sophia Tak Wing Chan, View of Porta Maggiore. Ink on paper. Summer, 1998.

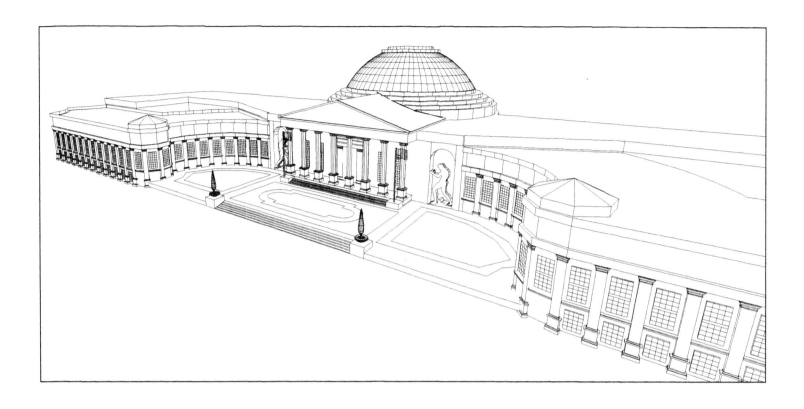

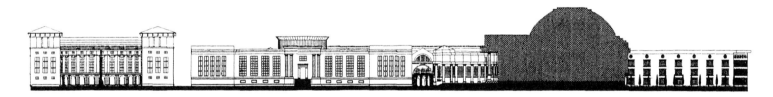

GRADUATE STUDIO PROJECT: "New Civic Center for The City of Guatemala." Warren Orbaugh, instructor. Fall, 1998.

TOP: Paula Bendfeldt, Perspective view. CAD drawing.

BOTTOM: Paula Bendfeldt, Site section. CAD drawing.

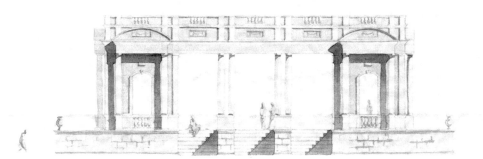

INTRODUCTION TO CLASSICAL ARCHITECTURE: "Design for a Garden Pavilion." J. François Gabriel, instructor. Fall, 1998.

LEFT: Matthew Dockery, Front elevation. Water color on paper.

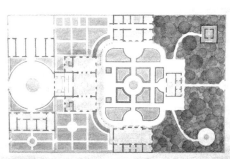

SECOND YEAR STUDIO: "A Study of the French Hotel Type." J. François Gabriel, Instructor. Fall 1997.

ABOVE LEFT: Joel Kline, Front elevation. Watercolor on paper.

LEFT: Jim Wisniewski, Rear elevation. Watercolor on paper.

ABOVE: Jim Wisniewski, Site plan. Watercolor on paper.

MAN DOES NOT BUILD FOR HIMSELF ANYMORE THAN HE SMILES FOR HIMSELF ALONE
THE FACADE IS DESIGNED OUT OF RESPECT FOR THE BEHOLDER A FORM OF
ARCHITECTURAL COURTESY TO THE MAN IN THE STREET
·HENRY HOPE REED·

The foundation course is a unique, intensive, one year full-time course for students who wish to pursue a career in architecture, the building crafts, or the fine applied arts. For those students without formal qualifications the course provides a recognized access route to higher education and leads to a Diploma in Architecture and the Building Arts. Strong emphasis is placed upon relating theory to practice. The students are also taught the principles and techniques of traditional building and how these might be used appropriately today. —The Prince's Foundation Catalog

FOUNDATION COURSE: "The Building Project." Ben Taylor, tutor. Spring, 1998.

During the 1998 academic year, the Foundation Course students learned about design, construction, and siting of buildings through the various strands of the curriculum. The ultimate test of this understanding came in the summer term when, over a five week period, they designed and constructed a simple building, working for a real client.

The Prince's Foundation was asked to build a loggia for a new housing development inside the market town of Shepton Mallet, Somerset. Working in close partnership with the District Council, the landowner, the Duchy of Cornwall, and the architect for the housing scheme, the students were able to undertake this project. Under the supervision of practicing architects, engineers, health and safety consultants, craftsmen, and a local building contractor, the project was completed in five weeks. In this way, the students were exposed to the entire process of building in a microcosm. The final design was composed of natural materials, including green oak and hand made tiles. The students worked as a team to prepare working drawings of the final design to ensure that they understood how the building would be constructed and finished. Once on site, the students cut the timber to the requisite sections out of the round and erected the oak frame on a stone plinth using traditional pegged joints. In just fourteen days, these eighteen students, none of whom had any significant building experience, produced this innovative structure.

ABOVE: Foundation course students working on site.

TOP RIGHT: The finished loggia.

BOTTOM RIGHT: Details of the finished loggia.

FOUNDATION COURSE: "Architectural Ornament." Dick Reid, tutor. Fall, 1998.

RIGHT: Christina Godiksen, Plaster cast.

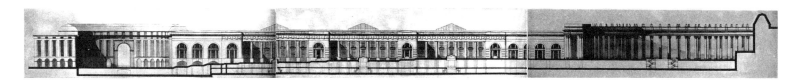

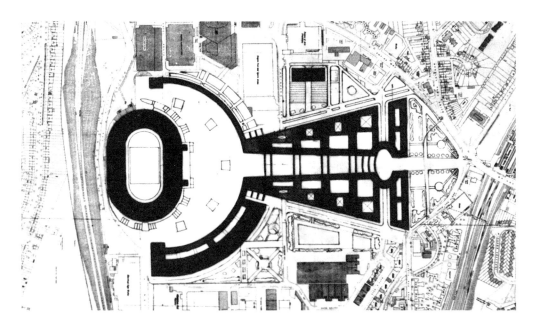

DIPLOMA PROJECT: "The Redevelopment of Wembley Park." Viacheslav Uhuv, professor. Fall, 1997.

"The Redevelopment of Wembley Park" was a one year diploma project submitted to the Architectural Department of The St. Petersburg Academy of Painting, Sculpture, and Architecture in fulfillment of the final architectural requirement for graduation. The work on this project was executed under the supervision of the Brent Council (Brent, London) and in association with The Prince's Foundation (London).

The focus of this project centers on the development and revitalization of Wembley Park, the area surrounding Wembley Stadium in the London borough of Brent. The design proposes a grand pedestrian artery which links the Wembley Park tube station to the stadium grounds. The splayed approach terminates in a grand piazza at the North end of the stadium. The plan includes an enfilade of shops, restaurants, and cafes as a means of supporting the stadium crowds and providing a much needed infusion of commerce into the surrounding area. The lower level of the design is dedicated to underground parking.

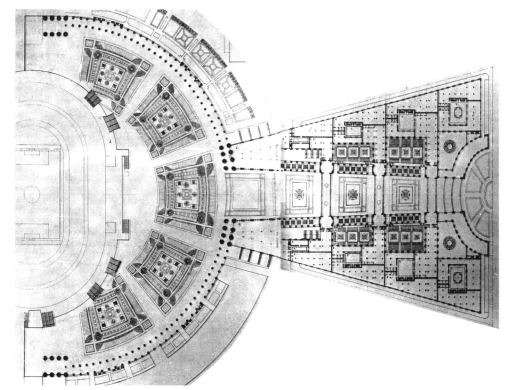

TOP: Anton Glikine, Section/Elevation. Watercolor on paper.

MIDDLE: Anton Glikine, Site plan. Watercolor on paper.

BOTTOM: Anton Glikine, Ground floor plan. Watercolor on paper.

INTERNATIONAL URBAN DESIGN STUDIO, ST PETERSBURG, RUSSIA: "The Reconstruction of Greek Square." Maxim Atayantz, Ben Bolgar, Marina Shirskaya, assistants. Summer 1996.

The 1996 International Urban Design Studio in St. Petersburg was originally conceived by HRH The Prince of Wales during his visit to The St. Petersburg Academy of Painting, Sculpture and Architecture in 1994. The program brief and organization was developed by Brian Hanson (The Prince of Wales's Project Office), Simeon Mikhailovsky (St. Petersburg Academy of Arts) and Thomas Gordon Smith (The University of Notre Dame School of Architecture).

Greek Square is situated in the south-eastern quadrant of St. Petersburg at the beginning of Ligovsky Prospekt. In 1861, the Greek Diaspora was given this piece of land for the building of a church. Under the design direction of the architect Roman Kuzmin, the church was completed and dedicated in 1864. In 1964, the church was demolished for the construction of the October Concert Hall. This modern edifice was erected in honor of the 50th anniversary of the October Revolution.

The participants of the 1996 studio were given the following tasks: Preserve the heart of the concert hall while increasing its usable space, replace the modern façade of the building with a contextually sensitive motif, and revitalize the square with the introduction of a hotel, shops, and a memorial chapel in commemoration of the Greek church. Professor Jean Verzhbitzky (St. Petersburg Academy of Arts), one of the original designers of the October Hall, served as consultant to the summer school.

TOP: Hotel elevation. Watercolor on paper.

NEAR RIGHT: Memorial chapel elevation. Watercolor on paper.

FAR RIGHT: Concert Hall elevation. Watercolor on paper.

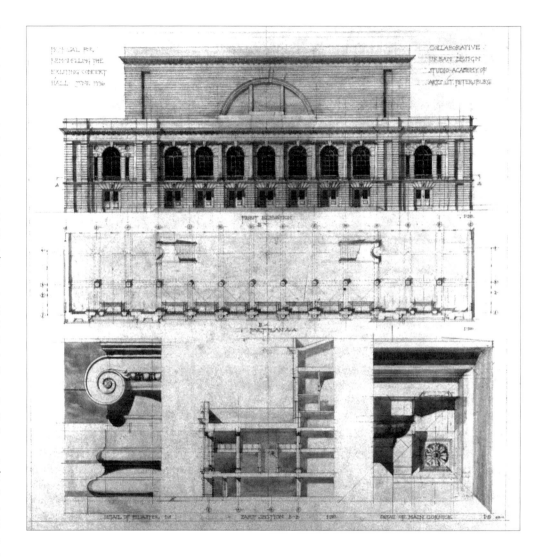

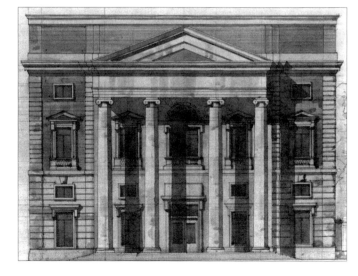

COMPETITIONS

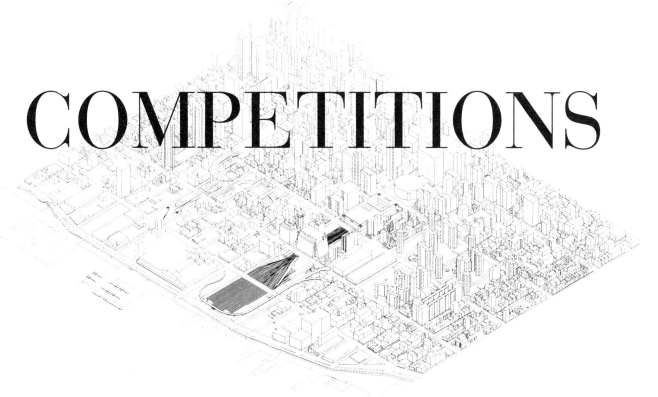

HERE ARE THE NEW URBANISTS!

In previous issues of *The Classicist,* the competitions section has highlighted many classical and traditional solutions entered in architectural and planning competitions. Whether the featured projects have been winners, as many have been, or not is in some respects unimportant, as the creative work that went into the projects has brought experience to the participating architects and inspiration to our readers. This year, however, we present the results of a closed competition in which the traditional/classical urbanists were not invited to participate. Included are images submitted by the invited participants of this competition, a counter-proposal from a pair of uninvited classicists, and a response from a noted traditional architect to the question *"Where are the New Urbanists?"*

In November of 1998, Phyllis Lambert, Founding Director and Chair of the Canadian Centre for Architecture (CCA) announced the creation of an international competition, intended to encourage innovative contributions to the design of cities. The competition, to be held every three years, focuses each time on a different site in one of the world's major cities, and offers a prize of $100,000. The competition has been established through the International Foundation for the CCA (IFCCA), a fundraising organization that supports CCA's mission of "making architecture a matter of public concern." Ms. Lambert describes the competition as one that "challenges the world's most forward-looking architects to think of the city of the twenty-first century as a place both vital and inspiring to their inhabitant… and to propose design solutions that bring together the large-scale infrastructure and the smaller urban spaces of everyday life."

For this first IFCCA competition, a large and vacuous site was selected in the center of New York City. Penn Station, Madison Square Garden, rail yards, bus storage, and the Lincoln Tunnel entrance define the complexity of the west Midtown site, an area sometimes referred to as "Hell's

Kitchen." In describing the potential development of the site, Ralph Lerner, Dean of the School of Architecture at Princeton University and Director of the first IFCCA Prize Competition stated that "existing urban development formulas would be ineffective. Competitors are, therefore, being encouraged to go beyond existing convention in their thinking. We're asking them to consider how to overcome the site's isolation, how to spark new forms of urban experience, and how to revitalize those forms that may have been overlooked…" According to Mr. Lerner, "the aim of the competition is to enhance and extend the public understanding of architecture's ability to offer bold re-examinations of existing models of urbanism."

The CCA selected five preeminent architects, none of which are classicists, to participate. They are Peter Eisenman, Thom Mayne of Morphosis, Cedric Price, Reiser+Umemoto, and Ben VanBerkel and Caroline Bos of UN Studio in the Netherlands. The first prize went to noted architect and protagonist, Peter Eisenman. Though the images and models by Eisenman (and all of the participants for that matter) appear seductive and polished as sculptural objects for architectural connoisseurs, the schemes lack the variety and complexity of elements that are necessary in the making of a viable humanist city. However successful the CCA has been in "making architecture a matter of public concern," it has actually done a disservice to the public by its failure to also include even one traditional architect, who would have presented a different approach to contemporary urbanism. Such an approach would certainly have contributed a more believable, enduring solution that engages rather than overwhelms or even terrifies the public. —M.F. & W.B.

ABOVE: Axonometric Site Plan of CCA competition

Ben Van Berkel and Caroline Bos : UN Studio, Amsterdam, The Netherlands

A CRITIQUE OF THE RECENT CANADIAN CENTER FOR ARCHITECTURE COMPETITION

BY ANDRES DUANY

Thom Mayne : Morphosis, Santa Monica, California

The victorious Peter Eisenman crows: and where are the New Urbanists? And so, alas, one of us must take the time to respond.

The short answer, of course, is that no New Urbanist was invited to participate in this competition, intended to develop an urbanism worthy of Manhattan. The entrants were selected ideologically, all five being at a minimum allergic to traditional urbanism. This editing was undoubtedly necessary. Had a New Urbanist project been included, the ensuing public discussion would have been heavily polarized, with a preponderance of popular support behind the NU design. An open, democratic process and a modernist megastructure are incompatible, and the CCA knows that.

The story in short is that the CCA, prolonging the seventy-year search for a workable modernist urbanism, stumbled upon a revival. As it happens, Rem Koolhaas with his XL Category has made megastructures fashionable again. But he is not stupid, so he supplies a caveat: not within the city. In *Delirious New York* he clearly states that the urban block must be the limit of each individual architectural ideology. The huge, multifunctional XL buildings are justified only to achieve critical mass in the unraveled infrastructure of suburban sprawl. It should be obvious that there is no need for a megastructure when there is a functioning urban grid. The street network is an automatic, synergetic integrator. Manhattan works because its small blocks break down activity for parallel

processing. The twenty-block, centralized architecture of the competition is as inefficient as an old mainframe.

The CCA designers camouflage their out-of-date conceptions with a fashionable stylistic complexity. It is this false complexity, no less than the monolithic urbanism that could prove vulnerable in the long run. Twenty blocks designed by a single architect is a monoculture, with all the fragility that the term implies. Whatever variety the single architect can muster cannot avoid being palpably inauthentic and ultimately boring, as in the Malibu Getty. One must imagine the relentless oppression of a style, when it falls out of fashion. Imagine twenty blocks of Pei, Johnson, or Roche. And should a single detail fail, the minor problem multiplied over 40 acres becomes a catastrophe.

An authentic urbanism would reorganize the single project into many individual ones. A restored urban grid and the 18 foot wide Manhattan lot would allow both the rowhouse and, in accretion, the block-long St. Patrick's Cathedral.

That is in general.

Now, some notes on the individual competition projects: Cedric Price's team of revelers seem to have invested not more than a few jolly hours, perhaps as in the old Architectural Association not entirely sober, throwing together a scrapbook of sardonic ideas. They cannot possibly be taken seriously.

Reiser and Umemoto display a superb analytical methodology, the results of which they then proceed to ignore. Their design, to be fashionable, pretty much follows the others, including that of Van Berkel & Bos. It is a symptom of the coercive homogenizing of the avant-garde, that from L.A. to Amsterdam the wavy megastructure is now de rigeur. Eisenman at least makes it clear that he has no need for an analytical methodology to identify the so-obvious imperatives of the Zeitgeist.

Reiser and Umemoto make a special error: their design brings the highway integrally into a megastructure and includes the garages. The result is that the user need not leave the building to ever set foot in the city.

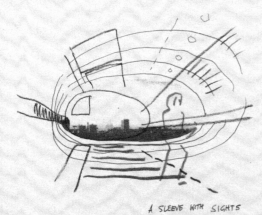

A SLEEVE WITH SIGHTS

This fulfills the suburbanite's dream of driving into Manhattan without engaging street traffic, parking conveniently, and using the facility while avoiding the messy sidewalks. It might as well be on the Jersey landfill.

Morphosis imposes their usual laid-back, L.A. informality. But must New York tolerate such bad manners, such unwarranted flaunting of the decorum that underlies Manhattan's mature urbanism? To support their playfulness they create a sort of baby talk that passes for terminology: snakes, conquistadors, pugs, floaters, crepes, linkers, noodles, missiles, warp holds, displays, bits, suspended objects unknown, and so on, to describe their design.

While Morphosis mangles the lexicon of urbanism for fun, Reiser and Umemoto ominously deploy language in order to control the discourse. They use semantically neutral terms like: "cluster," "void," and "critical package," when "block," "square," and "campus" would do (but calling a square a square is so square). They soothingly promise "mutability," "absences," "deficiencies," "deformations," "transformations," "potential," "diversity," "vicariousness," when in fact everything has been thoroughly designed and controlled.

Eisenman's project undermines the status quo, not verbally, but with a version of the kiasma, popularized by Holl at Helsinki: a sort of crossover warp that, just for starters, destabilizes the ground plane. However, Eisenman has become conservative and the twist is disciplined to a suave elegance so monolithic that

---

ABOVE: Cedric Price Architects, London, England.

RIGHT: Peter Eisenman: Eisenman Architects, New York. © Fondation Daniel Langlois.

the result may have troubled Speer. The building is totalitarian in syntax, as well as size. Its construction is a hermetic tectonic secret.

The apparent indeterminacy of all these projects is deceptive, as all of them, as megastructures, require a permanent management authority, effectively withdrawing from public discussion a large sector of Manhattan. Their administration must be a central bureaucracy—never a democracy, not even the democracy of competing economic interests.

The people of New York so ostentatiously invited to the viewing of the projects at Grand Central Terminal have in fact been presented only with the illusion of choice. Four of them are conceptually interchangeable and Price's entry is so depleted that only a nihilist (like Herbert Muschamp) could back it.

A New Urbanist proposal would present a third position, one between the absolute control of the megastructures and the abdication of Price. It would begin with the restoration of the tested, super-efficient Manhattan block pattern. This is radical compared to the too-obvious concept of a single big building for the single big site. The streets thus created would not be completely conventional as they could hump over the ridgeline of the railway tracks, in memory of the industrial geography. Only a few of the resulting twenty blocks would be permitted to conjoin, and then only in the event of a genuinely large user, perhaps at the

scale of a Rockefeller Center or a Yankee Stadium. Never more, because it is important to the vitality of the urban public realm to avoid internalizing activity.

The NU proposal would subdivide each block into many separate building sites. The architectural work would thus be decanted to dozens of architects, the five entrants to this competition not excluded. A sequential, incremental design would assure a self-correcting variety in programming, investment strategy, and architecture. The result would be infinitely more resilient, though it would lack the blockbuster quality of an Eisenman.

The CCA competition is not about urbanism. The four designs are no more than audaciously large architectural projects, and their only contribution to this benighted art is to add the horror of the gigantic to the nightmare of the irrational. As Goya warned, the sleep of reason creates monsters.

Andres Duany completed his undergraduate studies in architecture at Princeton, and received his M. Arch. from Yale University. He maintains an architectural and town planning practice with Elizabeth Plater-Zyberk in Miami, Duany Plater-Zyberk & Company, and teaches in the University of Miami's Master of Architecture Program for Suburb and Town Design. He is a member of the Advisory Council of The Institute of Classical Architecture.

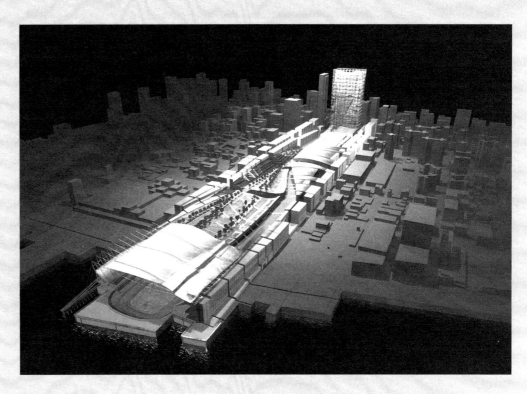

COUNTER-PROPOSAL FOR THE RECONSTRUCTION OF HELL'S KITCHEN

BY DINO MARCANTONIO AND RICCARDO VICENZINO

Our proposal begins with the restoration of the Manhattan block pattern. We expanded the original CCA competition area down to 23rd Street, and divided it into two quarters, each about a 10-minute walk from end to end. The more heavily trafficked streets mark the boundaries of the neighborhoods, 34th Street to the north, 23rd Street to the south, Eighth Avenue to the east, Tenth Avenue in between, and of course, the Hudson River and a new promenade to the west. Since Ninth and Eleventh Avenues pass through the center of each neighborhood, we interrupt them with a square, at once slowing down avenue traffic and emphasizing the importance of the square. The squares would serve as the conceptual centers of each neighborhood, and one can imagine them bounded by commercial and residential buildings, arcaded on the ground floor like those on Place des Vosges, for example. We thought the East Side Manhattan blocks, at 450 feet long, were much more hospitable to pedestrian traffic than the typical 800-foot long blocks of the West Side, so we halved the blocks on the competition site. These smaller blocks, about 350-375 feet by 200 feet, will not only make walking more comfortable, but will also increase commercial frontage and ease traffic in the north-south direction.

The proposed promenade on the Hudson would be built over the West Side Highway. It could incorporate a boardwalk and gardens reminiscent of Grant Park in Chicago. The promenade, a continuation of the planned procession that begins at Battery Park, would be punctuated where it meets 34th Street by a combination ferry terminal, naval museum, and recreational structure based on Magonigle's winning entry for the Robert Fulton Memorial of 1910. To the east it faces a public square, shown in the perspective on the cover of this issue. At the far end one can see a public building, perhaps a college or an art gallery, based on one of Hawksmoor's projects for All Souls. A new baseball stadium would anchor the southern edge of the square. The stadium is related axially to the west entrance of the newly renovated train station, currently the Post Office, designed by McKim, Mead and White. We have

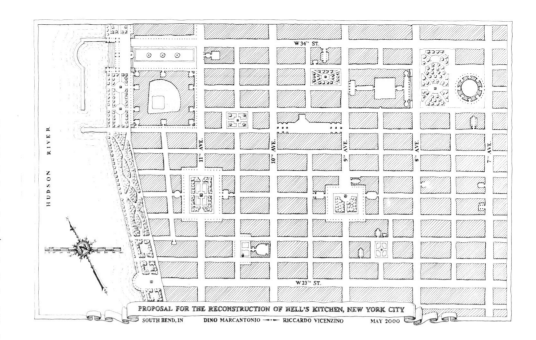

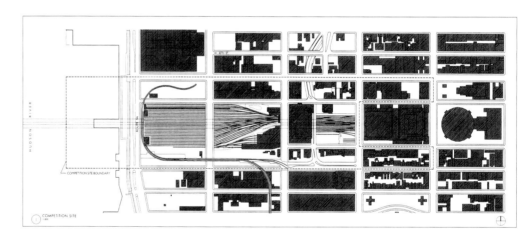

TOP: Proposed site plan, D. Marcantonio and R. Vicenzino.

BOTTOM: CCA site plan for comparison.

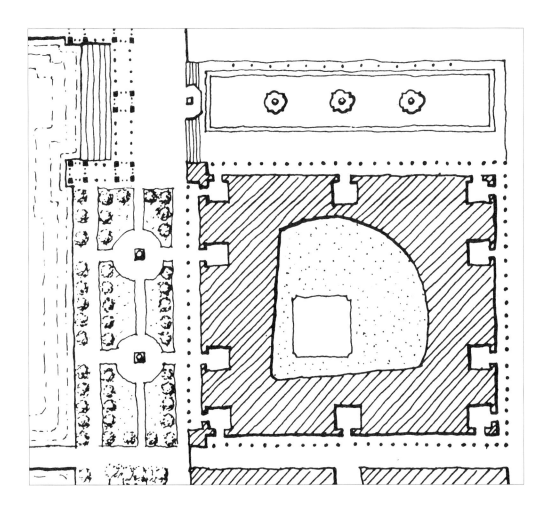

also extended the competition site to the east of the new train station. Additionally, in order to accommodate the increased traffic in and out of the building, and to give it a more civic setting, which is its due; Madison Square Garden gets pushed back to make way for a public square. This square would also extend up to 34th Street, so that the train station would be more clearly visible from that heavily trafficked street.

This plan strengthens the civic quality of the Manhattan urban landscape, first by increasing the number of squares. It draws from some of the more successful examples nearby, such as Gramercy Park and Tompkins Square, and from great European examples as well. Second, the plan gives priority to the pedestrian by keeping unimpeded avenue traffic to the edges of the neighborhoods, and by reducing block sizes. Third, the Hudson River becomes a point of reference and a close engagement with the city is emphasized.

Riccardo Vicenzino received his B. Arch. from Pratt Institute and M. Arch from the University of Notre Dame. He is a registered architect in New York State and is currently working in the office of Nasser Nakib Architect.

Dino Marcantonio received his M. Arch. from the University of Virginia, and has worked in the offices of Hartman-Cox Architects, Robert A. M. Stern Architects, and Ferguson Shamamian and Rattner Architects. He now teaches at the University of Notre Dame.

TOP: *Plan showing public square, baseball stadium, promenade, and ferry landing.*

BOTTOM: *Proposed public square, looking east from the Hudson River.*

MOULDING POSSIBILITIES

by Natalie Jacobs

As classical architects, our work at Ferguson Shamamian & Rattner Architects (FSR), like that of many traditional architects, is recognizable by the use of architectural mouldings. Although more than ornamental—providing structure to the composition of the building, protecting it and its inhabitants from sun, shedding rain water at joints and edges where building elements meet—moldings have symbolic significance that makes buildings meaningful. John Summerson, in *The Classical Language of Architecture,* credits the Romans with transporting the orders (and I take this to include all other ornament) from merely the sculptural equivalent in stone of earlier carpentry devices to this higher level.

" *...they raised architectural language to a new level....The orders are, in many Roman buildings, quite useless structurally, but they make their buildings expressive, they make them speak; they conduct the building, with sense and ceremony and often with great elegance, into the mind of the beholder."*

Our contemporary practice at FSR is largely limited to residences, and we use a variety of 'styles' of ornament depending on the client's taste and the context in which the building will be set. In many cases, we have followed the Georgian precedent of using elements more traditionally associated with public buildings to aggrandize a smaller or simpler

Painted interior representing architectural elements by Giambattista Zeloti and Paolo Veronese at Villa Emo.

volume. We use the language of public buildings, but clothed in less formal materials. When appropriate to the construction of a building

we prefer to use stone, but we find that we are often constrained by budget, time, and the unavailability of higher levels of building craftsmanship. So, we have found that we can construct mouldings in new and different materials, often finished to imitate stone, without losing their significance or language. Of course, as designers we are not unique in this pursuit. We have only to look to *Preservation Magazine,* July/August 2000, to find a letter from John Fitzhugh Millar, who reminds us that imitation of stone has been done with ingenuity as early as 1736:

"...when Anglo-American architect Peter Harrison, 20, designed his first building in America, the Portuguese Synagogue in the Dutch colonial port of Paramaribo in Guiana, South America...when the clients told him there was no limestone for thousands of miles around to build his design, Harrison quickly altered the specification to beveled planks representing stone."

The example quoted above refers to the creative use of a new material to achieve a form based on historical precedent. We do not in our practice resort to the use of imitative materials to produce the contrived, derivative, or wholly unsuitable forms that we sometimes see in architecture *á la* Las Vegas. The selection of the appropriate material is not in itself based upon historical correctness as much as it is based on budget, efficiency of fabrication and installa-

tectural educational process changed. Fortunately, there are many alternatives to stone.

Wood is easy to cut, carve, and support, and is appropriate as our office is often involved in residential construction projects that are structured with wood members. Stock shapes are readily available. Wood species that are best for exterior use are red cedar, Southern cypress, redwood, and mahogany. Each species has different characteristics—strength, resistance to twist, paintability—so we select a species based upon the intended use. Most wood species, with the exception of teak and old growth red cedars, must be protected from sunlight and moisture for longevity. Opaque stains or paint coatings must be applied and maintained, especially on the building exterior.

For some uses, composite materials can be a better alternative. Cast stone and terracotta have been used for centuries, but their weights are similar to natural stone, and newer and lighter materials have been found. Composites can be factory fabricated and include GFRC

tion, and sequence of construction. Yet, as we consider what might be available for a particular project, we avoid using methods or materials that cannot accurately represent the mouldings or which do not exhibit longevity in use.

With some exceptions, we consider the same alternative materials for both exterior and interior applications. Interior materials, however, can be selected and finished with less regard for durability and weathering. There is greater selection of stones and stone polishing techniques, wood species and exotic graining effects, as well as wood finish techniques that are available for interior moulding use. Mouldings can even become part of the decorative finish, using paints and plastering effects. Historical examples of decorative painting representing architectural elements include interiors as ancient as those revealed by the excavations at Pompeii. Another example

would be the particularly beautiful painted interior by Giambattista Zeloti and Paolo Veronese at Villa Emo.

When we look to the precedents of Greek and Roman buildings, stone was often used for both interior and exterior mouldings. For exterior mouldings, stone is still preferable on buildings with stone or other unit masonry veneer but it usually does not fit into today's budgets. As a raw material, stone is costly and supporting its weight requires careful detailing which then compounds the outlay. Further, carving is not only costly but often cannot be executed in an architecturally correct manner by the majority of stone carvers today. This is due largely to the fact that there was a 50-year period during which the time-honored tradition of transferring knowledge, methods, or techniques in the form of working apprenticeship was abandoned. This gap was a direct result of how the archi-

(glass fiber reinforced concrete), GFRG (glass fiber reinforced gypsum), and proprietary glass fiber reinforced exterior plaster mixes which can be layered into molds to create thin shells, and easily lifted into place and supported. The use of these composites does require skilled craftspeople, but it can be done away

TOP: Initial small-scale model of column capital at Ahmad Suleiman's shop.

ABOVE LEFT: Next the proportions of the elements are refined at full size.

ABOVE CENTER: Then the individual turnings are built and joined together.

ABOVE RIGHT: The Ionic element becomes more defined.

from the building site and within carefully controlled environments. The texture and color of the finished product can vary based on the materials used in the mix, the treatment of the mold prior to casting, and surface treatments applied after forms are stripped. The architect can direct and control the finished appearance of the composites through a sampling process.

For a recent project in Nashville, Tennessee, FSR specified double height Ionic columns for the entry portico. The three segments of the columns were fabricated from three different materials: the plinth block is stone, the shaft (including the torus and necking) is turned wood, and the capitol is glass fiber reinforced 'Design Cast,' a polymer modified cement. Ahmad Suleiman, an experienced craftsman who specializes in architectural sculpture, ornamental plaster, scagliola, period ceilings, and restoration fabricated the capitals for this project. Mr. Suleiman has provided his

layers of alternating fiberglass mat and cement to form the cast thickness and to provide the strength required to hold the final shape. The castings are only partially cured when the two halves are combined and glued and they are clamped together until curing is complete. The joint between halves is not perceptible in the final product. Ahmad does not suggest adding additional material to fully cured castings because the difference in curing conditions will create incompatibilities and applied material may delaminate.

For our purposes, we wanted the finished capitals to imitate limestone and the casting materials do just that. However, if alternative effects are required, cast surfaces can be treated during or after casting. Color pigments and colored aggregates can be added to the casting mix; veining can be imitated by partial mixing, or by layering within the mold with different color mixes. Aggregates can be sand, marble dust, crushed limestone, or marble. The texture can also be altered by washing the finished sur-

difficult to attain. There is also the uncertainty of curing. Exterior plasters are made with cements, and shrink as the mixture hydrates and cures.

To reduce costs, simplify the construction, and provide control of shop fabrication environments, we are contemplating executing a similar entablature detail with EIFS. EIFS is the acronym for Exterior Insulation and Finish System. Manufacturers of building materials have developed EIFS products that are sold through approved application contractors. The typical EIFS assembly incorporates a succession of layers applied over a rigid substrate. The layers are typically, 1) extruded polystyrene foam insulation; 2) inorganic or fiberglass reinforcing mesh; 3) acrylic emulsion primer or fiber reinforced Portland cement base coats; and 4) acrylic based emulsion finish coats, which may be colored and/or textured.

Extruded polystyrene foam is an inexpensive and easily sculpted back-up material. To execute a design, insulation can be shop sculpt-

expertise in sculpted ornament for many of FSR's projects from Suleiman Studios in Horsham, Pennsylvania.

Ahmad's first task was to make the model/prototype based on our drawings and his own knowledge of historical precedents. Ahmad modeled in clay and plaster the elements of the Ionic Order—necking, abacus, volutes, egg and dart, honeysuckle leaves—carefully considering their inter-relationship in the final dimensional product. He provided sample castings of each element for review as he proceeded and as each element was approved, they were combined to form the full capitol. Once the fully executed model was approved, a mold was made and cut diagonally to facilitate demolding.

The capital castings were then made in the completed molds. A quarter inch thickness of 'Cement Mix' is applied to the entire surface of the mold. This first layer is followed by multiple

face with muriatic acid solution. To imitate travertine, fabricators may use Bicarbonate of Soda (baking soda) to create voids in the finished surface.

The support for our capital was provided by the projecting necking of the wood shaft below, but an additional cornice or projecting molding would require support for its cantilever. Looking to the fabrication of terracotta for additional insights, structural steel members can be cast into the concealed surfaces and Ahmad suggests forming male and female ends at individual members of a running trim. The positive keying will restrict movement of adjacent members.

Site drawn plaster is also a traditional material for mouldings. At FSR we admire the curved plaster coved entablature at Lutyens' Salutation. But site drawn plasterwork can be expensive and requires a level of craftsmanship

ed to form the cove, eliminating the need to site install lathing across the eave line. Sculpted units can be installed over cast concrete, concrete block, or wood sheathing. The units are lightweight and easily installed with construction adhesives—there is no expense or time required for installing structural framing support. However, the lightweight, less dense characteristics of the polystyrene foam may have drawbacks. The foam is softer and less dense than wood or stone, so the shapes that are carved do not have the sharp corners, crisp edges, and reveals that can be achieved with the

LEFT: Egg and dart molded full-size in clay.

CENTER: Egg and dart elements in plaster.

RIGHT: Completed unit.

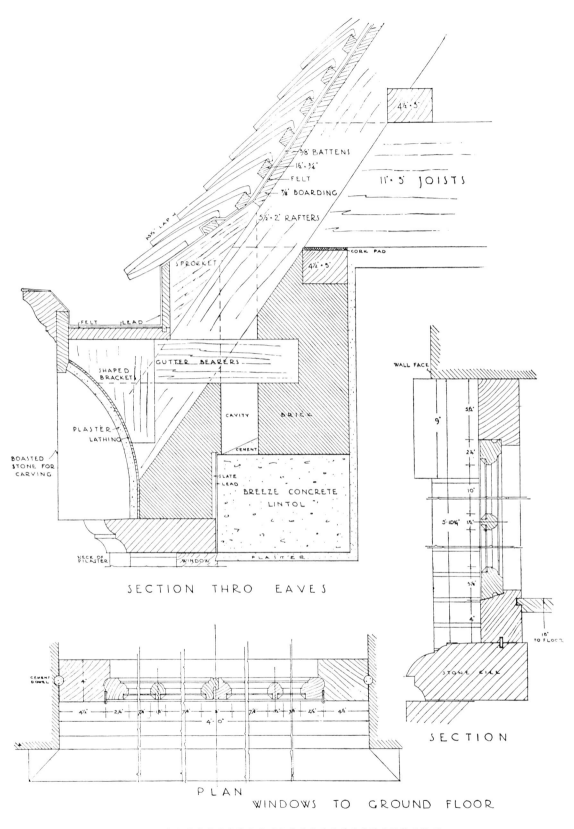

SECTION THRO EAVES

SECTION

PLAN

WINDOWS TO GROUND FLOOR

Coved entablature detail from Lutyens "Salutation." From The Domestic Architecture of Sir Edwin Lutyens, *by A.S.G. Butler, 1950.*

harder materials. Even after coating with base and finish materials, foam can be easily dented or abused, and so is inappropriate for use adjacent to the pedestrian or vehicular traffic expected at lower elevations of a building wall. The cove, on the other hand, would be a good, protected location on the building, and is a suitable shape for the use of foam.

After site erection, the insulation will be covered with a reinforcing mesh and a two-coat finish. By carefully specifying the coating mix, we hope to achieve a non-porous surface that will convincingly mimic exterior plaster and withstand weathering. The site installed coating will be continuous, eliminating the inevitable cracks where the typical joint lines would be. We have used this type of material on a residence in Florida, successfully creating cornice, rustication, and casings.

EIFS assemblies have been in use approximately 15-20 years, but the methods of installation for the earlier systems have been prone to failure. Wind-driven moisture was allowed to enter at cracks at joints between the EIFS finish and dissimilar materials and became trapped behind the non-breathable acrylic finish. The moisture damaged the wall back-up. Newer installation techniques now incorporate air cavities and weeps behind the finish to allow moisture to be evacuated. Wherever we are specifying acrylic coating, we are careful to consider its joint to adjacent materials.

The design and application of mouldings for contemporary classical architecture is enhanced by the availability of a wide variety of materials both natural and man-made. Historical reference and research are only the beginning steps that need not be a deterrent to creating what makes a building expressive and lends integrity to the overall design. The technical challenges are part of the process that must include consideration of cost, constructability advantages and disadvantages, and ultimately the selection of materials that are the most suitable. ⧫

Natalie Jacobs is a graduate of Carnegie-Mellon University. She is currently a practicing architect and associate at Ferguson Shamamian & Rattner Architects where she is responsible for technical oversight and specifications writing. It is her role to adapt current technology, materials, and building practices—along with researching older methods—to find solutions for the execution and realization of traditional architectural designs.

TOP: *Completed unit with Tom McManus of FSR (left) and Ahmad Suleiman.*

CENTER: *Column in place at the site.*

BOTTOM: *Cornice, rustication, and casings created with extruded polystyrene foam on the FSR designed residence in Florida.*

READYMADE IDEALS:

    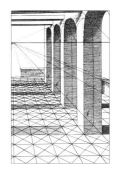

ELEMENTS OF ARCHITECTURE IN THE PAINTINGS OF CARLO MARIA MARIANI

by David Ebony

Carlo Maria Mariani is an internationally recognized painter known for compositions featuring meticulously rendered figures based on classical ideals of drawing and proportion. These figures inhabit imaginative spaces that are often punctuated by architectural forms. Sometimes the architecture is based on classical and neo-classical examples, the Greek orders, Doric, Ionic, and Corinthian make regular appearances, as do Renaissance, Baroque, or neo-classical models. Often the architectural elements are fragmented or in ruins. Frequently, the structures are complete inventions.

In his work, Mariani approaches historical style, philosophy, and architecture as if each were an elegant Marcel Duchamp "readymade." However, the schematic figures and architecture that appear in Mariani's work function as symbolic representations of the highest forms of human values, endeavors, and aspirations. While the artist uses traditional techniques of oil-on-canvas and ink and graphite on paper, and the paintings may conjure the heady atmosphere of antiquity, Mariani does not wish to elicit a nos-

"The past, present and future are one."

—*Carlo Maria Mariani*

talgic longing for the past. Instead, he aims to interject an argument for classical ideals into a discourse on contemporary artistic practice and values. In his witty compositions, the artist is as likely to refer to the German conceptualist Joseph Beuys as he is to Tintoretto.

Born in Rome's Trastévere district, Mariani was an only child. His father, a writer, and mother, a painter, helped him understand and appreciate the rich cultural heritage that surrounded him. He remembers as a young boy

visiting the famous museums, churches, villas and other treasure houses of Rome. The collections of the villas Farnesina, Doria Pamphili, Medici, and of the Vatican museum were familiar to him at an early age. Among his childhood memories are scenes of devastation wrought by bombs and shelling in and around Rome during World War II. In a recent drawing, *Assassination of the Divine,* Mariani evokes these images. The drawing shows the scattered ruins of the early Renaissance Church of San Lorenzo, which was bombed by American pilots. In the foreground a classical head is partly obscured by chunks of shattered stone. The drawing is enhanced by collaged pieces of torn and burnt paper that contain fragments of poems, a reference to the works of literature that have been lost due to the ravages of war.

Since childhood, Mariani has had a deep appreciation for literature, especially poetry. In his teens he immersed himself in the works of Goethe, Shelley, Baudelaire, Kierkegaard, and Carl Gustav Jung. Mariani was a precocious student at the Academy of Fine Arts in Rome, where he graduated early and with honors in 1955. The paintings he produced there reflect his thorough understanding of Italian modernists such as Modigliani, Morandi, and Carrá as well as artists of the Roman and Venetian Renaissance, including Raphael, Titian, Veronese, and Tintoretto.

Soon after graduation, Mariani's career abruptly ignited when his proposal for a mosaic was the surprise winner in a prestigious competition to decorate the apse of the Frosinone Cathedral. In a sense, the first public acceptance of his art was for work that was directly related to architecture. The success of this commission led to a string of new church projects. Though Mariani was raised as a Catholic, his interest in Catholicism did not extend much beyond an appreciation for the music and pageantry of church ritual. Intellectually, he was always more stimulated by the mythology of the Greco-Roman pantheon. He used the church commissions to support himself and his family for a number of years. However, while he worked on those projects by day, at night he produced a very different group of works in his studio.

Many of the early canvases are allegorical images that reflect the angst-ridden cacophony of the tumultuous 1960s. In *Triumph of the City* (1966), for example, a screaming woman holding a megaphone stands before towering skyscrapers made of Legos, the brightly colored plastic building blocks for children, which Mariani uses symbolically to refer to the dehumanizing aspects of modernist urban design that favors cheap materials and prefab uniformity. In key works of the period such as *Allegory of the Future* (1967), the artist juxtaposes structures made of Legos with fragments of classical architecture. The conflict of ideals represented by the classical marble and contemporary plastic, a theme Mariani returns to in a number of subsequent works, is already well underway here.

———

During a period of experimentation with conceptual works and performance art in the late 1960s and '70s, Mariani discovered a way to connect with and assimilate certain aspects of the distant past. Key to this revelation was a simple matrix he had invented for his work, which he explained with his now-famous proclamation, "I am not the painter. I am not the artist. I am the work." In art-historical terms, he assumed the techniques, attitudes, and, in a sense, the identities of well-known figures

from art history, ranging from Leonardo da Vinci, Raphael, Van Eyck, and Dürer to Angelica Kauffmann, Jacques-Louis David, and Anton Raphael Mengs. After much research, Mariani re-created lost originals by some of these artists, based on written accounts of them he had discovered in libraries. And, remaining true to the various artists' styles, Mariani made completed versions of works that they had left behind unfinished. He focused on the ideas of the neo-classical period of the late eighteenth and early nineteenth centuries, as exemplified by the writings of Goethe, Delècluze, and

Winckelmann, who famously wrote that "The only way to become great and, if possible, inimitable, is by imitating the ancients." Mariani felt a special comraderie with Mengs, whose tomb, Mariani later learned, is located in the church of his elementary school in Rome.

Mariani featured some of these works in a 1975 exhibition in Rome titled "Compendium of Painting." The show caused quite a stir. A number of critics declared it a pivotal moment in the emergence of "post-modernism." It anticipated the so-called appropriation art movement by more than a decade. For a 1976 exhibition in Rome, Mariani painted a large architectural study based on Baldassarre

Peruzzi's illusionistic renderings of a Doric colonnade executed in 1535 for the Palazzo Massimi alle Colonne in Rome. This palace is part of an older complex that housed Rome's first printing office, established in 1467 by the Germans Arnold Pannartz and Konrad Schweinheim, who were responsible for the some of the first printings of works by Cicero and other authors from antiquity.

Mariani's formidable canvas, in the shape of a tall arch, is currently ensconced in the artist's Bridgehampton studio. It was one of his first works featuring this Doric colonnade, a recurring motif in numerous subsequent works. Also on view in the show was Mariani's *History of Art,* a series of large images centered on Winckelmann's book of the same name. These blow-up details of body parts and drapery were executed according to the rules of proportion put forth by the author to illustrate and define classical beauty. Here, Mariani makes an equation between the idealized figure and the architectural elements. In a metaphorical sense,

———

ABOVE: "The Constellation of Leo," 1980-1, oil on canvas, 133 ¾" x 177".

"The Eye Does Not See, The Heart Does Not Hurt," 1990, oil on canvas, 76" x 71".

columns suggest stand-ins for the figure, a notion consistent with that of writers such as Frederich W. J. Schelling (1775-1854), who, elaborating upon Vitruvius's first century observations in his *Philosophy of Art*, finds architecture's parallel in music.

"Proportions are obtained in architecture primarily because of the allusion to the human body, whose beauty is based precisely on proportions," Schelling writes. "Architecture, which in the observance of rhythm yet preserves high and strict form and has truth as a goal, approaches organic beauty through the observance of the harmonious aspects: since in this regard it can only be allegorical, harmony is actually the ideal element of this art. Here, too, architecture conforms to music, such that a beautiful building is indeed nothing other than music perceived by the eye, a concert composed not in a temporal, but rather a (simultaneous) spatial sequence of harmonies and harmonic combinations."[1]

For Schelling, the Doric column establishes the basic rhythm of architectural form. To him the curving lines of the Ionic order allude to harmony, while the Corinthian order is primarily a melodic type. "The Corinthian order unites the rhythmic forms of the Doric and the harmonic softness of the Ionic." He also sees the Doric as the masculine form evolving through the softening contours of the Ionic order to become the quintessential feminine form in the Corinthian order. A similar sense of musical rhythm and harmony may be found in architectural elements that appear in Mariani's work, perhaps the seminal example being his re-creation of the Peruzzi colonnade.

Mariani's re-creations, re-inventions, and paraphrases of the old masters culminated in his 1980 canvas *Constellation of Leo* (page 92). This vast composition (140-by-177 inches), which took a year to complete, was based on Mengs's 1760-61 painting *Parnassus,* a work that was inspired by Raphael's *School of Athens*. Mariani in this canvas presents a new School of Rome. Seated at the heart of a mythical Rome, surrounded by many of the leading art-world figures of the day, Mariani himself holds center stage; he wears the green cape of the San Luca Academy, the garment that Canova and Thorvaldsen wore as presidents of that illustrious institution. When the painting was exhibited in Rome in 1981, "Documenta 7," in Kassel, Germany, and in New York the following year, it caused an international sensation. Reproduced in countless newspapers and journals, the work was instrumental in bringing about a return to figuration in avant-garde painting. According to some critics, it is a key work of post-modern painting that sparked a new interest among young artists and critics in the ideas of neo-classicism. One of Mariani's champions at the time, the writer Charles Jencks, stated that Mariani's work defined a post-modern trope—"an ironic comment on a comment on a comment which signals the distance; a new myth thrice removed from its originating ritual."[2]

Jencks and others sought to define a relationship between Mariani's work and the worldwide post-modern movement in architecture and other fields. Some critics saw the artist as the heroic savior of beauty in an art-world filled with tired neo-Dada gestures, *nth* generation *Arte Povera* and mediocre conceptual works. Mariani appreciated the attention, indeed, acclaim that his early 1980s works received, but the artist felt that the new and broad exposure brought with it a profound misunderstanding about his goals. He had always followed a unique and solitary path, but he suddenly found himself at the forefront of a movement he had no wish to lead. All along he has maintained that his art should initiate a discourse on classical notions of beauty within the contemporary art context and should not be seen as a force set in opposition to contemporary currents. | He insists that his art is not directly related to classicism, realism, super-realism, surrealism, magic realism or any other "ism," except, perhaps, conceptualism. Especially offensive to the artist are analogies that certain critics have made between his work and the empty heroics of fascist art or social-realist painting. For Mariani, his work simply proposes an argument for form rather than non-form, and his principle goal has to do with pursuing what the artist refers to as a sense of spiritual beauty. "I look at the artists of the past also with the subtlety of irony," Mariani has said. "The theme may be of the moment, but the form is eternal if it's classical. My form of classicism is represented in every century. I don't think that classicism is something that is only from the past. It's also modern because it comes from what I'm painting now."[3]

> "...the form is eternal if it's classical."
>
> —*Carlo Maria Mariani*

"Eclipse I," 1998, oil on canvas, 40" x 35".

Gradually, Mariani turned away from direct quotations of eighteenth and nineteenth century art history, and instead devoted himself to refining a kind of personal mythology in which he incorporates well-known works of modern and contemporary art. Pieces by artists such as Picasso, Brancusi, Duchamp, Calder, and Beuys make regular appearances in Mariani's art beginning in the mid-1980s. Around the same time, he met the American art director Carol Lane and began to spend part of each year in the United States. In the works of that period he continued to use classically perfect figures, and also references to classical architecture, but his imagery became ever more fanciful and quixotic.

A particularly striking work from 1989, *Ivory Tower* (page 97), shows a classically perfect male nude with a miniature figure of "Venus" standing on his shoulder. Flanked by towering white Doric columns, he ascends heavenward with the help of tiny billowing white flags borrowed from a de Chirico painting. Crashing down from above and all around him are crude stone slabs, components of a famous 1985 installation by Beuys titled *The End of the Twentieth Century.* In allegorical terms, the painting depicts the ultimate triumph and transcendence of beauty. The Peruzzi colonnade reappears in a number of canvases from the late '80s. *Composition 3* (1989) shows the sleek, sturdy pillars in stark contrast to the shifting elements of a black Calder mobile. *Composition 7* is another study of columns. The large canvas features a segment of Brancusi's endless column that traverses the height of the composition in the foreground. Three Doric columns loom in the background while a large reclining figure wedged in-between seems to meld into one of Bernini's twisted Baldacchino pillars from the Vatican.

The Eye Does Not See, The Heart Does Not Hurt (1990) is an elaborate, multi-panel composition featuring a dynamic play of architectural forms (page 93). Two panels in the shape of right triangles, abutting at the lower right, nearly form a square. A circular panel attached to the upper right presses against the lower left panel. On the right a Corinthian column soars toward the sky, while on the left a melancholy male nude closes his eyes as if daydreaming. A nude in the circular panel floats toward heaven and *God,* a 1918 sculpture by the American Dadaist Morton Schamberg ensconced in the cupola. In the painting, architectural elements play counterpoint to the fractured architectonic design of the multi-panel support. It is tempting to see in this work a connection with deconstructivist archi-

"Abyss—First Dream," 1991-2, oil on canvas, 84" x 63".

tecture in the way that the surface suggests a collision of discontinuous or incongruous planes. Most likely the work has even less to do with the style of architects such as Frank Gehry, than Mariani's earlier paintings had in common with post-modern structures like those of Michael Graves.

Increasingly wild architectural inventions sprang from Mariani's imagination throughout the 1990s. *Abyss-First Dream* (1991-92) features a youth sleeping in the shade of an anthropomorphic structure whose mouth serves as a doorway. A dangling pottery shard is an allusion to the distant past, while the spiraling pupil of one of the building's "eyes" appears as a misty apparition (below left).

A 1995-96 series of works by the artist centers on the image of a stone caryatid. According to George Hersey in *The Lost Meaning of Classical Architecture,* the caryatid refers to the Carians, Persian girls who were made slaves of the Greeks, and also to Carya, daughter of the king of Laconia, who was turned into a walnut tree by Dionysus when she refused to love him. As the first columns were likely carved tree trunks, the caryatid thus came to be used in classical architecture as roof support for porticos and terraces.[4] In Mariani's work, the caryatid, metaphorically at least, carries the weight of history upon her head, a prisoner of today's misunderstanding and neglect. In his *Caryatid III,* the stone figure bound with barbed wire seems to have hung herself rather than face eternity in despair. In Caryatid II, she hangs from the ceiling of a grand, arched hallway. The mysterious folds of her tunic indicate her androgyny. A red carnation lying at her feet may have been left there by a sole mourner or an only admirer, the artist, perhaps?

Another recurring motif in Mariani's recent paintings and works on paper is a schematic rendering of the floor plan of the Accademia in Venice. Situated in the former convent of Santa Maria della Carità, with additions by Palladio and murals painted by Veronese in 1573, the building, for Mariani, is emblematic of architectural perfection and the harmonic integration of art and architecture. In works such as *The Kite,* the quatrefoil Accademia motif appears on the billowing white canopy of

> "In Mariani's work, the caryatid, metaphorically at least, carries the weight of history upon her head...."
>
> —*David Ebony*

an airborne kite. The kite carries aloft a ghostly classical figure that hovers far above a stormy sea. Glittering globes floating upon the waves hint at otherworldly places, where perhaps the figure may thrive once more. *The Kite I* and *Kite II* each show a solitary classical figure flying a kite that bears the Accademia symbol. In the former, part of the kite's tail displays an image based on Carravaggio's *Medusa;* in the latter, a figure with a green hand, perhaps a reference to a painting by Max Ernst, holds the string of a kite in which a cutout version of the Accademia design encompasses a classical profile.

During a trip to Germany in 1997, Mariani took a number of photos of buildings in Weimar and Berlin that were to reappear in a series of 1998-99 paintings in which the nude or partly clothed figure of Psyche flies or falls out of a building. Accompanied by her attribute, the butterfly, Psyche appears in these works as a symbol for the soul or spirit. In *Eclipse I* (page 94) she flies from the darkened interior of an elegant baroque structure. The two caryatids that frame the building's tall window hint at the captivity from which she has fled. *The Empty Night* (page 96) shows the figure of Psyche hovering in mid-air between Ionic columns flanked by large, classical stone heads. Raising her hand in a gesture of both resignation and defiance, Psyche recalls a figure from Poussin's *Rape of the Sabines.* In *Eclipse III,* Psyche may be flying onto or out of an elaborate Romanesque portico resembling the colonnade of a monastery courtyard. Here, she was unable to save Apollo; the head of the sun god hangs upside down, suspended by a rope attached to the vaulted ceiling.

Mariani's most recent paintings feature architectural elements based on the interior of Goethe's house at Weimar. One recent work, *The Miracle,* shows a statue of Apollo seated, placed to the left of an expansive and eerie interior space lined with tall blue-green columns. An enormous sprig of coral spouts from the figure's hair. The statue is visited by a band of sculptural figures with Picassoid heads. These identical, mass-produced modernist objects resemble the giant stone monuments of Rano Raraku on Easter Island. However, in Mariani's painting they appear to be humble

"The Empty Night," 1999, oil on canvas, 40" x 40".

and diminutive suppliants as they pay homage to the formidable, ancient god. In this enigmatic composition, Mariani presents a hushed and solemn image of eternity.

Architectural elements in Mariani's work function symbolically to enhance his overall project. His work offers an alternative to the discord and strife of the present cacophonous era. But rather than turn away from the relentless chaos, nihilism, violence, rhetorical conformity, and aggressive commercialism of today, the artist faces the situation head on. He produces an art of clarity and balance that is provocative in its silence and serenity. ❧

Carlo Maria Mariani has held numerous exhibitions in the U.S. and abroad. A museum retrospective of his work was organized by the Mathildenhohe, Darmstadt, Germany, in 1991, and traveled to the Los Angeles County Museum of Art in 1992. Another museum survey is currently being organized by the Bologna Museum of Modern Art, Italy, for 2001. His most recent gallery exhibition was held at Hackett-Freedman in San Francisco in 1999.

David Ebony is associate managing editor of Art in America. He also contributes to the on-line magazine artnet.com. His monograph on Carlo Maria Mariani is forthcoming from Volker Huber Editions, Frankfurt.

ENDNOTES

1. This and following Schelling quotation from Friedrich W.J. Schelling, The Philosophy of Art, Minneapolis, University of Minnesota, 1989, pp. TK–TK.

2. Charles Jencks, What is Post-Modernism?, London, Academy Editions, 1996, p. 41.

3. Mariani interviewed by Hugh Cumming in The Classical Sensibility, London, Art & Design/Academy, 1988, p. 18.

4. The Lost Meaning of Classical Architecture by George Hersey, Cambridge, MIT, 1988, pp. 71-72.

"Ivory Tower (Turris Eburneous)," 1989-90, oil on canvas, 90½" x 74¾".

DISCOVERING *the* AMERICAN MONOGRAPH

In the past, *The Classicist's* Ex Libris section has covered the language of architecture, its grammar; the interior; and treatises laying out the rules of drawing and composition. However, one important component of the education of a classical architect has not yet been addressed—precedent. Imitation, or mimesis, is one of the foundation principles in classical architecture. Students of architecture study what has been done before, sketching, photographing, reading descriptions of buildings long gone, and they attempt to reconstruct the building. By studying its elements and relationships to the whole, one learns about the architect's intentions, and about the inventiveness of the classical language.

One of the best ways to learn is to look at monographs of other architects. By examining many buildings by one architect one may observe trends in the architect's work and study his or her development. In the early years of the twentieth century, monographs were often collections of working drawings and photographs of buildings—excellent learning tools. More recently, monographs are often biographies of the architect, illustrated with glossy photographs and a few drawings, and are useful in a different way. In this issue of *The Classicist*, the Ex Libris editors have supplied a list of volumes that covers the range of books devoted to American architects—exhibition catalogs, monographs of work, biographies, and tribute books. All are worthy of investigation as the distinctiveness of American architecture varies from region to region and periods of time. There has never been a rigid American classical or traditional style as architects in the United States have adopted and adapted architectural language from every major civilization in the world. This gives architects one of the most richly varied architectural histories to draw upon. American cities are as likely to have an entire city center designed in one language, sometimes by one architect, as they are to have the rich tapestry of urban fabric like that of a European city.

Our section in this edition has several features to distinguish it from previous ones. First, we have an essay by Seth Joseph Weine to address the essential nature of the monograph. A Fellow of the Institute of Classical Architecture and the original art director for this publication, Mr. Weine gives us the elements of an ideal monograph, once considered just a portfolio, and enumerates the different types of monographs available today.

Next, in the Bookshelf section, a selection of monographs is divided into regions, giving readers a sampling of the variety of architecture across the country. Though only a brief cross section of architects, we aim to acquaint readers with many talented architects who are almost unknown outside of their particular region. And lastly, we are pleased to bring back our "Briefly Noted" section, with recent publications of distinction.

The editors note that there are many excellent architects—both regional and nationally known architects or firms—who lack monographs of any sort. We hope the following list spurs readers to research these architects including Cárrere & Hastings, Delano & Aldrich, Warren & Wetmore, York & Sawyer, Peabody & Sterns, Hertz & Tallent, Clinton & Russell, Arthur Brown (Bakewell & Brown), Henry Bacon, Bruce Price, and Horace Trumbauer. Readers may also note the paucity of women or minorities in these lists. It was difficult for either of these groups to gain clients in the early part of the century, and their work was rarely published. We urge readers to explore their libraries, their hometowns, and other sources for architects who have contributed to the architectural heritage of our country. *The Classicist* looks forward to years to come, as more talented architects are discovered, and are shared with the rest of the world. —S.J.T.

ABOVE: Proposal for a skyscraper (unbuilt), New York, 1932. John Russell Pope, Architect.

Dear Editor,

Thanks for asking me to review the Pope monograph. Unfortunately, I found so much that was inadequate or troubling in this book that a conventional review would end up as just a litany of complaints—which is ultimately neither illuminating nor interesting to read. The only way to make the citation of faults meaningful was to put them into a context, and use them as a positive opportunity: an opportunity to contrast the book with what a "model" monograph could really be.

What do architects want? *Most architects I know are busy—extremely busy. What we want are books that will help us become better architects. Period. Not academic texts, but books that will open to us the practical & aesthetic thinking processes of designers we admire—and deliver that information in a highly graphic way. For a number of years I've been thinking about the nature of architectural monographs, and why they so often (and frustratingly) fail to deliver what a serious practitioner wants to know. More and more luxuriously produced books are offered, almost all of which miss the mark.*

The state of monograph publishing needs to be reformed. This review-essay clearly outlines an anatomy for the ideal monograph. It could offer publishers a model to aspire to—one that's "as clear as a checklist". The world of design publishing is a small one; perhaps word will get around.

Respectfully yours,

S. J. Weine

• • •

JOHN RUSSELL POPE, ARCHITECT OF EMPIRE
By Steven McLeod Bedford
Introduction by William L. MacDonald
With new photography by Jonathan Wallen
240 pages, 250 illustrations, 100 in color.
Rizzoli, N.Y., 1998

We are presented here with something of a puzzle. A book—focused on an important subject, sumptuously produced, scrupulously researched, labored at over many years and in many lands, and underwritten by distinguished institutions—for which one can imagine hardly any readers! There may be general readers who would like to know more about an architect as important as John Russell Pope, but this book is too long and ponderous for a limited commitment. It is almost useless for the design professional as its visual materials are too incomplete to be a resource to learn from. Who's left? Perhaps a few graduate students who need some of the information to do their doctoral dissertations. Perhaps their professors, who need to check a date for an article they're preparing. That totals about a dozen people a year. For the rest of us, we are left with a muscular mammoth, large and impressive, but hard to chew and impossible to digest.

How could this impressive project have yielded such unsatisfying results? The situation is not confined to this single example, for the infelicitous presentation of architects' work is to be found in the majority of monographs on the market. There is an origin to this wasteful phenomenon: The avoidance of the most basic questions that a publisher should ask when considering a new monograph project: What kind of monograph am I creating, for whom, and what will the readers get out of it? In my view there are six possible approaches.

Popular: If the book's purpose is to make an architect better known and appreciated by a cultured (but largely non-professional) audience, the book should not be burdened by a lengthy, detailed text. It would need to rely on large reproductions of seductive renderings and luscious photography. These would be put in context by a brief introduction and chapter openings, supplemented by informative captions.

Professional: If the goal is to produce something useful to practicing designers and planners, the level and quantity of visual material must change radically. Photos may be effective at giving a feeling for a building in its setting, but a book composed mainly of photographs leaves one with the feeling of having gone through a stack of shelter magazines. There remains the impression of a pleasant collage of images—*but nothing sticks!* What educates (and penetrates) deeply are drawings, drawings, drawings of elevations, sections, site plans, and details.

Definitive: If an author aims to produce the ultimate work on his subject, then other standards apply. Some architects are subject to an endless series of monographs. Nearly every year we are offered a new work on Palladio or Adam. Frank Lloyd Wright is practically a cottage industry. Incredibly, this is the first monograph on Pope and is published 60 years after his death! Once a book is out, most architects, if they ever get written about again, are lucky to be reassessed once a generation. In light of this, one quickly arrives at what I call the "single bullet theory" of monographs: If you have only one chance, you better get *everything* into your book: Every date, every client, every anecdote, every bit of juvenilia, and the story of each project. Moreover, each fact and facet would be reflected in a comprehensive pictorial record. For example, if a project evolved through several schemes, each would be offered for visual comparison.

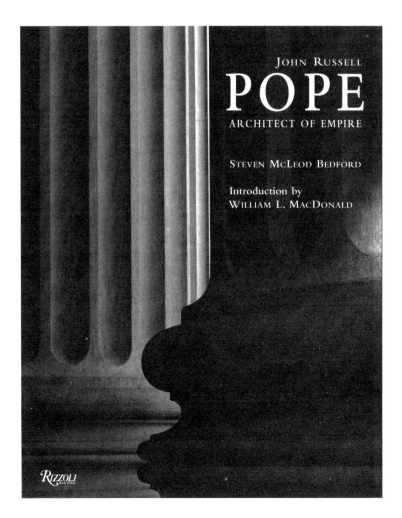

Such studies would be gargantuan, and few publishers will have the means to support such productions—though the advent of the CD ROM may change all that—but the results will be a timeless resource for anyone attempting to learn about the career of a creator.

Catalog *Raisonné:* Here the goal is to offer a complete record of the architects' work. Each project is cataloged, vital information is supplied, and a few paragraphs of description, history, and commentary are provided (the focus, however, is on the visual). Organization is generally chronological. In its ultimate version, every available sketch, rendering, image, plan, and document is shown with a caption that explains how each reveals an aspect of the design.

Portfolios: These are usually large-format productions, often offered as loose plates in a custom-designed case. They are generally published and edited by the architect's own firm, a tradition reaching back through the Adam brothers (the classic exemplar of this kind) unto the lost, legendary project treatises of the ancient Greeks. Though they are called "monographs," they actually bear as much relation to a serious, objective study as any self-portrait or memoir. It's important to remember their motivating purpose: To present the subject in the best light, either for impressing potential clients or for soothing the anxious ego of the architect who is unsure of his place in history. This is not to say that they are without value. Portfolios are often the only generally available source of information about a designer's output (the one that Pope's office produced was the sole collection of his designs for decades until Bedford's book came out). The Adam brothers set a high standard, and some self-published monographs like those of Platt, Lutyens, or Mellor, Meigs & Howe, include a rich abundance of detailed drawings to compliment their photographic presentation.

Biographical: Here, narrative is all: the drama and the incidents of the subject's life make up the bulk of the text, with formal criticism of the architect's work secondary to the flow of the story. A sliver of illustrations is usually provided, as reference points for the narrative.

· · ·

I regret to inform John Russell Pope's admirers that the book under review cannot claim success as any of these types. To understand the extent of the failure, let us compare the author's performance against the standards for an ideal monograph. These can be stated as a set of prescriptions:

1. Be "properly introduced": Abruptly starting up the slope of reviewing a life's work is hard, especially since we are generally expected to trudge through a chapter or two on family history, early education, and the politics of the time before we get to "the good stuff". What's needed to get our biographic-voyeuristic juices flowing, is a spirited, appreciative, overview. Someone must be found to author a Forward, someone who is esteemed in his profession, and has a resonance for the subject. William L. MacDonald's Forward shows that he has a deep respect for Pope. As practicing classicists, however, we only hope that when he says, "As an architect of monumental American buildings, Pope was the last of that long line of classical interpreters. . ." he is ultimately proved to be wrong.

2. Formgiving: I once helped organize an exhibition of the architectural work of a late friend. As I unrolled drawing after drawing, I wondered how to give coherence to her lifetime's rich production. Show it chronologically? By building type? By parti? Each approach simultaneously clarifies *and* obscures. All monograph authors are faced with the categorical imperative of giving form to a great mass of material. Bedford's

solution is an elegant compromise. He examines buildings by types in the time sequence that each type became a prominent part of Pope's career. Within the type he looks at each commission chronologically. When a particular type contains a large number of examples over a span of years (Pope's monumental commissions for instance), the author returns to it with a later chapter.

3. Formats that don't annoy the reader: Books are published with valuable content that will never be read, or, once started, will not be finished. The fault lies not in their words but in their design. Among the most common problems are:

· Book designers that are more committed to conforming to typographic fashions than to making pages that are easy to read. Witness the vogue for using the eye-unfriendly *Bodoni* typeface for the text of entire books.

· Spreads that are laid out with double-columns on each page, giving the reader an oppressive feeling that they are facing two open books side-by-side.

· Segregating illustrations to the back (or center) of the book, forcing the reader into an eternal (and tiresome) flip-flop as he tries to find an image that corresponds to the text.

· The sparse use of sub-heads. They are invaluable in breaking up painfully long spans of text (and help distinguish where the author starts talking about a new commission).

· Publishers (and a public) that sometimes act like children attracted to shiny objects, hence the choice of glossy paper over matte. This is a sad choice for long texts, as the glare from those pages reduces reading to a dreadful task. Moreover, photographs reproduced on glossy paper are not necessarily better. After all, reality generally doesn't have a high-gloss look.

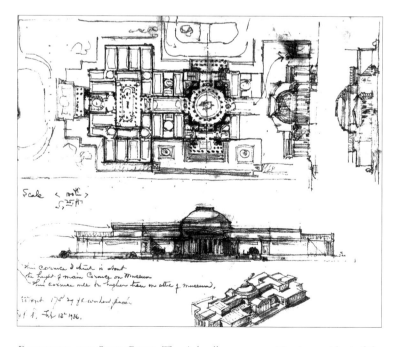

REMEMBER THE SEED GERM: *There's hardly a more exciting image (short of the finished building) than an early sketch that shows the designer crystallizing his idea. Monographs should include these clues to the architect's thinking. (Pope's drawing courtesy of the Gallery Archives, National Gallery of Art, Washington, D.C.)*

• Making no distinction between what content should be in footnotes versus endnotes. Often, juicy tidbits (and keen observations) are hidden in endnotes, buried among the source citations. Conversely, dry citations are needless at the foot of a page.

These are *not* trivial matters, for the "readability" of a text will profoundly affect the size of its audience. The Pope book has several format faults, but the chief one is using a weak (or under-inked) typeface. Against the bright white paper it cannot hold the reader's eye.

4. Give us the key: When there's an important person, moment, or object in the subject's life, show it. For Pope, it was certainly the Theater of Marcellus, which he measured during his student days while traveling on the Rome Prize. Pope returned to the theater's Ionic order relentlessly throughout his career, and Bedford points out each use, but strangely does not mention it during his description of Pope's education, nor does he illustrate it (which is especially to be wondered at, since a copy of the drawing is extant).

5. To psychologize—or not: Attributing the actions of one's subject to dark, moist motivations is an ever-popular game, but there's the pitfall of finding that your psychological system is going out of fashion. Authors share a further danger: Their theories are permanently rendered in print. Legions of biographers now bear the embarrassment of seeing their deep Freudian interpretations derided by a world that no longer widely validates such a system. Still, a monograph that did not delve below the surface would be shirking its duty. To plumb your subject's feelings while not giving in to current (and soon-to-be-passé) therapeutic modes of dissection is a difficult dance. The wisest analytic course is to stick to the "classics" of human behavior. The ones that are universal: Guilt, jealousy, compassion, and so on. Bedford only indulges in psychologizing once, when he says of Pope "…this tenacious adherence to classicism may also have been an expression of insecurity…" but gives little proof for this gratuitously offered notion.

6. Give us the anecdotes: Discovering how the offices of the great worked—how the business got done so that the buildings we admire could be created—is like finding gold. Testimony to the importance of this subject is the fact that *Pencil Points*—the greatest architectural magazine ever published in America, and the one that was dominant during Pope's career—was devoted to being an aid to the art and business of running a practice. (As a publication, it became steadily less interesting as it strayed from that purpose.) Most monographs devote only a page or two to this topic of consuming interest to practitioners, and the flavor of the office is usually conveyed through anecdotes. However many are told, we always want more, for these are the incidents that put blood in the corpse of history. Bedford tells us that Pope's tendency to distance himself from clients forced junior employees into awkward client contact; and that he acted brusquely with some employees and warmly with others. I wonder what stories he heard that made him make these generalizations and instantly wish that the readers could hear them too.

7. Show us the man: Something changes forever when you meet the creator of a work you've read about or walked through. When the subject has passed from this existence, photos will have to do, and the more, the better. We can look into a person *when we are shown multiple views*. The snapshots of Harold Van Doren Shaw in costume for a local theatrical, Mies clowning with a paper flower at a party, or the many shots of a smilingly sunny Lars Sonck round out our sense of the subject. Further, when an author has included photos of his subject at various ages, we can see him mature as his work does. Bedford's book contains a single photograph

of his subject. A large photo portrait of Pope stares out at us from the frontispiece—strong and forthright, but not forbidding or unattractive—clearly a studio shot. Surely there must be other views, however slight, that would show us other facets of this man in his time.

8. Behind the scenes: Anyone who has ever worked in an office knows that the great name is only as good as the staff that brings the projects from concept stage to constructed reality, and this was no less so with Pope's office. Bedford gives capsule profiles of Pope's indispensable adjutants, Otto Eggers and Daniel Higgins. They served him for years, but remain shadows in this book and deserve more coverage. An approach that gives some credit and dignity to the troops would be to have an appendix that gives an employee list, and highlights the most important ones with concise biographies and photos. This can be taken further (as it was by Charles Baldwin in his biography of Stanford White) by including profiles of collaborating artists, patrons, and other associates.

9. Inside the hothouse: One of the pleasures of paging through old volumes of *Pencil Points* is coming across group shots of the office staffs of architects you admire. All the members of the firms are seen together in the drafting room and these photos are windows into their working lives. Questions are answered that give you a sense of the life of the office: What's the age range? Are the tables crowded together, and what equipment did they have? What was the lighting like? Is the atelier spartan or cluttered, and, if cluttered, with what? Drawings? Ornamental fragments? Risqué cartoons? I don't know if such a photo exists for Pope's office, but any monograph that would tell the world about the conditions of creation and production should try to include such a shot.

10. It's the little things: Everyone who's seen the photographs of Freud's Vienna offices gazes with fascination at the multitude of curious objects. Dozens of examples of primitive art are crowding his desk. Do we perceive more about the man from seeing this? You betcha'. Monograph writers could include such evidence as a way of building our picture of an architect. Whether it be a set of Burnham's title blocks (the name changes show the firm's evolution), Schinkel's deft design for a damask napkin border, or Le Corbusier's passport, each adds a clue.

11. Be generous with reference images: The unforgivable sin for authors of art and architecture books is to refer to works and then not show them. I wonder how many of us were turned off art history by trying to struggle through *Gardner's Art Through The Ages* (the predominant art textbook during my youth). Its author repeatedly compared the painting or sculpture she was analyzing with something that was not pictured. My frustration would build until throwing the book at the nearest art teacher seemed the best thing to do. Bedford boils us in the same pot. He eruditely compares Pope's projects and motifs to works from all the riches of architecture's history, but nary an image is offered. It's fair for an author to imagine he has an educated readership, but impractical to assume that he shares so much of the same knowledge base that illustrating his references is unnecessary. At times this lack of images seems cruel, for the reader continually, naggingly, wonders what he's missing. Postage stamp sized shots of the referenced work would be more than sufficient. Venturi showed us this long ago, when he used them, like visual buckshot, to persuasively back up each of his points in *Complexity and Contradiction*. The lack of reference images becomes ever more vexing, as Bedford mentions a number of Pope's works that do not appear in a single illustration. Even minor works tell us something about a career, and deserve a look.

12. Verifiable opinions: It's not enough to check facts; judgements can also be tested. Pope tried his hand at several high-rise office building

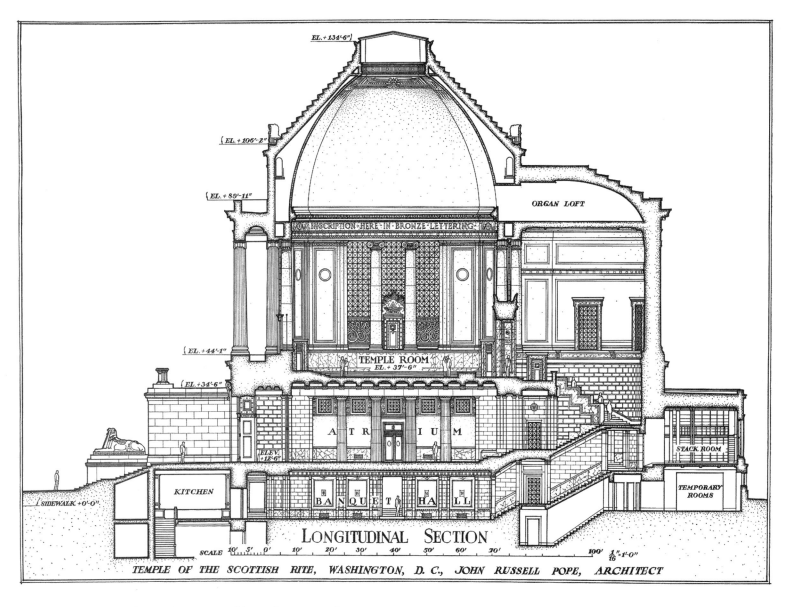

EL. + 134'-6"

EL. + 106'-2"

EL. + 89'-11"

ORGAN LOFT

INSCRIPTION·HERE·IN·BRONZE·LETTERING

EL. + 44'-1"

EL. + 34'-6"

TEMPLE ROOM
EL. + 37'-6"

A T R I U M

ELEV.
+ 12'-6"

STACK ROOM

KITCHEN

BANQUET HALL

TEMPORARY
ROOMS

SIDEWALK +0'-0"

LONGITUDINAL SECTION

SCALE 10' 5' 0'   10'   20'   30'   40'   50'   60'   70'   100' $\frac{1}{16}$"=1'-0"

TEMPLE OF THE SCOTTISH RITE, WASHINGTON, D. C., JOHN RUSSELL POPE, ARCHITECT

designs, and Bedford fingers the questionable results. He may be correct with his verdict on Pope, but, when he speaks of the "…incompatibility of the essentially horizontal classical mode with the verticality of the sky-scraper," Bedford instantly invalidates great chunks of the commercial core of our cities—thousands of buildings that inventively engage classical design with the high-rise building type. Clearly such a judgement cannot be sustained, as a short stroll through any downtown will show.

13. Hearing voices: The opinion of clients, users (often not the same thing) builders, engineers, and collaborators all add to our faceted vision of the work. The words of design critics, whether they are curmudgeonly carping or the warmest encomium, bring relief to the otherwise monotone voice of a monograph's author. Even those that have added to, renovated (or demolished) an architect's work may have views that illuminate the oeuvre.

14. Take your supplements: If it's disruptive to include extended quotes or critical texts in the body of the book, appendices can be an ideal site for them. Such an editorial policy can be extended to the inclusion of

valuable but hard-to-find texts, such as Pierce Rice's devastating critique of Pope's National Gallery—a unique essay that examines the building on its own terms, and finds it greatly wanting. Bruce Kamerling's monograph on Irving Gill can be commended for including Gill's only two known published essays. Similarly, a book on Bertram Goodhue would benefit from reprinting the architect's delightful musings on office management from a 1924 *Pencil Points*.

15. Do ask, do tell: Nobody's perfect, not even architects. It's not the author's job to manufacture an icon, and including the less palatable side of his subject is fulfilling a duty to Clio. Shannon Irish, in her study

ABOVE: The Kindest Cut: *The inclusion of sections, like this one of Pope's Temple of the Scottish Rite in Washington, tells the reader about the organization of spaces, as well as the processional experience of the building. Unfortunately, such informative material is often omitted from monographs. (Image from American Masterpieces)*

of Cass Gilbert, doesn't flinch when revealing that her subject shared in the endemic anti-Semitism of the times. Bedford forthrightly shows Pope providing segregated facilities in a major project, as well as noting his sometimes difficult relations with employees.

16. Writing that moves: Bedford's prose is clear and serviceable, but largely emotionless—one can only wonder what a stylist like John Summerson would have done with the material. [Where can the writer find passion to inject into his voice? By returning to the sense of wonder and curiosity that motivated him to begin his study.] Only once does Bedford's text well with energy. During his account of Pope's alternative schemes for the Lincoln Memorial, his descriptions are mouthwatering. I've seen the drawings and Bedford is right: They're knockouts! But his book offers no pictures of them, which brings us to…

17. Less talk, more show: Why provide detailed descriptions, when a photo or elevation would let us see the point with directness and power? Bedford makes us sail oceans of words, when we thirst for the

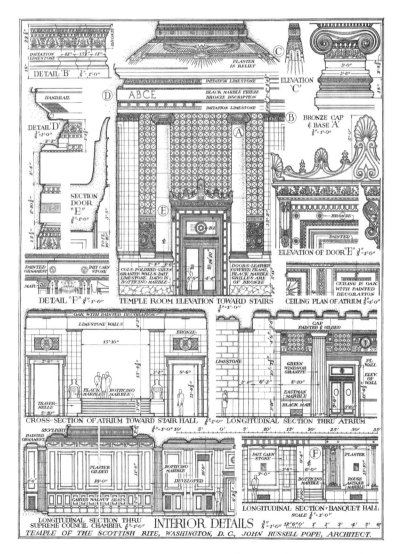

sweet water of plans and elevations. Why the strong emphasis on drawings? *Because that's how an architect thinks.* Decree: All monograph authors shall have the phrase "show it" boldly printed on their mouse pad.

18. Context is all: Designs respond to their environment. Now there's a home truth, but you'd never know it from looking at this book. The reader is hardly ever presented with a site plan; a street map, north arrow, scale indication, or anything that would tell you how the project fits into the world.

19. The big picture: Filmmakers often open scenes with an "establishing shot," an overall view that helps the audience understand the environment and the character's place in it. Such an approach would have helped in this book. Some of the most significant projects, like the Frick Museum, are presented to us in fragmented views. A "long shot" would have helped us gain a sense of the 'wholeness' of the project.

20. More than the obvious: Beyond the general views, almost every project has a unique, telling (and sometimes quirky) detail that would delight the reader. Give it to us. For example, we are shown an impressive obelisk: Pope's Macdonough Memorial. Just over the edge of the hill one can detect some amazing carving at the monument's base, and Bedford takes time to describe it. We're intrigued and want to see it up close—but where is a picture? We are denied the pleasure. Similarly, the book offers a close-up shot of a Corinthian capital from one of the luxurious homes that Pope created. It's a nice photo but a very average capital. Surely the house had something more interesting, more revealing, to expend page space on.

21. Density creates context: Sometimes an architect's designs so saturate a city that his oeuvre begins to transform the metropolis. This can certainly be said for McKim Mead and White's work in New York, and an even stronger case could be made for Pope's impact on the nation's capital. Describing the projects in a city one-by-one, as the book does, allows us to see the merits of each—but denies us a sense of the whole. Monographs could easily cure this tunnel vision by providing a city map with each of the architect's buildings indicated and keyed. The ubiquity of the work would quickly and powerfully be seen.

22. Image versus reality: Ever since Plato articulated the philosophy of ultimate and perfect Forms, the West has been deeply haunted by the contrast between our inner vision and the concreteness of life. Architects play with this tension every time they prepare a rendering for a client's review. (If anything, the computer's ability to depict a variety of highly persuasive "realities" has aggravated the problem.) Pope's office (through the hand of Otto Eggers) created some of the most compelling architectural renderings of modern times. The pencilwork is bewitching, and we get to see a nice selection in the book. Bedford occasionally offers us something that monograph authors should do for every project: Show us the rendering *and* the final built results (preferably side-by-side, photographed from the same point of view), so that the ideal and the real can be compared. William Mitchell's Neil Reid monograph is particularly good in this regard.

23. Captions as opportunities: Bedford shows a beautiful photograph of one the many palaces for the elite that Pope created, but what are we looking at? Is this the facade that faces the ocean? Did Pope design that fountain in the garden too? And this interior shot: Are we looking back toward the entrance? What's that intriguing paneling detail on the left? The reader may never know, for the author is often mute about such things. Captions are monograph-land's most unexploited natural resource, and that should change. Contemporary book designers prize "white space" in their page layouts. Fear not: The ample margins of most books could absorb captions of three times today's average length without a sacrifice in the overall readability of the page. Let us have extended captions. They can offer more than a simple identification. Each is a chance to clarify an orientation, to share another insight, to point out a unique detail. David Lowe's books take advantage of this chance to tell more of the story and it's like getting an unexpected bonus.

24. Full sets: To an architect-reader there's nothing as frustrating as being shown *one* floor plan of a building. They want to view every floor to see how the space planning was handled at each level. Just because the upper floors of a building "only" has sleeping quarters or offices does not make it less revealing of the designer's skill. Moreover, secondary spaces often reveal much about the life lived in them: Whether the offices have facilities for both genders, or how much privacy the bedrooms allow, speak to us about the clients, the architect, and their society. The number of projects in this book that have plans (and show multiple levels or sections) are in the minority. Moreover, when offered a plan, it's not always the most interesting one: We are shown an upper library level of the National Archives building, where most of the space is devoted to stacks. But what of the main level, where Pope provided a processional spatial sequence wherein our country's founding documents are approached with reverence? Further, can a building be understood without a section? This is particularly significant in Pope's oeuvre. His monumental/institutional commissions relied on the play of vaults, ceiling heights, and the experience of ascent (he was truly a master at creating cascades of exterior stairs).

25. Size does matter: When we are shown plans, they must be big enough to be readable. I'm delighted to see a full page view of a charming lounge in Pope's *Ward Home for Aged and Respectable Bachelors* (I wouldn't mind ending up there myself), but readers would be better served by a larger reproduction of the facility's plan, which is printed too small to read without a magnifying glass.

26. Deeper, please: Perhaps the paucity of plans and other drawings can be attributed to the disappearance of most of Pope's papers. This however is not the case with the National Gallery of Art; Pope's most famous building. Here's the opportunity—not taken by the author—to show through drawings the complete development of a project from *early sketch to detailed contract drawing*. A copy of Pope's brilliant, stunningly concise sketch (showing the entire concept of the museum crystallized on one sheet) does exist but mysteriously does not rate an appearance in the book.

Ideally, every monograph would, at least once, devote a whole chapter to fully documenting a single project. After showing the development stages of the design, a *complete* set of plans, sections, and elevations, would be reproduced at a scale convenient for study. Finally, a portfolio of representative contract drawings would be included so that one can see how the grand concept is ultimately manifest at the tectonic and sensual level of details.

27. Chronology: A list of buildings can be so much more potent than the dry enumeration of projects at the back of the Pope book. Ideally it would offer a mini-dossier on each work, including the following information:
- Client
- Building type and concise description
- When it came to the office
- Office job number
- Primary partner and staff
- When construction was begun and completed
- Complete address, including street number (or cross-street)
- Gross square footage and cost
- Primary materials and structural system
- Present status
- A general view (preferably a photo, taken at middle distance)
- A plan of the primary floor
- A comment from a contemporary source (newspaper, the client, etc.)
- Bibliographical references

The inclusion of the set of floor plans can be especially illuminating, as it allows us to develop a typology of the architect's approach to planning. This is important with Pope. Bedford perceptively notes that Pope relied on a limited set of partis, and a collection of small plans for comparison would make this readily evident. To be fair, Bedford cannot be completely blamed for the lack of this information. Pope's office records were largely destroyed or lost, and it is a tribute to the author's doggedness that he pieced together a largely comprehensive list of Pope's projects. Still, the ideal project list is not an unrealizable fantasy. Chappell's monograph on the work of Graham, Anderson, Probst and White goes far to fulfill it, and even the old Blom edition of the works of McKim Mead and White gives adequate notes for each project.

28. Give us the glory: Finally, if there is one project that is transcendent, share it with joy. Pope's *Temple of the Scottish Rite* may be America's most splendid classical pile! This book gives us some glossy color photos of it, but not one shows how it rises like a mountain in its tree-lined Washington neighborhood. Readers are offered a shot of the entry hall, but this foreshortened view does not convey its expanse, nor is the thrilling verticality of the main sanctuary revealed in the other photo shown. Though John Wallen has made a superb portfolio of new photographs for this book, here one feels that he did not understand the building. Also, specially drafted presentation drawings of this project were created by Pope's office and the inclusion of them here would have enhanced the reader's experience of Pope's best building.

• • •

In summary, what are we left with when considering this first monograph on Pope? A text that is clear but not compelling, photography that is lovely but sometimes unrevealing, project profiles that are word rich but visually impoverished, and—ultimately—a book that we are glad exists, but which will sit on the shelf, largely unused. Bedford's book is a tribute to the author's years of diligent search and research, yet it exemplifies many of the faults of today's monographs. Pope is an architect that today's classicists could learn from. He (and his potential students) deserve more.

Seth Joseph Weine, a 20-year veteran of the Architecture Wars, is a New York based designer. His work has included architecture, furniture, graphics, and teaching; and he was the founding art director of The Classicist. *He wants to grow up to be a Regency architect.*

THE CLASSICIST'S BOOKSHELF
THE AMERICAN MONOGRAPH

As usual, we are pleased to present a partial list of monographs for your perusal. This is not intended to be an exhaustive list, but one to expose the reader to prominent and successful architects of the various regions of our country. We have focused our selections on the late nineteenth and early twentieth century. During this time period, architecture became a profession, and the influence of the Ecole des Beaux Arts is seen in office organization and education. This is the beginning of the 'American Renaissance', and we hope to express the inter-relationships of these architects. Titles and architects were chosen for their interest and talent, therefore expanding on a traditional view of large firms being the only ones to complete successful projects. There is a mix of residential, public, religious, commercial, and institutional work among these architects. Books range from the biographic to the wholly graphic. Alternate titles have been suggested for some architects. Though many of the volumes are still available, some are rare or out of print. Many of these titles are ripe for reprinting. We hope that our efforts may introduce you to one or two previously unknown masters. —S.J.T., P.J.D., S.J.W.

NORTHEAST

Grossman, Elizabeth Greenwell. **The Civic Architecture of Paul Cret,** *Boston: Cambridge University Press, 1996.*

Paul Cret (1876-1945) is one of the towering architects of the past century. Though never a strictly classical architect, Cret was able to unite his personal tastes in architecture with the over-riding vision of the public society. During his career, Cret produced work throughout the country in both public and private realms. His work appears in many previously published volumes, but is rarely shown as a whole. Grossman's book focuses on six of Cret's public commissions, and is less a monograph than a study of the projects and Cret's struggle to design and complete them. Each work is surveyed in a dedicated chapter, and Grossman attempts to draw a parallel between Cret's personal ambition and public architecture.

Other works better illustrate Cret's architecture, although they do not give us a wide range of his work. *Paul Cret at Texas* is an excellent book of Cret's work and drawings at the University of Texas, and is an exhibition

catalog. *Paul Phillippe Cret, Architect and Teacher,* by Theo White combines essays of Cret as an educator and architect with a wide range of images of his work. Finally, *The Folger Shakespeare Library* (published for the Trustees of Amherst College in 1933) is a monograph of one building in Cret's career, and is an excellent volume giving insight into the design and detail of Paul Cret's transformation of a strictly classical language into a more modern sensibility.

Dana, Richard H., Jr., Introduction by Harmon H. Goldstone. **Richard Henry Dana, 1879-1933, Architect,** *New York, NY, 1965.*

Richard Henry Dana (1879-1933) was educated at Harvard and Columbia Schools of Architecture, and went on to study at the Ecole des Beaux-Arts in Paris. He returned to New York and worked in the offices of Delano & Aldrich and Welles Bosworth. He opened a practice with Henry Killam Murphy in 1908 (Murphy & Dana), which closed in 1920. During that time, the firm worked on the Yale in China school, and designed several additional educational buildings in China. After the partnership dissolved, the next 12 years were spent in his own practice, primarily in the Northeast, and consisted of many private estates, schools, and renovations. The work exhibited in the monograph is a collection of plates illustrating Dana's various solutions to similar types of problems. He is best known for his refinement of Colonial and Georgian elements in his work, as well as for being the editor of *Georgian Homes.* The oeuvre of his work exhibits a quiet dignity and refinement, as well as an element of inventiveness in his details.

A limited printing of only 500 copies makes this edition hard to come by, but well worth the effort and expense if one can find it. A list of his houses, renovations, and other projects is found at the rear of the book.

Price, Chester. **Delano & Aldrich: A Portrait of Ten Country Houses,** *Introduction by Royal Cortissoz, New York: 1924.*

The work displayed in this monograph covers the years between 1912 to the early 1920s, and captures a vital portion of Delano & Aldrich's portfolio. The work in this phase of the firm's development is derived from McKim, Mead and White's houses, but brings a new level of design to the American country house and estate. A rigid symmetry of design and romanticism did not drive the design, instead, we see the beginnings of free plans, and elements of restraint and quiet elegance are brought into the designs, along with an overriding linearity. The estates are shown integrated into the landscape as well.

This volume was available in both a student edition and a full folio, the difference between them in the binding and a few extra plates. The drawings by Chester Price are exquisite and influenced a generation of illustrators. Anyone, from student to practitioner to layman can learn as much from the illustrations as from the houses themselves. Each country house is illustrated in plan and a series of perspectives, providing a rich understanding of the design.

Bacon, Mardges. **Ernest Flagg: Beaux Arts Architect and Urban Reformer,** *New York: American Monograph Series, Architectural History Foundation, 1986.*

Of all the Americans of his generation for whom study at the Ecole des Beaux-Arts marked the mecca of architectural training, Ernest Flagg (1857-1947) would seem to be the paradigm. Here was an architect whose work represented the broadest range of Beaux-Arts theory and practice in America. There is a refreshing originality about his work, as he was particularly taken by the decorative use of exposed iron and glass. His work includes the Corcoran Gallery of Art in Washington, the U.S. Naval Academy at Annapolis, and the now demolished Singer Tower—one of the most memorable early skyscrapers in Manhattan.

In this groundbreaking study Mardges Bacon carefully documents the work of Flagg, both as a proponent of academic classicism and as an ardent promoter of urban reform. This well written monograph is descriptive in character, and provides biographical and contextual information that offers the reader an invaluable insight into the work of this often overlooked architect.

Forster, Frank J. **Country Houses: The Work of Frank J. Forster,** *New York: William Helburn, Inc. 1931.*

Frank J. Forster (1886-1948) was the nation's leading exponent of the French Provincial Style. He believed that this playful and picturesque form of vernacular architecture was the most suitable and malleable for domestic work. Grounded in sound logical design and appropriate use of natural materials, specific features included steeply pitched roofs, the use of dormers and towers, and a diversity of roof levels, chimneys, and window openings.

In 1931, Forster published his monograph *Country Houses,* illustrated with photographs, renderings, and plans. This portfolio of work is a testament to Forster's considerable talents as an architect committed to creating an enduring architecture of simplicity, amenity, and delight.

Oliver, Richard. **Bertram Grosvenor Goodhue,** *New York: The Architectural History Foundation, 1983.*

Bertram Grosvenor Goodhue (1869-1924) was one of the most talented architects of the twentieth century. His draftsmanship and design abilities are extremely wide ranging, leading to distinctly different styles of design in each region of the country. All of them are imbued with a quality, however, that make them instantly recognizable as a Goodhue creation. Goodhue was a self-educated architect who gained his experience through apprenticeship. Incredibly artistic and talented, Goodhue held the view that the Beaux-Arts was too rule-bound and dry. In the early years of his career, he was a draftsman, but after winning a competition for a church, he associated himself with Cram & Wentworth. During his association with Cram, many churches and projects at West Point were completed, as well as institutional work at the William Rice Institute. After the dissolution of his partnership, Goodhue pursued work on his own. He is most noted for churches and public buildings—including the Nebraska State Capitol and the Los Angeles Public Library.

The Oliver monograph is an excellent study of Goodhue's life and work. From architectural composition to detail, to book design and typography, Goodhue was an accomplished, innovative designer. His ability to work in many styles, and unify many different arts in his architectural compositions make him one of the greatest American architects we have yet seen. For those interested in more of his drawings, *Bertram Grosvenor Goodhue, Architect and Master of Many Arts* is recommended.

Stein, Susan. **The Architecture of Richard Morris Hunt,** *Chicago: University of Chicago Press, 1986.*

Richard Morris Hunt (1827-1895) is one of the great presences in American architecture. He was the first American to be trained at the Ecole des Beaux-Arts, and it was Hunt's influence that brought the French monumental character to American Architecture at the end of the nineteenth century. Hunt's social position and his architectural training garnered him many commissions, resulting in houses, museums, libraries, and other public works. Included in this list is the New York Metropolitan Museum of Art.

This was the first volume to be published specifically on Hunt's architecture. It accompanied an exhibition of his work, and is divided into several essays on various aspects of his life and education. The essays also cover the relationship of his architecture to landscape, specific buildings, and the role of detail and ornament. Illustrations are numerous, in both black and white and color.

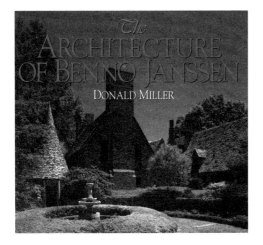

Miller, Donald. **The Architecture of Benno Jansen,** *Pittsburgh, PA: Carnegie Mellon University, 1997.*

Benno Jansen (1874-1964) is perhaps Pittsburgh's finest architect of the classic period. This gifted and versatile designer is best known for his reserved public buildings, as well as exquisite country estates in an English-influenced romantic style. In all his work, Jansen sought an aesthetic of simple, serene design grounded in the pleasures of everyday life. This philosophy is immediately apparent in his fairy tale Norman manor "La Tourelle", and the extraordinary Tudor Gothic mansion of "Elm Court" - both of which rank among the most beautiful domestic buildings ever to grace the American landscape.

This stunning monograph, lavishly illustrated with photographs by Edward Massey, is the first comprehensive study of this significant regional architect. Donald Miller provides a wonderfully written dialogue that introduces us to the work of Benno Jansen, and offers a rare insight into the tastes, interests, and values of early twentieth century Pittsburgh.

Hewitt, Mark Alan. **Domestic Architecture of H.T. Lindeberg,** *New York: Acanthus Press, 1996.*

Harrie Thomas Lindeberg (1880-1959) was probably the most prolific and widely known residential architect of the eclectic era, designing refined country houses for an elite clientele. He first served as an assistant to Stanford White, before establishing a reputation as an emerging innovator of romantic country house design. His language was from the vernacular—the colonial dwelling, the rural cottage, the village hamlet, the barn—and the timeless pattern of materials and craft. Building and designing with simplicity was his creed. As his career progressed he refined this design philosophy to incorporate art deco and early modernism.

The republication of this beautiful 1940 monograph provides a valuable retrospective that chronicles the work of this enigmatic architect. In a new introduction Mark Alan Hewitt presents a first-class interpretation of Lindeberg as a traditionalist with a fresh and lively sense of innovation.

Wilson, Richard Guy. **The Architecture of McKim, Mead and White,** *New York: Dover, 1990.*

The impact of Charles Follen McKim (1847-1909), William Rutherford Mead (1846-1923), and Stanford White (1853-1906) is profound, as together they redirected the course of civic architecture in America. They had a vision of a Golden City Beautiful, reminiscent of the masterpieces of ancient Rome and the Italian Renaissance and distinctively expressive of a new national building tradition.

The firm of McKim, Mead and White rose to prominence with the design of large "shingle style" country houses for the resorts along the shores of New Jersey, Newport, and Long Island. Yet by the end of the 1880's their focus had shifted towards the reshaping of America's urban landscape, and in particular that of New York City. During the next forty years McKim, Mead and White became the preeminent office in America. The Boston Public Library, Pennsylvania Station in New York, and the campus of Columbia University are among the national landmarks they designed. As important as the buildings themselves was the next generation of architects who were trained in the firm's drafting rooms. Their notable alumni included Cass Gilbert, Henry Bacon, H.T. Lindeberg, John Russell Pope, John Mervern Carrere, and Thomas Hastings.

The Architecture of McKim, Mead and White is a condensed reprint of the four-volume folio initially published between 1915 and 1920. This superb anthology of photographs, plans, and elevations of their major work remains an essential reference source and inspiration for anyone interested in architecture. A new introduction by Richard Guy Wilson appraises the enduring legacy of the firm.

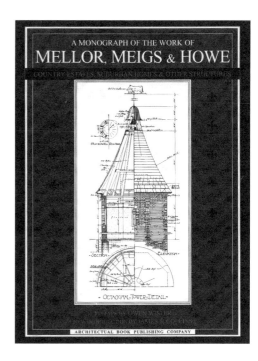

Also Noted:

White, Samuel G. **The Houses of McKim, Mead and White,** *New York: Rizzoli, 1998.*

This stunning photographic survey focuses on the residential work of McKim, Mead and White. The text is by architect Samuel G. White, the great-grandson of Stanford White, who as such is able to provide a uniquely personal appraisal of the firm's sumptuous country houses.

Collins, James S. **A Monograph of the Work of Mellor, Meigs and Howe,** *New York: Architectural Book Publishing Co., 2000.*

The architectural firm of Mellor, Meigs and Howe produced work of such vitality and principle that it remains today a hallmark in the evolution of American domestic architecture. By combining Philadelphia culture, scale, and building traditions with the picturesque architecture of rural England and France they created a new romantic American vernacular style for suburban country houses and their gardens. Their monograph, first published in 1923, became one of the most influential books on American domestic design, and as a result, the Newbold Estate and High Hollow became two of the most emulated buildings in America.

In this republication of the original monograph, architect James S. Collins provides an insightful new introduction that explores the evolution of the firm's highly personal and distinctive synthesis of styles. This lavish monograph, which records their corpus of over one hundred projects, is illustrated with large evocative photographic plates and measured drawings that were once the basis for study by students, architects and the public at large.

Cortissoz, Royal. **The Architecture of Charles Platt,** *New Introduction by Charles Warren; New York: Acanthus Press, 1999.*

Charles Platt (1861-1933) is considered by many to be one of the most talented American architects. His work spanned the country, encompassed public and private work, and was notable for its unique detailing and the care

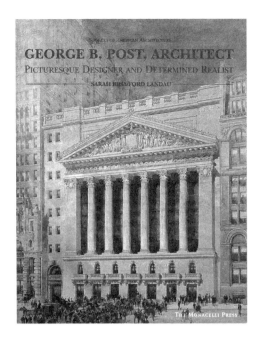

with which architecture and landscape were combined. This derived from Platt's career, which began as an artist, and developed into an appreciation of architecture during a study and tour of Italian gardens. Platt's work extended the house into the landscape through the introduction of pergolas, loggias, and pavilions that defined the views and edges of the estates. These were often influenced by the Italian sensibility he studied. Platt's work seems to be driven by personal taste and inventiveness, rather than by an adherence to learned classicism.

This reprint of the original monograph is eminently readable, with an excellent introduction by Charles Warren and foreword by Robert Stern. The reproductions are clear and the volume is easy to read. (However, if one can locate the larger original, there is something to be said for the larger format, which truly captures Platt's talent for detail.) Unfortunately, this monograph focuses on his houses, illustrating few public works. For a more biographical, wider view of Charles Platt, one should see *Charles Platt: The Artist as Architect,* by Keith Morgan. Other volumes are available highlighting Platt's Italian garden tour and his artwork.

Bedford, Steven McLeod. **John Russell Pope, Architect of Empire,** *New York: Rizzoli, 1998.*

Washington is Pope's city; in as much as any one architect can claim to have had the greatest cumulative effect on America's capital. His Jefferson Memorial, National Archives, Temple of the Scottish Rite, National Gallery of Art, Constitution Hall, and several prominent residences helped create the radiant classical image that we identify with the center of government. John Russell Pope (1874-1937), despite his impact, has been an unclaimed orphan on the sea of architectural writing. Other than Royal Cortissoz's introduction to a portfolio of his work (pub. 1925-30) and a few more recent essays (by Pierce Rice and Duncan Stroik), very little has been published that reflected on his career and design aims.

Into this gap sails a luxuriously produced monograph by Steven Bedford, who—despite the dispersion or disappearance of office records—meticulously researched Pope's life and career, and offers us his results after a decade of work. His text is complimented by the specially commissioned color photographs by Jonathan Wallen, and set off with a good introduction by William L.

MacDonald. The book will be welcomed by scholars studying this period of building, but is limited in what it offers to design professionals—a situation more fully dealt with in the review/essay that precedes The Bookshelf.

Landau, Sarah Bradford. **George B. Post, Architect, Picturesque Designer and Determined Realist,** *New York: The Monacelli Press, 1999.*

The career of George Browne Post (1837-1913) is synonymous with the rise of the skyscraper. Educated in the atelier of Richard Morris Hunt, Post was able to combine superb technical and engineering skills to advance the art of skyscraper design, and was responsible for the Equitable Building in New York—the first office building to use elevators. Among his other notable works were the vast Manufacturers and Liberal Arts Building at the 1893 Worlds Colombian Exposition in Chicago, the New York Stock Exchange, and the majestic Wisconsin State Capital.

This fascinating monograph provides a long overdue opportunity to reappraise the legacy of this underappreciated architect and engineer. Illustrated with archival drawings and photographs, Sarah Bradford Landau's text perceptively emphasizes Post's role as an innovator, whose achievements were nothing short of seminal. Noted New York architect Robert A.M. Stern writes the introduction.

Thomas, George E. **William L. Price: Arts and Crafts to Modern Design,** *New York: Princeton Architectural Press, 2000.*

Though William L. Price (1862-1916) left a legacy of exquisite Arts and Crafts houses in the suburbs of his native Philadelphia, he is best known for establishing the architectural character in the seaside resort of Atlantic City. An architect who valued richness and diversity over purity, Price's work best represented the social vitality and changing tastes of the roaring twenties. His acclaimed masterpieces—the now demolished Traymore and Blenheim Hotels—attest to the vigor of his ideals and his importance in the shaping of iconic architecture in American urban culture.

In this lavishly illustrated monograph, George Thomas eloquently describes the various evolutions and complexities of Price's work. This new insightful biography provides a unique opportunity to rediscover the work of this largely forgotten architect, and is a valuable contribution to the study of American architecture.

Betsky, Aaron. **James Gamble Rogers and the Architecture of Pragmatism,** *New York: The Architectural History Foundation, 1994.*

James Gamble Rogers (1867-1947) was raised in Chicago and was educated at Yale and the Ecole des Beaux-Arts. His early training combined with his education and social position placed him in an enviable position among American architects—he was able to design sophisticated buildings in any number of styles for clients he chose! Whether the commissions were private residences, townhouses, or institutions, Rogers always gave his buildings a solid, contextual essence, letting his own style and genius evolve in the details. Among his best-known works are the college campuses of Yale University, Northwestern, and the University of Chicago.

Part of the Architectural History Book Series, this is a study of Roger's work rather than a monograph. It is still a fascinating study of the architect's work at Yale and other campuses that demonstrates his range and diversity, as well as illustrating his profound imagination and ability to design. This book gives the reader an extensive look at Rogers' entire career, and truly makes apparent the power and ability of this architect to realize all the building types he undertook. Interested readers should also try to track

down *Sparing No Detail: The Drawings of James Gamble Rogers for Yale University, 1913-1935* (an exhibition catalog from Yale University).

Ruttenbaum, Steven. **Mansions in the Clouds: The Skyscraper Palazzi of Emery Roth,** *New York: The Balsam Press, 1986.*

Most readers will associate the name Emery Roth with the endless and undistinguished variations on the international style metal and glass skyscrapers that have occupied our cities. Those works are the spawn of Mr. Roth's successors. The original Emery Roth (1871-1948) was a fine traditional architect, who authored a series of beautiful and inventive solutions for urban housing. This monograph gives us the career of an architect that changed the skyline of New York. Though we are shown examples of the range of his practice (residences, houses of worship, offices, etc.), the book concentrates on the well-planned and elegantly detailed apartment houses that made up the bulk of his oeuvre. The familiar profiles of his El Dorado apartments, the San Remo, the Ritz Tower, and others have become an integral part of our image of the twentieth century classical city.

The author gives a thorough and lively account of Roth's career, and full treatments of his major projects. The book is visually rich, containing an abundance of photographs and presentation renderings. Its only failings are the lack of full sets of floor plans, and a paucity of construction documents.

Hewitt, Mark Alan. **The Architecture of Mott Schmidt,** *New York: Rizzoli, 1991.*

One of the few traditional architects who practiced and preserved his principles throughout the twentieth century, Mott Schmidt (1889-1977) is best known for his work in New York City and Westchester County. Schmidt's work included townhouses, suburban homes, and apartment buildings as well as public buildings. His work is almost exclusively in the American Georgian tradition, although the monograph illustrates some interesting departures. Many of his buildings are extant, and all display a solid design and quiet dignity that characterize his work. We see this especially in the attention to detail that jumps out at the observer from the background of the Georgian buildings.

An extensive essay on Mott Schmidt's life by the author is supplemented by illustrations of Schmidt's work in plans and period photographs. Sixteen new color plates showing details of his buildings add to the appreciation of his work. Finally, a very valuable bibliography and list of projects is included.

Royal Barry Wills Associates, (ed.). **Houses for Good Living,** *Architectural Book Publishing Co., Stamford, 1993.*

Even today, decades after his death, real estate agents still describe houses as being "Royal Barry Wills style" in an effort to attract buyers. Wills' (1895-1962) practice centered in New England, but through articles, good photography, and a series of books, he became very widely known as the masterful exponent of the "Cape Cod" style. It is a tribute to his skill that he was able to build a significant body of attractive houses for a predominantly middle-class clientele—offering them designs that extended the centuries-old north-eastern tradition of trim and practical building.

This book, edited by the firm that carries on his work, is an extension of Wills' own 1946 edition. It brings together many photos of his designs, supplemented by brief descriptions. Though hardly a comprehensive study of Wills' multi-decade oeuvre, it does display the gracious, comfortable (and comforting) built work that brought him success during his lifetime and remains successful today. People looking for design prototypes for detached middle-priced housing need look no further.

MID-ATLANTIC

O'Neal, William and Christopher Weeks. **The Work of William Lawrence Bottomley in Richmond,** *Charlottesville, VA: University of Virginia Press, 1985.*

William Lawrence Bottomley (1883-1951) is best remembered as one of the foremost architects of the American country house. An architect of wide vision, and in keeping with the prevailing eclecticism of his day, his work reflects Mediterranean and Tudor influences. He is, however, best remembered for Neo-Georgian houses that provide a poetic reminder of a felicitous period in the history of English building yet removed to the leafy suburbs

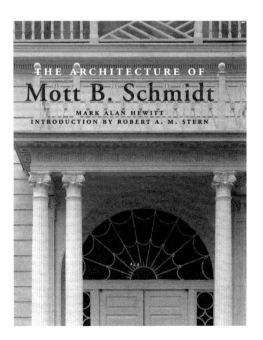

of Richmond, Virginia. Among Bottomley's work, Nordley, Canterbury, and Milburne, represent the finest examples of Georgian domestic architecture built in the 1920s and 1930s.

This beautifully photographed monograph is well researched and written in an unpretentious manner by O'Neal and Weeks that clearly demonstrates Bottomley's versatility, knowledge, and mastery of form. Always eloquent, Jaquelin T. Robertson has written the foreword.

SOUTH

Fatio, Alexandra, editor. **Maurice Fatio, Architect,** *New York, Palm Beach: Self-published, 1992.*

When the architecture of Florida is mentioned, the name of Mizner comes to most lips. Less well known—but perhaps more deserving of acclaim—is the work of Maurice Fatio (1897-1943). During his brief but prolific career, Fatio designed and had built over a hundred houses, some of which are among the most splendid residences of Palm Beach. He drew from history's riches to design in a multiplicity of styles, peppering the semi-tropical landscape with Spanish-style haciendas and Tuscan towers. His deft touch and excellent planning made his houses into sought-after stages for the lifestyle of a summering elite, and Cole Porter immortalized his affection for these environments with the lyric: "I want to live on Maurice Fatio's patio."

This monograph includes a collection of mostly period photographs of built work, softly suggesting the atmosphere of a passed elegance. Unfortunately, other than some renderings reproduced in the margins, there are no drawings. Its most interesting feature is the body of the text, which is composed of Fatio's letters from the last two decades of his active life. We see—from the architect's own point of view—his world of work, family, and the society he moved through and built for.

The Florida Architecture of Addison Mizner, *Appreciation by Ida M. Tarbell, Foreword by Paris Singer. New Introduction by James Curl. New York: Dover Publications, 1992. (Reprint of 1928 edition, published by William Helburn, Inc., New York.)*

Addison Mizner (1872-1933) was one of the finest architects in the United States during the early part of the twentieth century. At the beginning of his career, he produced some of the most original architecture in Florida for wealthy patrons in Boca Raton and Palm Beach. His later commissions included private clubs, residences, and commercial work. He transformed Florida architecture from the banal into the Spanish Colonial style that influenced architects of his time, and still does today. His architecture can be admired as a fine adaptation of architecture to a specific place and time. Though many of Mizner's finest commissions are no longer standing, they are captured in this inexpensive reprint. An introduction by James Curl addresses a career marked by personal tragedy and further historical context is provided throughout the book.

This volume is a valuable addition to anyone's library. An exact reprint of the 1928 edition, it contains photographs of over 30 of Mizner's works in Florida. For further reading on Addison Mizner and his architecture, you may wish to read *Mizner's Florida*, by James Curl.

Mitchell, William R. **J. Neel Reid, Architect, of Hentz, Reid and Adler,** *Savannah, Georgia: Golden Coast Publishing Company, 1997.*

Joseph Neel Reid (1885-1926) has long had a prestigious reputation in his native Georgia, where he is widely regarded as Atlanta's finest architect. A classicist in the old school tradition of the Beaux-Arts, Reid was a master of the grander aspects of classical design that well served the

aspirations of the Atlanta elite. There is a romantic aspect immediately apparent in all of his work that looks to the past for inspiration, thus creating Renaissance, American Georgian, Federal, Greek Revival, Baroque, and Italian estates of unequaled beauty. A Southern icon, and legendary hero of the Georgia School of Classicists, it is fair to say that Reid established a level of aesthetic quality that has not since been equaled. His buildings are so much beloved that two of them have been dismantled, moved elsewhere, and lovingly re-erected in their entirety or in part. An early death, at age forty-one, contributes towards the romantic appeal of Reid and the endearing legacy of his work.

With the publication of this monograph, author William Mitchell establishes Neel Reid as one of the most accomplished and influential architects of his day, and portrays the firm of Hentz, Reid and Adler as a Beaux-Arts Atelier, whose alumni included Lewis Edmund Crook, Philip Trammel Shutze, and James Means. This publication is by far the finest architectural monograph to be recently published, and is the standard for all others to emulate. Neel Reid's genius positively shines in this sumptuously illustrated and thoughtfully written monograph, and as such provides inspiration for the generations of classical architects that revere his legend.

Author Bill Mitchell and photographer Van Jones Martin are currently working on a new monograph on the Georgia architect James Means, which the editors of *The Classicist* eagerly await to review in our next volume.

Dowling, Elizabeth. **American Classicist: the Architecture of Philip Trammel Shutze,** *New York: Rizzoli, 1989.*

Philip Trammel Shutze (1890-1982) was by temperament and breeding a gentleman of the South. Though he worked briefly with both Mott Schmidt and F. Burrall Hoffman (architect of the Villa Vizcaya in Miami), Shutze is best known through his collaboration with his mentor, eminent Atlanta classicist Neel Reid. Moving from one manner of the classical to another with an idiosyncratic originality, Shutze helped introduce Atlanta to an elegance and refinement of design that epitomized his long career. His finest work is unquestionably the opulent Swan House, a masterpiece in American domestic architecture and a quintessential example of classical landscape design.

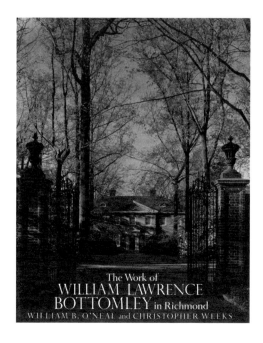

In this groundbreaking study Elizabeth Dowling chronicles the exceptional talent of Philip Trammel Shutze. This handsomely produced monograph is a fascinating account and is full of unexpected episodes. Of particular note is how Dowling unequivocally tackles the debate over the authorship of the Andrew Calhoun House—it is emphatically placed on the front cover. The preface and introduction are by Henry Hope Reed and Vincent Scully.

Mitchell, William R. **Edward Vason Jones: Architect, Connoisseur and Collector,** *Savannah, Georgia: Golden Coast Publishing Company, 1995.*

Though not formally trained as an architect, Edward Vason Jones (1909-1980) became one of America's greatest classical designers and a connoisseur of the decorative arts. Jones developed a Beaux-Arts approach towards architecture while working with Georgia classicist Philip Trammel Shutze. Practicing in a period when classicism was out of favor, Jones sought to revive and cultivate the tradition of building from eighteenth and nineteenth century America. Even though his considerable talents earned him wide fame, Jones was undeniably a product of his hometown, Albany, Georgia, where he designed and restored numerous great houses. He is, however, best known for his restrained and elegant period rooms in the U.S. Department of State and the White House.

In this beautifully produced monograph, William Mitchell provides a definitive account of Jones' devotion to the classical tradition of the South. A visual feast of sketches and working drawings, alongside exquisite photographs by Van Jones Martin, documents a well-mannered originality towards classical architecture and the decorative arts. This is another excellent architectural monograph to be recently published, and promises to become a standard for the serious student of the classical tradition.

MIDWEST

Pratt, Richard. **David Adler, The Architect and his Work,** *Chicago: The Art Institute of Chicago, 1970.*

David Adler (1882-1949) was "the house architect for the Chicago establishment" during the late 1910s and 1920s. By looking back, comparing, and selecting with care, then assembling and improving with consummate taste, Adler produced inspired designs of harmony and authenticity. Indisputably one of the most original and creative architects of his time, Adler was able to create graceful and meticulously detailed interiors of compelling grace and unity. Built in the manner of Sir Christopher Wren, the majestic Castle Hill is Adler's undisputed masterpiece.

Though not a scholarly or detailed account, this visually rich monograph by Richard Pratt does provide an enthusiastic and rare insight into the work of David Adler and includes a valuable inventory of the books in Adler's library.

Hines, Thomas S. **Burnham of Chicago,** *Chicago: University of Chicago, 1974.*

Daniel Hudson Burnham (1850-1892) thought in monumental terms, and the scale of his accomplishments match his intentions. His firm was prolific in design as well as innovative in construction, sprinkling buildings across the land, including Washington, D.C.'s Union Station, New York's Flatiron Building, Chicago's Field Museum, and Monadnock, Rookery, and Marshall Field buildings. Many of these buildings were designed with partner John Wellborn Root (1850-1892), and are among the most prominent works produced under Burnham's leadership. He also led the design and planning team of the 1897 World's Colombian Exhibition, which

EDWARD VASON JONES

ARCHITECT, CONNOISSEUR, AND COLLECTOR
by William R. Mitchell, Jr.
photography by Van Jones Martin   foreword by Clement E. Conger

changed how Americans envisioned their cities for a half a century. Perhaps only Hunt rivaled him for relentless civic activity.

Two major books on Burnhan exist, and the first one by Charles Moore has the merit of being done by an author who knew his subject (and his milieu) personally. The more recent study by Thomas Hines benefits from the objectivity that passing time can give—as well as the careful eye that a professional historian brings to analyzing the data of Burnham's life and work. Although the Hines book has more illustrations than the earlier study, it is still text oriented, and lacks the appeal of a more visual monograph. Burnham's greatness calls for a new edition of the book, enhanced by copious photos and drawings—a volume that would be welcomed by the architectural community.

Irish, Shannon. **Cass Gilbert, Architect: Modern Traditionalist,** *New York: The Monacelli Press, 1999.*

Working within the boundaries of established architectural vocabularies, Cass Gilbert became one of the preeminent figures in American architecture. Gilbert synthesized a diverse architecture that represented American democracy and enterprise. His work is second to none in its command of composition and detail in a variety of differing architectural styles. This diversity is illustrated by his monumental Beaux-Arts masterpiece, the lavishly embellished U.S. Custom House in New York, which is just a stone's throw away from the equally flamboyant Gothic Woolworth Building, designated the cathedral of commerce. Amongst Gilbert's other commissions that defined the architectural continuum of his generation include the New York Life Insurance Building, the Minnesota State Capital in St. Paul, the U.S. Supreme Court in Washington, the Detroit Public Library, and the Louisiana Purchase Exposition.

This is the first monograph devoted to the work of Cass Gilbert, and is an invaluable reference source. Wonderfully illustrated with archival photographs and drawings, this scholarly account by Shannon Irish reflects on the impressive and beautiful legacy of Gilbert's residential, civic, and commercial work. Robert A.M. Stern writes the introduction.

Chappell, Sally A. Kitt. **The Architecture and Planning of Graham, Anderson, Probst and White 1912-1936,** *Chicago: The University of Chicago, 1992.*

The prolific nature of Graham, Anderson, Probst and White, as well as the significance of their best known work, made this firm one of the most important in the development of American Architecture. The firm epitomized the ideals of urban civility and private enterprise and, as successors to Daniel H. Burnham, was involved with the design of large urban schemes, notably in Cleveland, Philadelphia, and Chicago. Adapting Beaux Arts principles with great imagination and refinement, their work includes Thirtieth Street Station in Philadelphia, Union Station in Washington, the Field Museum of Natural History, and the Wrigley Building, both in Chicago.

In this thoughtfully written monograph, Sally Chappell focuses on the legacy of Graham, Anderson, Probst and White's urban interventions, and reflects on how they continue to nourish present-day civic spirit. Richly illustrated with archival photographs and drawings, this is an essential contribution to understanding how architecture can alter our urban hierarchy and reflect the changing values of society.

Robert Bruegman. **Holabird & Roche/Holabird & Root: An Illustrated Catalog of Works, 1880-1940,** *New York & London: Garland Publishing, Inc., 1991.*

The three volumes of this survey show that this firm was one of the most prolific and talented in America's history. It would be difficult to find a building type that they didn't tackle. Their design work included the full range of structures that a growing and industrializing country needs: barracks, banks, residences, offices, factories, showrooms, theatres, a power station—all done in a variety of traditional (and evolving) styles—until the enticements of modernism show in their late work. (Bruegman's diligence in bringing this body of material together has resulted in a separately published monograph that gives his analytical and critical history of the firm.)

After a historical introduction, each building is shown chronologically. The profiles of information on each (location, date, condition, client, description, etc.) are a model of completeness. The author gives deeper treatment to significant structures (Chicago's Marquette Building for example—the only building whose excellence both modernists and classicists agree on!), with multiple illustrations and in-depth analysis. Useful appendices include lists by building-type, and maps showing concentrations of work. Unfortunately, illustrations are reproduced too small. Though the reader gets a grand impression of the firm's awesome potency, one struggles to gain anything by studying the individual designs (had the book's designers reduced the excessive leading, pictures might have been larger).

Mulfinger, Dale. **The Architecture of Edwin Lundie,** *St Paul: Minnesota Historical Society Press, 1995.*

Edwin Lundie (1886-1972) was born in Iowa and began his career in St. Paul, Minnesota. He was one of the last architects to successfully practice without obtaining a formal education. As a young man he gained experience by working his way though a number of offices, including that of Cass Gilbert. Once on his own, his early work consisted of several church commissions, which he inherited from his last employer, but after 1923 Lundie began to focus on residential practice. His craftsmanship and attention to detail are clearly presented in this book. The quirky details and repetitive motifs tie his designs together, and allow us to recognize a Lundie House. Lundie is a noteworthy regional architect whose work deserves a larger audience.

The book is well written, and well organized. There are three main sections, with accompanying essays focusing upon his historical context, his life, and his work. His designs are shown comprehensively, and are illustrated with plans and original drawings, as well as with photographs.

Greene, Virginia A. **The Architecture of Harold Van Doren Shaw,** *Chicago Review Press, 1999.*

Harold Van Doren Shaw (1869-1926) is a Mid-Western architect whose career spanned from 1894 to 1927. Generally unknown outside of his region, his work does turn up excerpted in many books, including the *American Vitruvius.* Fortunately, this new book examines Shaw's career and his enormous number of completed projects (over 200 built in his lifetime!). Most impressive is the wide range of work. Shaw is notable for his institutional work, churches, commercial, residential, and urban planning projects. Few architects can lay claim to this breadth, and we are pleased to see over 100 projects illustrated in this volume.

An essay on his career, along with an introduction by Stuart Cohen, sets the stage for this monograph. We are then treated to views of his many projects. Often the photographs are historical, showing the buildings recently completed. Occasionally there are original sketches and plans. This is the one weakness of the monograph; due to the archival nature of the illustrations, details are sometimes murky and hard to distinguish, and it is hard to grasp the beauty of some of the compositions without supplemental drawings. However, the photographs do allow us to see the building in the original context, and without the obstruction of modern buildings and utilities. This is an excellent addition to the annals of American architectural monographs.

Johannesen, Eric. **A Cleveland Legacy: The Architecture of Walker and Weeks,** *Ohio: The Kent State University Press, 1999.*

Walker & Weeks was one of the Mid-West's premier classical firms from 1911 to 1949. Located in Cleveland, the two partners created an architectural firm modeled on the organization of Daniel Burnham's office, which was also copied by McKim, Mead and White. They were able to pursue almost every major public building project in Cleveland in addition to houses, churches, and later commercial work. Harry Weeks (1871-1935) and Frank Walker (1877-1949) both graduated from M.I.T., and worked in several offices before re-locating to Cleveland at the suggestion of John Carrere, of Carrere & Hastings. They worked for J. Milton Dyer before starting their own

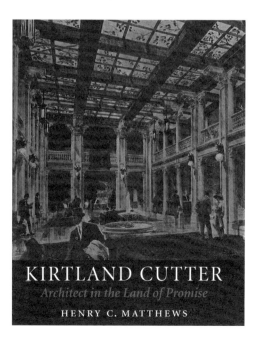

firm. The work began with small suburban residences, and gradually grew to more public buildings. In 1912, an unassuming bank built in Akron, Ohio led the way for Walker & Weeks to become the primary bank architects for the Mid-West. Over 100 banks alone in their repertoire, the bank designs led to commissions for churches, schools, courthouses, the Cleveland Public Library, Cleveland Auditorium, the Indiana World War Memorial, and others. This book traces the development of Walker & Weeks' work from their eclectic house styles, to high classical, to 'Moderne', as the architects struggled with the country's desire for a new architecture.

This monograph contains excellent anecdotes of the firm and its organization, many photographs of the projects, and a good selection of original elevation drawings. However, too few plan drawings are included. The book is organized into sections dealing with each type of work done—residential, bank, commercial, institutional, public, and engineering. There is a complete catalog of commissions with a description and location of each at the end of the book. It is an excellent monograph of a firm whose work deserves more study by any serious architect.

PACIFIC NORTHWEST

Matthews, Henry. **Kirtland Cutter: Architect in the land of Promise,** *Seattle, WA: University of Washington Press, 1998.*

The work of Kirtland Kelsey Cutter (1860-1939) provides a fascinating insight into the evolution of eclectic architecture. Primarily working within the city of Spokane, Cutter fully explored an astonishing range of styles and types, freely adapting them to meet the transition from frontier settlement to modern city. This is best exemplified by his design for the Davenport Hotel, which reflects the newfound affluence and civic spirit of Spokane and the Pacific North West Region.

This recently published monograph by Henry Matthews comes after exhaustive research that fully documents Cutter's work. Biographical in character, this essential reference source is accompanied by a scattering of archival photographs and drawings that offer a fascinating and comprehensive study of this largely undiscovered regional architect.

WEST COAST

Jay, Robert. **Charles W. Dickey: Hawaii and California,** *Honolulu, Hawaii: The University of Hawaii Press, 1992.*

Called "Hawaii's Dean of Architecture", for many years, Charles William Dickey (1871-1942) was one of the Island's preeminent architects. From the intimate tropical bungalows he designed in Waikiki to the large-scale commercial projects that dominated his California years, Dickey's work exhibits both eclecticism and diversity. Though schooled in the Beaux-Arts, Dickey fully explored and cultivated the vernacular architectural traditions of the Tropics. This unique blending of generous roof overhangs, broad shady porches, and intimate courtyards formed the basis for his work and became a signature of his style.

This monograph provides not only a study of Dickey's finest work but also includes a convenient overview of much of Hawaii's architectural history. In particular, Robert Jay highlights the significant contribution Dickey made towards Honolulu's urban development, and the enduring impact his architecture still has today.

Kamerling, Bruce. **Irving Gill, Architect,** *San Diego, San Diego Historical Society, 1999.*

During their architectural educations, many of our readers were force-fed the tendentious imaginings of canonical modern historians. In the teleological universe of Pevsner, Gideon, et. al., all righteous design aims toward the purity of the late Bauhaus. They anointed several figures as proto-modernists, and the American they named was Gill. It's time Irving Gill (1870-1936) was taken back from these architect-nappers, and Kamerling has come to the rescue with a monograph that reveals the full range of Gill's talent as a designer who drew from the mission vernacular to create homes (and other building types) for Southern California's growing population. This book is rich in illustrations showing Gill's ability as a planner and as a skillful composer of volumes that play well in the bright California sun. Plans, elevations, and photography evidence a lifetime of work that drew upon tradition and met the requirements of a new century with innovation.

The book reviews Gill's career from his earliest built work of the 1890s through projects completed at the end of his life. Period photographs show many of the buildings in their original state. Also included are project lists, reprints of the architect's known published writings, and a full bibliography.

Partridge, Loren W. **John Galen Howard and the Berkeley Campus: Beaux-Arts Architecture in the "Athens of the West,"** *Berkeley: Berkeley Architectural Heritage Association, 1978.*

John Galen Howard (1864-1931) is perhaps one of the most exceptional regional architects in the United States. Almost all his work was completed at the University of California at Berkeley, in the town of Berkeley, or in San Francisco. Despite the fact that he was responsible for one of the most complete, built Beaux-Arts ensembles in the country, he remains relatively unknown. Howard was both architect and educator at the University of California at Berkeley, and single-handedly oversaw its development from the Hearst Plan (1901) until his dismissal in 1924. During his tenure he completed more than 20 buildings based upon Greco-Roman and Beaux-Arts precedents. The diversity of style and exceptional detail are a testimony to his architectural talent. Howard was educated at M.I.T., worked in the offices of H.H. Richardson and McKim, Mead and White, and attended the Ecole des Beaux-Arts before settling in California. At Berkeley, Howard was appointed the supervising architect of the campus in 1901, and in 1903 he was appointed head of the architecture department. Under his tutelage, many important contributors to American architecture were trained. Howard was a proponent of the Beaux-Arts system, but encouraged stylistic diversity and independence in his students.

This small book focuses on Howard's relationship with the Berkeley campus from both a historical and an analytical standpoint. The master plan is addressed from its conception to implementation, as well as Howard's role and continued influence. In addition to that, five of Howard's buildings are analyzed. The book contains many illustrations of these projects, and the master plan competition. An extensive bibliography and a list of projects round out the information provided.

Belloi, Jay (ed.). **Myron Hunt, 1868-1952. The Search for a Regional Architecture,** *Santa Monica: Hennessey & Ingalls, 1984.*

Another regional architect similar to Wallace Neff, Myron Hunt (1868-1952) did not begin his career in California. Rather, he began in the Boston offices of Shepley Ryan & Coolidge. He moved to Chicago, where he was a contemporary of Frank Lloyd Wright (in his Oak Park era),

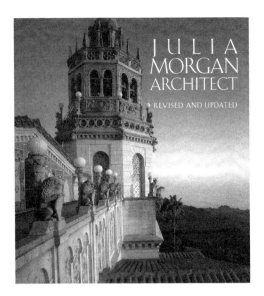

and designed and built over 40 houses by 1902. Following that, Hunt moved on to California where he eventually became the architect for Caltech, Pomona and Occidental Colleges. Other public commissions included the Rose Bowl and the Pasadena Library. Hunt's projects during his career also included churches and houses. Though he struggled with regionalism, revivalism, and the rise of the International Style, there is a very unified quality to all of Hunt's work. His public and private commissions, however, remain stylistically very different and reflect his search for a 'California' style.

This volume is a collection of essays; each addressing various aspects if Myron Hunt's work. The reader is treated to photographs and drawings of his work that give an overall appreciation of his entire career. At the back of the book is a partial list of Hunt's commissions. The lack of illustrations showing more detail is the only disappointment.

Woodbridge, Sally. **Bernard Maybeck, Visionary Architect,** *New York: Abbeville Press, 1992.*

Raised in New York, and educated at the Ecole des Beaux-Arts, Bernard Maybeck (1862-1957) was an incredibly innovative and talented architect. Instead of remaining in the Northeast to practice he chose to settle in Northern California. The majority of his work is residential, but the Palace of Fine Arts in San Francisco and the First Church of Christ Scientist in Berkeley stand out as masterpieces even in his own oeuvre of work. Maybeck's projects are notable for their originality and attention to detail. From the overall plan to furniture and lighting, Maybeck would use plays of color and form, as well as material and texture to create a unified composition.

This monograph is photographed by Richard Barnes, whose images give a richness to Maybeck's work previously not widely available to the public. Woodbridge's text is excellently written and is comprehensive. Plans and some of Maybecks sketches supplement the photographs. A list of Maybeck's commissions is added at the end of the volume.

Boutelle, Sara. **Julia Morgan, Architect,** *New York: Abbeville Press, 1995.*

One of the few recognized female architects of the early twentieth century Julia Morgan (1872-1957) was in fact the first woman to receive a certificate in architecture from the Ecole des Beaux-Arts. Morgan's practice cen-

tered in California, and in the early part of her career she associated with other architects, including Bernard Maybeck. She designed buildings of all sizes and types, including clubs, schools, residences, and churches. Morgan was an incredibly prolific architect, producing over 700 built projects in her lifetime with size, scale, and detailing varying from project to project. She is known for works that range in style from a simple Arts & Crafts, to a Mediterranean vernacular, to the highly decorative California classical. It is this style which distinguishes her most famous commission, the Hearst Castle at San Simeon.

This volume is very well written and researched, and lavishly photographed by Richard Barnes. Historic photographs and images of original drawings and sketches supplement the more recent images. The monograph provides the reader with an excellent description of the full range of Morgan's work and an appreciation of her skill in overall planning and detailing. A list of buildings designed by Morgan, as well as an extensive bibliography round out the wealth of information provided by Boutelle. Interested readers can also track down *Julia Morgan, Architect of Dreams* by Ginger Wordsworth.

Belloi, Jay, (ed.). **Wallace Neff, 1895-1982, The Romance of Regional Architecture,** *Santa Monica: Hennessey & Ingalls, 1998.*

Wallace Neff (1895-1982) was a regional architect in California who embraced the romanticism of the area. His architecture has remained largely unknown to the rest of the country, though several books exist on his work. Neff began his architectural career in 1922 after receiving his education at M.I.T and traveling in Europe. Much of his work is done in a Mediterranean vernacular, but it reflects elements of other cultures as well. With each of his projects Neff attempted to create architecture appropriate for California and that remained true to the project. His designs are recognizable by the sensibility in composition, taste, and detail. As Robert Stern states in his preface, "No one project stands out—it is rather the sum of Neff's work which is greater than its parts." Much of the work seen in this catalog is residential in nature, though Wallace Neff completed other types of buildings during his career.

This catalog consists of five sections, each with an essay focusing on a separate aspect of Neff's career and development. In this volume, Neff's style is termed Regional Eclecticism, and this is a theme throughout the five articles. Photographs, sketches, and some working drawings are provided as illustration. Also included is a partial list of Neff's buildings and clients. Interested readers should also investigate: *Architecture of Southern California: A Selection of Photographs, Plans, and Scale Details from the Work of Wallace Neff,* and also *Wallace Neff: Architect of California's Golden Age* (both by Wallace Neff Jr. and Alson Clark, 1986).

Hudson, Karen E. **Paul R. Williams, Architect: A Legacy of Style,** *New York: Rizzoli, 1993.*

If you couldn't be a movie star, what would be your second choice? Well—if your talent showed more on the drawing board than the screen—it would probably be to design the homes of the stars. Paul Williams (1894-1980), in a four decade career centered in Southern California, was the architect to some of Hollywood's firmament. Williams was America's most successful black architect—and what a success he was! He worked in a range of styles and applied his skill to a wide variety of building types in addition to designing the residences of some of filmdom's elite. Whether he was evoking the regions' Hispanic past, applying a Regency palette, or using newer forms, Williams showed the sure touch of an architect well grounded in traditional building and composition.

This monograph has the high level of sharp images that we associate with the golden age of Hollywood photography; well printed in a large format. Unfortunately each project, beyond several excellent views, is treated superficially, with little text and no floor plans or other drawings. This is partially compensated for by livening the pages with quotes from the architect's own writings, a portfolio of construction drawings from one of his 1920s houses, and introductory texts by both the author and David Gebhard.

SOUTHWEST

Carl D. Sheppard. **Creator of the Santa Fe Style: Isaac Hamilton Rapp, Architect,** *New Mexico, University of New Mexico, 1988.*

A few years ago, the Santa Fe style became one in the succession of fashionable "looks" for the au courant designer. Though it has a thousand years of history rooted in Native American and Spanish Colonial building practice, the forms of the southwest entered the vocabulary of American architects through the work of Isaac Hamilton Rapp (1854-1933). As this book shows, Rapp was a talented designer in all of the many styles practiced by turn-of-the-century architects, and was equally at home in a robust Romanesque or a civil Georgian mode. Stylistically flexible, Rapp will be remembered for initiating the use of bold, soft adobe forms in building types as diverse as exhibit spaces, offices, resort, and warehouse structures.

This welcome volume gives a broad view of Rapp's career, with photographs of many of his built works leavened by several examples of construction drawings. Hopefully future studies—with multiple views and drawings of his well-built structures—will be offered to his admirers.

Barnstone, Howard. **The Architecture of John F. Staub: Houston and the South,** *Austin, Texas: The University of Texas, 1979.*

John F. Staub (1892-1981) produced one of the largest oeuvres of any eclectic architect during the twentieth century. Having spent his apprenticeship with H.T. Lindeberg in New York, Staub eventually set up practice in Houston, where he soon became the city's foremost residential architect. Designing for the elite of Houston, Staub is probably best known for his commissions in the exclusive garden suburb of River Oaks. His formal Georgian compositions command an air of gentle serenity, and his picturesque English Arts and Crafts style designs subtly allude to an enduring sense of harmony and beauty.

This well illustrated volume by Howard Barnstone contains a concise and comprehensive study of Staub's finest work. This fascinating monograph provides a stimulating mixture of the architectural history of Houston and the contribution John F. Staub made towards its evolution from the small town society of the twenties to the sophisticated community of today.

BOOKS BRIEFLY NOTED
A Selection of Recently published titles

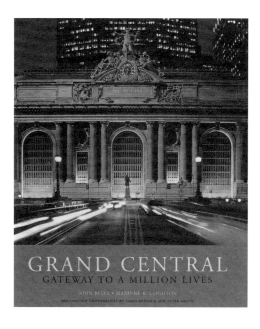

- *Various authors,* **The Campus Guide Series,** *New York, Princeton Architectural Press, 1999-2000;* Yale University, *Patrick Pinnell;* University of Virginia, *Richard Guy Wilson;* Stanford University, *Richard Joncas;* Princeton University, *Raymond Rhinehart.*

- *Belle, John and Maxine R. Leighton.* **Grand Central, Gateway to a Million Lives,** *New York: W.W. Norton and Company, 2000.*

- *Congress for the New Urbanism.* **Charter for the New Urbanism,** *New York: McGraw Hill, 2000.*

- *Crowe, Norman, Richard Economakis and Michel Lykoudis, editors.* **Building Cities,** *London: ArtMedia Press, 1999.*

- *Duany, Andres and Elizabeth Plater-Zyberk and Jeff Speck.* **Suburban Nation: The Rise of Sprawl and the Decline of the American Dream, DPZ,** *NorthPoint Press, 2000.*

- *Du Prey, Pierre de la Ruffiniere.* **Hawksmoor's London Churches: Architecture and Theology,** *Chicago: The University of Chicago Press, 2000.*

- *Good, Albert, H.* **Park and Recreation Structures,** *New York: Princeton Architectural Press, reprinted 1999.*

- *Greenberg, Alan.* **George Washington Architect,** *Kilbees Farm, England: Andreas Papadakis Publisher, 1999.*

- *Heilbrub, Margaret, editor.* **Inventing the Skyline: The Architecture of Cass Gilbert,** *New York: Columbia University Press, 2000.*

- *Hurwit, Jeffrey.* **The Athenian Acropolis: History, Mythology and Archaeology,** *Boston: Cambridge University Press, 2000.*

- *Longstreth, Richard.* **On the Edge of the World: Four Architects in San Francisco at the Turn of the Century,** *University of California Press, reprinted 1999.*

- *Marder, Todd A.* **Bernini and the Art of Architecture,** *New York: Abbeville Press, 1999.*

- **Porphyrios Associates, Recent Works.** *Kilbees Farm, England: Andreas Papadakis Publisher, 1999.*

- *Quill, Sarah.* **Ruskin's Venice: The Stones Revisited,** *Ashgate Publishing Company, 2000.*

- *Rowland, Ingrid D. and Thomas Noble Howe.* **Vitruvius: Ten Books on Architecture,** *New York: Cambridge University Press, 2000.*

- *Scott, Geoffrey.* **The Architecture of Humanism,** *New York: W.W. Norton and Company, reprinted 1999.*

- *Stamp, Gavin.* **Alexander 'Greek' Thompson,** *Laurence King Publishers, 1999.*

- *Tavernor, Robert.* **On Alberti and the Art of Building,** *New Haven, Yale University Press, 1999.*

- *Wyllie, Romy.* **CalTech's Architectural Heritage, From Spanish Tile to Modern Stone,** *Balcony Press, 2000.*

- *Younes, Samir.* **Quatremere De Quincy's Historical Dictionary of Architecture: The True, the Fictive and the Real,** *London: Andreas Papadakis Publishers, 2000.*

Sean Jefferson Tobin is a designer and architectural historian currently residing in Brooklyn, New York. After receiving his joint BA in Architecture and Art History at Yale University, he eventually found his way to the University of Notre Dame, where he received his Master's Degree in Architecture. He is currently preoccupied with writing a monograph on a lesser-known American architect, while working for Robert A.M. Stern, Architects.

Phillip James Dodd, a Native of Manchester, England, received his undergraduate education at Manchester School of Architecture. He continued his studies at the Prince of Wales' Institute before receiving his Master's Degree in Architecture from the University of Notre Dame. He currently works in New York City for Fairfax & Sammons, Architects, and has also taught design studio for the ICA Summer Program.

Seth Joseph Weine, designer and reviewer: See bio on page 104.

NEWS OF THE INSTITUTE

BOARD OF DIRECTORS AND ADMINISTRATION

NEW MEMBERS, NEW MISSION

The Institute's Board of Directors has had a busy two years as it has, among other things, added new members, assessed the Institute's mission and direction, and participated in two Board retreats. Gilbert P. Schafer, III was elected as the new president and The Institute Board of Directors elected four new members: Christopher H. Browne, Christine Franck, Peter Pennoyer, and Roy Zeluck. Mr. Browne will serve as the Board's Treasurer. Mrs. Franck, former Executive Director of The Institute, will represent the Advisory Council to the Board. Additionally, The Advisory Council is pleased to have Jaquelin T. Robertson as a new member.

During the Institute's first Board retreat in the fall of 1999, the Board met for two days with a facilitator to discuss the history of the Institute, review its goals, and to draft a new mission statement. The Board adopted the following mission statement to help guide its activities: *"The Institute teaches the fundamentals of architecture through the study and exploration of the classical tradition. It exists to perpetuate the cultural memory of the past as a resource for architectural issues in the present."* At the retreat the Board also decided to adjust the Institute's name from the Institute for the Study of Classical Architecture to the Institute of Classical Architecture or The ICA. The Board felt that this new name would more accurately reflect the full scope of the Institute's activities.

The Institute's Board Retreat was so successful that a Board meeting was held in Atlanta—a city rich in the classical tradition—hosted by Board members Rodney Cook and Jeffrey Davis. Kicking off a weekend-long tour, Board member Bunny Williams gave a public lecture at the Fernbank Museum on the classical influences in her interiors and garden design. The group also visited some of Atlanta's finest classical buildings including a number of houses by Philip Schutze and William Banks' extraordinary federal period plantation, Bankshaven. The Institute is fortunate to have an active and supportive Board assisting in the growth of the organization.

The Institute's new President Gilbert P. Schafer, III with new Executive Director, Aida della Longa.

NEW EXECUTIVE DIRECTOR, NEW LOCATION, NEW MEMBERSHIP PROGRAM, NEW LOGO

One of the most significant developments of the past year has been the appointment of Aida della Longa to the position of Executive Director. With over twenty years of experience in fundraising, development, and special-events organization for non-profits, Ms. della Longa is a considerable asset to the Institute. Under her direction the Institute moved into its new office and classroom at 225 Lafayette Street on October 15th, 1999. For the first time in its history, the Institute has classroom space on the same premises as its administrative offices.

In addition to this change of locale, Ms. della Longa has overseen the very successful launch of the "Friends of the Institute" membership program campaign. In conjunction with this new initiative, the Institute felt it was appropriate to formulate a logo and graphic identity for the Institute, which has been created by Dyad Communications of Philadelphia. The new Institute logo is the silhouette of Diana, Roman goddess of the hunt, adapted from the sculpture by Augustus St. Gaudens originally designed to crown McKim, Mead & White's Madison Square Garden. The ICA Diana symbolizes the importance of a dialogue between the arts and architecture in the classical tradition and suggests the vitality of the Institute's refocused mission and its participants.

FELLOWS

NEW MEMBER, FELLOWS EMERITUS

Over the past year the Fellows have been active in refining their governing procedures, evaluating their status as Fellows, and formalizing their responsibilities. Melissa Del Vecchio, a graduate of the University of Notre Dame and Yale University, was elected to Fellowship in recognition of her volunteer work with the Institute's newly formed Program committee. Several Fellows have become Fellow Emeritus, having distinguished themselves as volunteers in the past but who are no longer able to be active. These include Grace Hinton, Victor Deupi, and Laurence Dumoff.

DEVELOPMENT

NEW MEMBERSHIP, LIBRARY

In an effort to build upon the Institute's new growth, as well as to ensure its future, the Board of Directors launched a membership program in November of 1999. After years of having no formal means of membership, the Institute has created a structure that will make it easier for its friends to join the Institute and support its mission.

Another major development for the Institute during the past year has been establishing the cornerstone for an Institute Library—the acquisition by Board member Christopher H. Browne of some 2,200 volumes on architecture, decorative arts, ornament, and furniture design. Thanks to the happy convergence of Barry Cenower's decision to close his bookstore, Acanthus Books, and the generosity of Mr. Browne, this significant collection of both general reference works and rare titles will become a valuable resource when Mr. Browne donates the collection outright to the ICA. The books are presently being catalogued, and plans for housing the collection and making it available to the Institute's learning community are being developed.

ACADEMIC PROGRAMS

SUMMER PROGRAMS

Under the direction of Richard Wilson Cameron as Chairman of Programs, the Institute's academic programs have undergone significant review and have been strengthened and refined over the past two years. Since the publication of *The Classicist No. 5* the Institute has offered three Summer Programs designed to introduce students to classical architecture as well as continuing education programs for its professional audience.

Each summer the Institute hosts an intensive six-week training program where students learn the fundamentals of the classical language of architecture through drawing and lecture classes, sketching tours, and visits to architectural offices and fabricators of building components and crafts. These core classes then culminate in a studio design project that allows students to integrate all of the lessons that they have learned.

Students participating in the 1998 Summer Program included a sculptor, set designer, an architect, several architecture students, and a manufacturer of moldings. The students were primarily American, but two students traveled from as far away as Romania and the Philippines. In the measured drawing portion of the program students studied the entry pavilions at the Grand Army Plaza entrance to Prospect Park. In keeping with the location of the measured drawing project, students then went on to design a structure to cover the farmer's market that occurs every weekend at Grand Army Plaza. The studio instructors were Steve Bass and Christine Franck. Scholarships were graciously given by Chadsworth's 1.800.Columns and Curtis & Windham Architects.

In the following year, from June 5 through July 17, 1999, the Institute hosted its sixth Summer Program. Nine exceptionally talented students and professionals from around the world studied under the direction of Summer Program Director Christine Franck. The students came from as far away as Japan, Brazil and Venezuela, and as close as New York State. During the course of the program students first surveyed the entrance of the Merchant's House Museum in New York and then completed a design project for three empty lots adjacent to the Old Merchant's House Museum. Melissa Del Vecchio and James A. Tinson served as

BELOW LEFT: Summer Program student Ben Johnson measures one of McKim, Mead & White's entry pavilions at Grand Army Plaza as part of the 1998 Summer Program measured drawing project.

BELOW RIGHT: Students of the 2000 Summer Program, Kate Bridgewater and Colin Tinsley work on an analysis drawing for their studio design project.

BOTTOM: Students and faculty from the 1999 Summer Program celebrate their graduation at the home of Institute Board member Christopher Browne.

studio instructors. Scholarships for the 1999 students were provided by Chadsworth's 1.800.Columns, Curtis & Windham Architects, Eric J. Smith, Architects, and David Anthony Easton, Inc. Thanks to the sponsorship of the I. Grace Company, the Summer Programs of 1998 and 1999 used studio space at the American Institute of Graphic Arts.

Most recently, once again under the direction of Program Director Christine Franck, who was assisted by studio faculty Phillip Dodd and Richard John, the Institute undertook its first community-based planning project during the Summer 2000 Program. This new approach to the studio project exposed the students to an urban context with real, neighborhood-based issues. In just four short weeks, the students actively engaged the community, soliciting their input, and produced an in-depth analysis of Manhattan's historic Meatpacking District, culminating in a proposal for the future growth of this neighborhood. At the conclusion of the program, the Summer 2000 students produced an impressive presentation for the general public at a neighborhood community center. Coming both from within the U.S. and from as far away as Venezuela, Australia, and Turkey, some of the students were assisted with scholarships given by Chadsworth's 1.800.Columns, Curtis & Windham Architects, Eric J. Smith, Architects and David Anthony Easton, Inc. The Summer 2000 students were the first class of summer students to enjoy the Institute's new studio space.

The Summer Programs' instructors included Steve Bass, Martin Brandwein, Richard Cameron, Stephen Chrisman, John Kelley, Rocco Leonardis, Leonard Porter, Richard Sammons, Peter Talty, and Andy Taylor. Without instruction in literature, theory, proportion, drawing, sculpting, materials and construction, the elements of classical architecture and traditional urbanism, the students would not be able to take on the challenging studio projects presented to them.

CONTINUING EDUCATION

The Institute has continued to offer AIA/CE registered continuing education courses. New offerings include the addition of short courses, such as ones by Peter Talty on *Detailing Doors and Windows* and *Masonry Construction Techniques,* as well as one on *Proportion* taught by Richard Sammons. For the first time in its history, the Institute is now able to offer all of its academic classes in its own classroom space,

thanks to the generosity of the I. Grace Company and the design skills of Cameron Cameron & Taylor, Design Associates. In the Fall of 2000 the Institute will add two courses on *Design Strategies for the Classical Interior* and a one-evening lecture on the design and project management of university projects, to be offered at Robert A. M. Stern Architects and underwritten by Manning Windows.

TRAVEL PROGRAMS

The Institute sponsored its first travel program, an Architectural Drawing Tour of Rome, July 23 through August 7, 1998. The ten program participants included an international body of architects, designers, students, and one set decorator. Under the instruction of Richard Cameron, Christine Franck, and Fellow-in-Residence, Leonard Porter, the students studied the architecture and urbanism of Rome through analytical drawings, measured drawings, and sketches. The Institute held its next Architectural Drawing Tour of Rome in October of 2000, for which architect and Friend of the Institute, William H. Bates III, created the Edward Vason Jones Scholarship. Named in honor of the great American classicist and fellow Georgia native, Mr. Bates believes the scholarship will bring some much needed recognition to Jones' work and underscore the importance of drawing in classical design.

Another Institute venture into travel-oriented programs was *The English Country House and Garden* (May 23 through June 2, 2000). The Institute was pleased to offer this ten-day itinerary focusing on the country houses and gardens of England in conjunction with the Sotheby's Institute of Art. Led by Tom Savage, Vice-President and Director of Sotheby's Institute of Art, the tour visited many houses rarely open to the public. Nancy Lancaster's Ditchley Park and Hasley Court, Cockerel's Greek Revival masterpiece, Oakly Park, and a private tour at Magdalen College, Oxford were among the highlights of this trip.

TOP LEFT: Institute Fellow-in-Residence Leonard Porter instructs students in perspective during a private visit to the Villa Aldobrandini in Frascati.

BOTTOM LEFT: Participants of the 1998 Architectural Drawing Tour in Rome study the exposed structure of the portico of the Pantheon.

ABOVE: During the May 2000 English Country House Tour, Lord Niedpath shows participants his garden.

NEXT PAGE, TOP: Institute Vice President, Richard Cameron (left) discusses the "Truth of the Matter" with Salon lecturer Demetri Porphyrios (right).

NEXT PAGE, BOTTOM: Attendees of the Second Hastings Council gather on the steps of the Charleston City Hall.

PUBLIC PROGRAMS

SALONS AND LECTURES

Headed by Fellow Courtney Coleman, the Institute's Public Programs have continued to offer Salons and Lectures on various topics. At the Union Club on Wednesday, April 28, 1998, featured speaker Richard Jenrette spoke about his passion for preserving and restoring classical American houses including Edgewater, Milford Plantation, and the Roper House. On December 6, 1999, the well-appointed Penn Club served as the backdrop for Dr. Demetri Porphyrios' illustrated talk entitled "The Truth of the Matter." He spoke about architecture in general and his work more specifically. Sponsored by Xhema of New York and hosted by Christopher Browne, the evening was a spectacular success for the Institute and was our best attended salon to date.

A cold evening the following February did not keep the Institute's fans from attending a talk by Priscilla Roosevelt, author of *Life on the Russian Country Estate*. Ms. Roosevelt's animated lecture, "Serfdom and Splendor," was accompanied by slides in the beautiful ballroom of the Russian Consulate on 91st Street in New York. Sponsored by The I. Grace Company, the evening was an elegant event and participants enjoyed caviar provided by David Netto, a Fellow of the Institute.

Most recently, at the Colony Club on May 18, 2000, New York interior decorator Thomas Jayne and his client Robert Falk spoke about their collaboration for the design of Mr. Falk's Westchester residence. Institute Vice-President, Richard Cameron, who was the design architect for the project while an Associate at Ferguson Murray & Shamamian Architects, moderated the evening, which explored the challenges and rewards of creating an appropriate setting for an important collection of American Federal antique furniture and Asian artifacts. The evening included surprise guest, antiques dealer Leigh Keno, who spoke briefly about the Falks' collection. This event was sponsored by Xhema of New York.

The Institute also sponsored two Summer Lecture Series in conjunction with both the 1999 and 2000 Summer Programs in Classical Architecture. Speakers in 1999 included Professor Norman Crowe of the University of Notre Dame; Dr. Richard John of the University of Miami; and David Ligare, Ted Schmidt, John Kelley, and Leonard Porter who participated in a painter's symposium. The "Young Architects Forum" featured the work of Cameron Cameron & Taylor Design Associates, Fairfax & Sammons Architects, and Catherine Johnson.

The Summer 2000 Lecture Series was co-sponsored by the Institute and Sotheby's Institute of Art and held at Sotheby's new headquarters in New York. Organized by Institute Fellows Steven Semes and Courtney Coleman, and Sotheby's Tom Savage, the series was a "Grand Tour of Classicism in Four American Cities". Berkeley urban geologist Gray Brechin spoke on San Francisco; University of Virginia architectural historian Maurie McGuiness spoke on Charleston; and architects Norman Askins and Robert A.M. Stern each spoke about their hometowns, Atlanta and New York, respectively.

COMMUNICATIONS

WEBSITE AND NEWSLETTER

Under the direction of Leonard Porter and with assistance from William Bates, Katherine Cheng, and Tony Goldsby the Web Site has continued to be an integral part of the Institute's programs and marketing by reaching out to an ever-expanding audience. New to the Institute's web site, www.classicist.org, is a bulletin board where debates and discussions can take place. Also new is a calendar of events that lists upcoming activities of the Institute as well as those of other related organizations.

Future plans for the web site include an effort to make *The Classicist Nos. 1* and *3* available on the web site, as they are now out of print.

As a benefit to the members of the Institute, a newsletter, *The Forum*, will be published three times a year and sent to all members. *The Forum* is edited by a team of volunteers that include Ben Pentreath, Christiane Fashek, Gil Schafer, and Jim Taylor.

SECOND HASTING'S COUNCIL MEETING

Following the success of the first Hastings Council Meeting, held in Hastings-on-Hudson in April 1998, the Institute organized another meeting of the Hastings Council in Charleston, South Carolina. The event was graciously hosted by the City of Charleston and The I'On Company. During a day-long meeting the Hastings Council explored ways that a consortium of Universities, Schools of Architecture, and Institutions dedicated to teaching classical and traditional architecture and urbanism could work together to benefit each other's activities. Institutions including the University of Notre Dame, the University of Miami, Syracuse University, the College of Charleston, the Classical Architecture League, Classical America, and the Institute also updated each other on developments since the last meeting. The Hastings Council was pleased to have in attendance Mr. Andres Duany, who announced plans for a new institute, the Institute of Traditional Architecture, dedicated to training professionals in traditional architecture. The Mayor of Charleston, Joseph P. Riley also addressed the Hastings Council, and visits were arranged to the College of Charleston by Ralph Muldrow and to Milford Plantation by Thomas Gordon Smith.

For regular updates on ICA activities and events please visit our website at **www.classicist.org.**

THE CLASSICIST NO. 1
1994-95★
ISBN 1-56000-804-0

THE CLASSICIST NO. 2
1995-96
ISBN 1-56000-850-4

SELECTIONS FROM THIS ISSUE »
Essays: Ingrid Rowland on THE NEW VITRUVIUS; David Watkin on C.R. COCKERELL AND THE GREEK REVIVAL; Christopher Thomas on FRANCIS BACON; Hugh Petter on BUILDING ROMA CAPITALE; Projects by: Arthur May, Appleton & Associates, Ernesto Buch, and Leon Krier; Competition entries for New York's PATH System, the Augusta Monument, and the Acropolis Museum; The sketchbooks of David Anthony Easton; Student work from the Art Institute of Chicago, Tulane, and Virginia Commonwealth University.

THE CLASSICIST NO. 4
1997-98
148pp., 165 illus., paper.
ISBN 1-7658-0459-X

SELECTIONS FROM THIS ISSUE »
Essays: Elizabeth Meredith Dowling on PHILIP SHUTZE'S DRAWING TECHNIQUES; John Stamper on THE CRITICS OF CLASSICISM; J.-François Gabriel on the ECOLE DES BEAUX-ARTS; Projects by: Curtis & Windham, Dwyer & Sae-Eng, Julian Bicknell and Norman Askins; Competition entries for Governors Island, New York and Glenwood, Illinois; The sketchbooks of Frank Montana; Allied Arts: Contemporary Classical Sculpture; A bibliography of books on the classical orders of Architecture.

THE CLASSICIST NO. 5
1998-99
166 pp., 203 illus., paper.
ISBN 0-7658-0492-1

SELECTIONS FROM THIS ISSUE »
Essays: Leon Krier on AYN RAND; Robert Gilkey Dyck on PLEČNIK; Catesby Leigh on GOETHE AND THE ORGANIC FALLACY. Projects by: Cooper Robertson, Eric Watson, Carden & Godfrey, and Robert A. M. Stern. Competition entries for: the New Town Center for the Village of Plainfield, IL, the Oklahoma City Memorial, and the Royal Oak Center. The Sketchbooks of Milton Grenfell; Kanchan Limaye on the STATE OF THE ALLIED ARTS; A bibliography of literature on the classical interior.

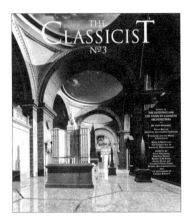

THE CLASSICIST NO. 3
1996-97★
136pp., 150 illus., paper.
ISBN 1-56000-936-5

★*These issues are now out of print.*

Previous issues of the journal are available at $39.95 (price as of November, 2000) per copy, plus $5.00 shipping for the first volume and $2.00 for each additional volume. To order back issues of The Classicist, *send your order, payment, and shipping information directly to the Institute. The Institute can accept cash, money orders, and checks drawn only on a U.S. bank (no foreign checks, currency, or money orders please).*

THE CLASSICIST ANNOUNCES ONGOING CALL FOR PAPERS AND PROJECTS

The editors of *The Classicist* announce an ongoing call for papers and projects to be published in forthcoming issues. The work may be related to any theoretical or practical aspect of classical architecture and its allied disciplines, which include painting, sculpture, and the decorative arts. Contributions to the journal are welcome from architects, artists, landscape designers, interior designers and decorators, educators, builders, craftspersons, and students. Generally, submissions received by January 15 will be considered for the issue to be published that year.

All papers must be accompanied by an abstract. Illustrations should be 8½" x 11" photocopies. If selected for publication, authors will be required to resubmit on computer disk. Architectural projects may be built or unrealized, professional or student work, involve new construction or rehabilitation of existing structures. Project submissions should be accompanied by written documentation concerning site, program, etc. Drawings submitted must be REPRODUCTIONS ONLY and NO LARGER THAN 11" x 17". DO NOT SEND ORIGINAL MATERIALS OR ROLLED DRAWINGS!!! Photographs may be prints up to 8" x 10" in size or 35mm slides. Materials for papers or projects will be returned only if a self-addressed and stamped envelope is provided.

THE INSTITUTE OF
CLASSICAL ARCHITECTURE

Susan Marcus
G. D. Markey
John Massengale
Mark McClure
Robert B. McNeill
William R. Mitchell Jr.
Charles Morris Mount
Bruce Nicols
Edwin Peissis
Anthony M. Pucillo, AIA
George Punnoose
Thomas Rajkovich
William Randle
Paul Stuart Rankin
A. Miles Redd
Katia Rubio
Stephen Salny
Frances Schultz
Edward Siegel
Joseph Singer
Llewellyn Sinkler
Phillip Sleep
F. Clifton Smith
L. Caesar Stair, III
Superior Building & Painting of NY
Mia Taradash
Andre Tchelistcheff
M. Thomas Construction
Thomas Jayne Studio
Collin Tinsley
S. Nancy Upham
Douglas A. Vanderhorn
Ward Architectural Products
Mr & Mrs. James K. Warren
Lamar T. Webb
Dr. & Mrs. Robert D. Wickham

MEMBERS
David Anderson
Colleen Babington
Marc Bailly
Elliott Banfield
Marco Battistotti
D. Troy Beasley
David A. Beckwith
E. Albert Berol
Marguerite P. Bierman
F.L. Bissinger, Inc.
Jennifer Black
Cornelis J. de Boer
Larry E. Boerder
Glen B. Boggs, II
Raffaello Borello
Holland Brady, Jr.
Martin Brandwein
Jay Bretton
Bill Breyer
Harry P. Broom, Jr.
Dennis Buettner
Martin D. Bush
Richard Buchsieb, Jr.
Allison A. Caccoma
Deborah Campbell
Ellen M. Cheever
Stephen Chrisman
Joseph Connors
Morgan A. Conolly, AIA
Michael Cook
Cindi Crain
David Creech
Glen B. Dabaghian
Robert M. Del Gatto
Melissa Del Vecchio
Dickson Architects & Associates
Matthew Dockery
Richard Dragisic
Robert G. Dyck
Cuyler Feagles

J.C.V. Ferrusi
Ruth Frangopoulos
Andrew Friedman
J. Wilson Fuqua
Todd Furgason
Kaja Gam
Patty Gay
Anton Glikin
Wayne L. Good, AIA
Jessica Goodyear
Susan Goulder
Carson Gross
Peter Louis Guidetti
Tamara E. Hadley
Gregory M. Hall
Peter B. Hansel
Stephen Harby
Thomas Rex Hardy
Kevin Harris
Julian Hartzog
Ralph Harvard
Paul Hastings
Thomas Hayes
Keren He
Jack Hillbrand
Lorin Hodges
Carter Hord
Benjamin NNA Igwebuike
William B. Irvine, III
Davis Jahncke, Jr.
Michael C.D. Javelos
Patricia Jean
Laura Jereski
Andrew Berrien Jones
David Jones
Gary William Justiss
Kaja Gam Design
Thomas Kaufmann
Kazumasa Oda
John Kelley
Bruce C. King
Thomas A. Koloski
Brent A. Kovalchik
Kirk E. Kreuzwieser
Salem Richard Lahood
Asheton Langdon
Alan Liddle, F.A.I.A.
William Malmstedt
Richard Manion
Van Jones Martin
Dennis C. McGlade
Patrick S. McDonough
Denis McNamara
Diane Fasce Meleski
Marcelo C. Mendez
Manuel Mergal
Jeffrey Miller
Daniel Millette
Matthew Mosca
Beverly B. Mosch
Gail Winkler & Roger Moss
Mull & Weithman Architects
Robin Muto
Dr. Donald J. Neely
J. Mark Nelson
David Netto
Kaz Oda
Kevin K. Ohlinger
Ottavino Corp.
Richard Paulson, Jr.
Hugh Petter
Dr. and Mrs. Anthony Picaro
Christopher Podstawski
Mary Pynenburg
George A. Radwan
Paul Rankin
Ellen Rauch
Michael Rouchell

William Rutledge
Kenneth Ryden
Ray Sawhill
Schwartz's Forge and Metalworks, Inc.
Sandra Seligman
Lauren and Bruce Sherman
Shield & Co.
Scott Shonk
Jeffrey Shopoff
Brian Shore
Margaret Shrader
Michael Simeone
L.M. Silkworth, AIA
John Sinopoli
Howe K. Sipes, III
Daniel K. Slone
Demetra Canna Smith
Stephen R. Sonnenberg
Jeffrey P. Soons
John Steigerwald
David W. Stirling, AIA
David Stocker
Mark Stromdahl
Anthony Seto
Stephen M. Talasnik
Andy Taylor
Carole Teller
Christie H. Teller
Daniel Teske
Claire Theobald
Julie Thompson
John B. Tittmann
Sean J. Tobin
Paul R. Tritch
Claire Trubald
Darius Toraby
Luis Van Couthem
Sandra Vitzhum
James Waite
Phil Walden
M.L. Waller
Francis Ward
Seth Joseph Weine
Mark Wenger
Elaine White
Frederick Wilbur
William S. White
Charles B. Wood, III
Eric Woodard
Arlene A. Wright
Douglas C. Wright
Mei Wu
Gregory L. Wyatt
Ryan M. Yamada
Arthur Zabarkes

SPECIAL SPONSORS OF THE INSTITUTE

2000 SUMMER PROGRAM
Christoher H. Browne
Cameron Cameron & Taylor
Chadsworth Inc.
Curtis & Windham Architects
David Anthony Easton, Inc.
Ben Krupinski Builder
Eric J. Smith Architects
The I. Grace Company, Inc.
White River Hardwoods
Xhema of New York

OFFICES AND CLASSROOM
E.R. Butler & Co.
Cameron Cameron & Taylor
Jet Pak Electric
Mead & Josepovich

Rama Interiors
Gilbert P. Schafer III
The I.Grace Company, Inc.

LECTURE SERIES
E.R. Butler & Co.
Peter Cosola

ROME PROGRAM
William H. Bates, III

SALONS
David Netto
The I. Grace Company, Inc.
Xhema of New York

THE CLASSICIST NO. 6
The Institute of Classical Architecture and The Classicist *gratefully acknowledge the generous support from the following sponsors. Thank you for making* The Classicist, No. 6 *possible.*

Architectural Sculpture
Archivia
Balmer Studios
Brennan Brothers Co.
E. R. Butler
Case CDE Corp
Chadsworth's Columns
Curtis & Windham Architects
David Anthony Easton, Inc.
David Pearson Design
Delphi Restoration
Eisenhardt Mills Inc.
Eric J. Smith, Architects
Fairfax & Sammons Architects
Jacob Froehlich
FJ Hakimian
Lincoln Center/List Collection
LMC Corp.
Lumiere/Raj Gallery
Madison Cox Design
Mead & Josipovich
Michael Reilly Design
John B. Murray, Architect
Naill Smith Antiques
Nasser Nakib, Architect
National Reprographics
J.E. O'Donnell
Peter Pennoyer, Architects, P.C.
Leonard Porter
Procopters
Stanley Schoen Inc.
Andrew Skurman, Architect
Thomas Gordon Smith, Architects
Traditional Building Magazine
Traditional Cut Stone
Robert A.M. Stern
Ahmad Suleiman
Ken Tate, Architect
The I. Grace Company, Inc.
Thomas Jayne Studio
Tradewood
Travers
Hilton-VanderHorn, Architects
Waterworks
WhiteRiver
Bunny Williams, Inc.
Xhema of New York
Zeluck Windows & Doors

As of December 31, 2000

Bunny Williams
Incorporated

306 East 61st Street, Fifth Floor
New York, New York 10021-8752

Tel. (212) 207-4040
Fax (212) 207-4353

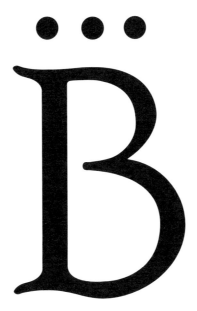

E. R. BUTLER & CO.

NEW YORK

Mead & Josipovich Inc

ARCHITECTURAL WOODWORKING

FABRICATORS OF FINE ARCHITECTURAL

Woodwork AND Furniture

140 58TH STREET, BROOKLYN, NY 11220

718 492-7373

Residence in Montecito, California

Robert A.M. Stern Architects

460 West 34th Street, New York NY 10001 Tel 212 967 5100 Fax 212 967 5588

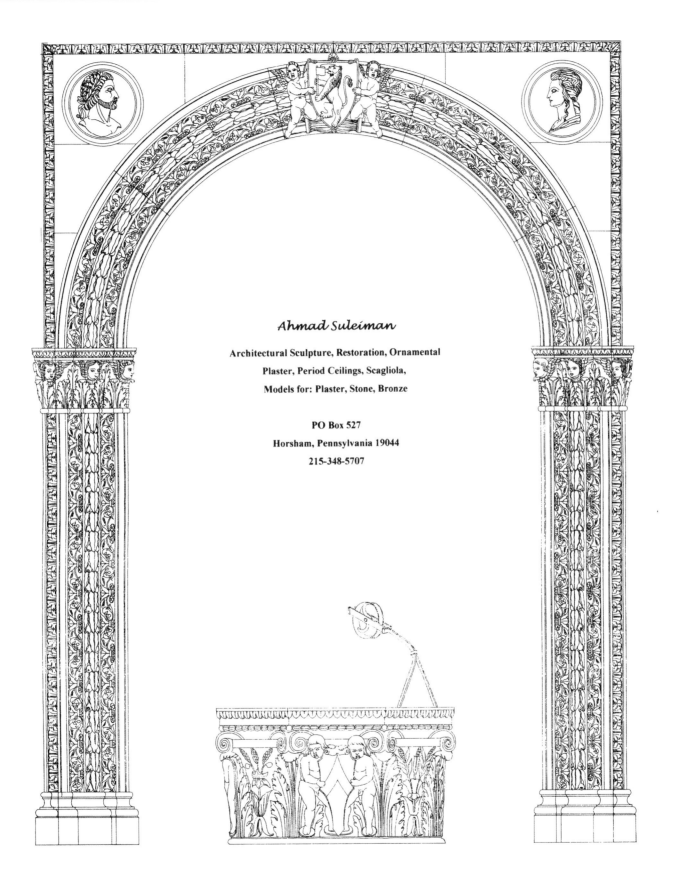

Ahmad Suleiman

**Architectural Sculpture, Restoration, Ornamental
Plaster, Period Ceilings, Scagliola,
Models for: Plaster, Stone, Bronze**

**PO Box 527
Horsham, Pennsylvania 19044
215-348-5707**

ERIC J. SMITH ARCHITECTS

Professional Corporation

72 SPRING STREET

SEVENTH FLOOR

NEW YORK NY 10012

(212) 334-3993

DAVID
ANTHONY
EASTON
INCORPORATED

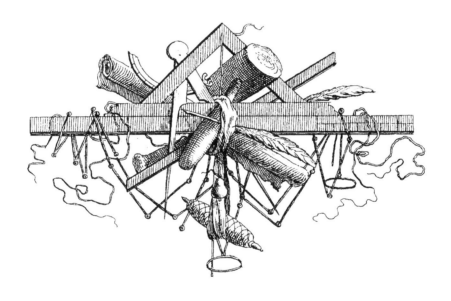

72 SPRING STREET

7TH FLOOR

NEW YORK, NEW YORK 10012

TELEPHONE: 212.334.3820

5300 KINGS HIGHWAY
BROOKLYN, NEW YORK 11234
NY:(718)251-8060 OUTSIDE NY:(800)233-0101
E-MAIL: RZZ@MINDSPRING.COM

OTHER OFFICES IN

CALIFORNIA   FLORIDA   ILLINOIS   WASHINGTON D.C.

NIALL SMITH
ANTIQUES & DECORATIONS

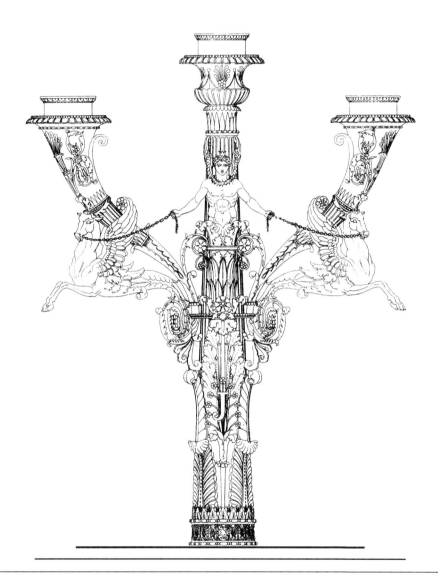

344 BLEECKER STREET • NEW YORK • NY • 10014 • (212) 255-0660

96 GRAND STREET • NEW YORK • NY • 10013 • (212) 941-7354

MERCURY ANTIQUE MIRRORS AND GLASS VENETIAN AND BAMBOO BLINDS GLASS
TOPS WINDOW SHADES VERTICAL BLINDS PICTURE FRAMES AND TABLE TOPS
BATHTUB ENCLOSURES MERCURY ANTIQUE MIRRORS AND GLASS VENETIAN AND
BAMBOO BLINDS GLASS TOPS WINDOW SHADES VERTICAL BLINDS PICTURE FRAMES
AND TABLE TOPS BATHTUB ENCLOSURES MERCURY ANTIQUE MIRRORS AND GLASS
VENETIAN AND BAMBOO BLINDS GLASS TOPS WINDOW SHADES VERTICAL BLINDS
PICTURE FRAMES AND TABLE TOPS BATHTUB ENCLOSURES MERCURY ANTIQUE
MIRRORS AND GLASS VENETIAN AND BAMBOO BLINDS GLASS TOPS WINDOW SHADES
VERTICAL BLINDS PICTURE FRAMES AND TABLE TOPS BATHTUB ENCLOSURES

STANLEY SCHOEN INC

MERCURY ANTIQUE MIRRORS AND GLASS VENETIAN AND BAMBOO BLINDS GLASS

MIRRORS AND GLASS

MERCURY ANTIQUE MIRRORS AND GLASS VENETIAN AND BAMBOO BLINDS GLASS

BATHTUB ENCLOSURES MERCURY ANTIQUE MIRRORS AND GLASS VENETIAN AND

BAMBOO BLINDS GLASS TOPS WINDOW SHADES VERTICAL BLINDS PICTURE FRAMES

AND TABLE TOPS BATHTUB ENCLOSURES MERCURY ANTIQUE MIRRORS AND GLASS

VENETIAN AND BAMBOO BLINDS GLASS TOPS WINDOW SHADES VERTICAL BLINDS

PICTURE FRAMES AND TABLE TOPS BATHTUB ENCLOSURES MERCURY ANTIQUE

MIRRORS AND GLASS VENETIAN AND BAMBOO BLINDS GLASS TOPS WINDOW SHADES

VERTICAL BLINDS PICTURE FRAMES AND TABLE TOPS BATHTUB ENCLOSURES GLASS

ARTHUR BALSKY AND SHELDON FEINSTEIN

1693 FIRST AVENUE BETWEEN 87TH AND 88TH STREETS, NEW YORK, NEW YORK 10128

212-EN9-0320 TELEPHONE, 212-369-1836 TELEFAX

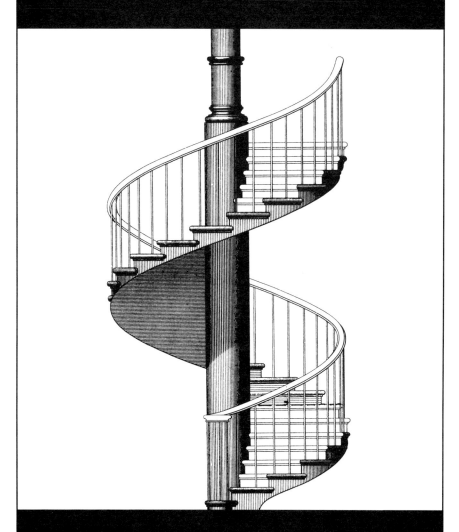

TIMELESS DESIGN
FROM A CLASSICAL PERSPECTIVE.

Exterior / Interior Concept & Design

DAVID
PEARSON
DESIGN

NAPLES   NEW YORK   ORLANDO   PALM BEACH   VOX 407.895.0444   FAX 407.895.0512   davidpearsondesign.com

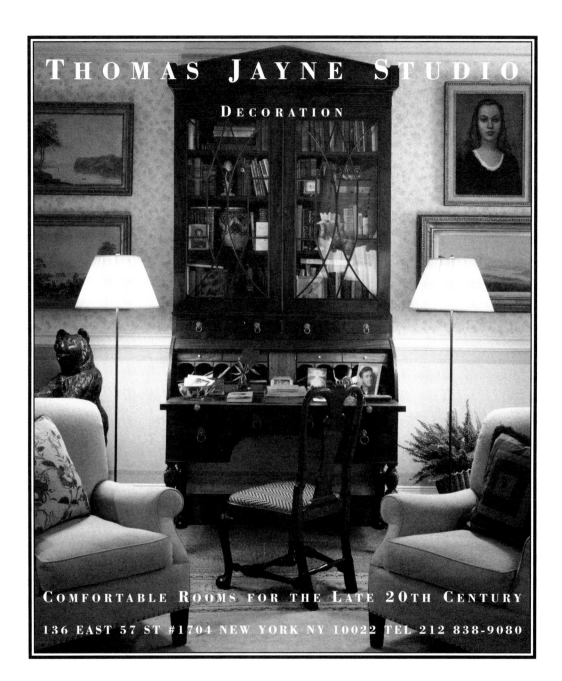

Classic...Timeless...Style...Elegance...Craftsmanship...Integrity

...words to describe over 40 years of manufacturing exceptional architectural wood windows and doors. The demonstrated capabilities of Tradewood's research, design and technical support team allow for uncompromising execution of the most demanding architectural projects. The element of conscious design incorporated into all of our products truly complements the distinctiveness associated with the evolution of building design through the ages, from classical to contemporary.

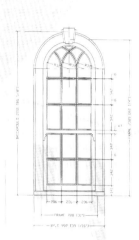 

ARCHITECTURAL WOOD WINDOWS & DOORS

Tradewood ensures aesthetic flexibility and style continuity through the careful planning of primary architectural elements and the small – but significant – details such as hardware, hinges and ornamental moldings.

Conscious design, aesthetic flexibility, structural integrity. The hallmarks of Tradewood Industries.

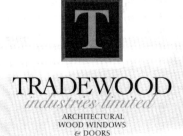

TRADEWOOD
industries limited
ARCHITECTURAL
WOOD WINDOWS
& DOORS

1-800-410-0268

JACOB FROEHLICH CABINET WORKS
ARCHITECTURAL WOODWORK

SIMPLY THE FINEST ~ SINCE 1865
TELEPHONE 718.893.1300

18th Century Aubusson, 15'5" x 15'1" (470m x 462m), Directoire Period, Circa 1795

F. J. HAKIMIAN

Distinctive European and Oriental Carpets
Antique Rugs *(18th Century to Art Deco)*
Period Tapestries
Expert Restoration and Conservation

136 East 57th Street
New York, New York 10022
Tel: 212.371.6900 Fax: 212.753.0277
www.fjhakimian.com

*"Colligationes Nostras Extollimus"**

We Are Proud of Our Connections®

BRENNAN BROS. CO., INC.

PLUMBING – HEATING – FIRE SUPPRESSION

JOHN A. BRENNAN
NYC LIC. NO. 12127
NYC FIRE SUPPRESSION
LIC. NO. 0179B

BRIAN FREER
NYC LIC. NO. 1545

JOHN K. BRENNAN
NYC LIC. NO. 1540

TERENCE P. BRENNAN
NY STATE BACKFLOW
PREVENTION TESTER
CERT. NO. 02209

Liscensed in New York City, New Jersey, Connecticut, Westchester & Rockland Counties

PEARL RIVER, NY OFFICE
PHONE: 914 735-4433
PAGER: 917 899-8048

NYC OFFICE
PHONE: 718 549-7860
FAX: 718 601-8352

The

I·GRACE

COMPANY, INC.

*Commissioned Private
Residences*

**A TRADITION OF BUILDING FINE
HOMES OF ENDURING VALUE**

403 EAST 91ST STREET NEW YORK NY 10128 *tel* 212.987.1900 *fax* 212.987.0900

10 SENECA PLACE GREENWICH CT 06830 *tel* 203.422.5550 *fax* 203.422.5552

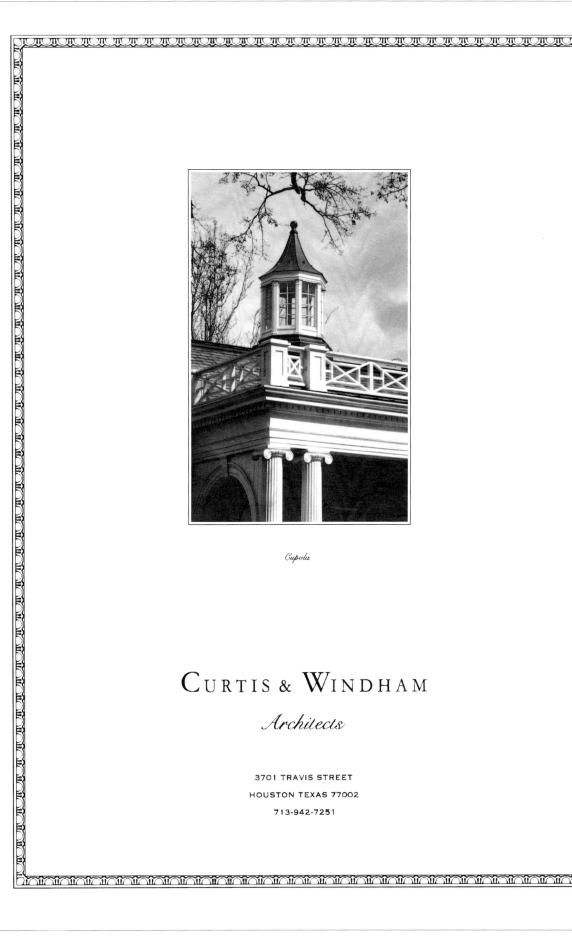

Cupola

CURTIS & WINDHAM

Architects

3701 TRAVIS STREET

HOUSTON TEXAS 77002

713-942-7251

"Windy Hill"   *Garden design by René Francen*

KEN TATE ARCHITECT,

New Orleans , Louisiana
(504) 845 8181

J.E. O'DONNELL

CONSTRUCTION CO. INC.

Builders of Fine Homes and Estates

173 WATERSIDE AVENUE • NORTHPORT, NEW YORK 11768

516.754.1144 office • 516.754.9762 fax

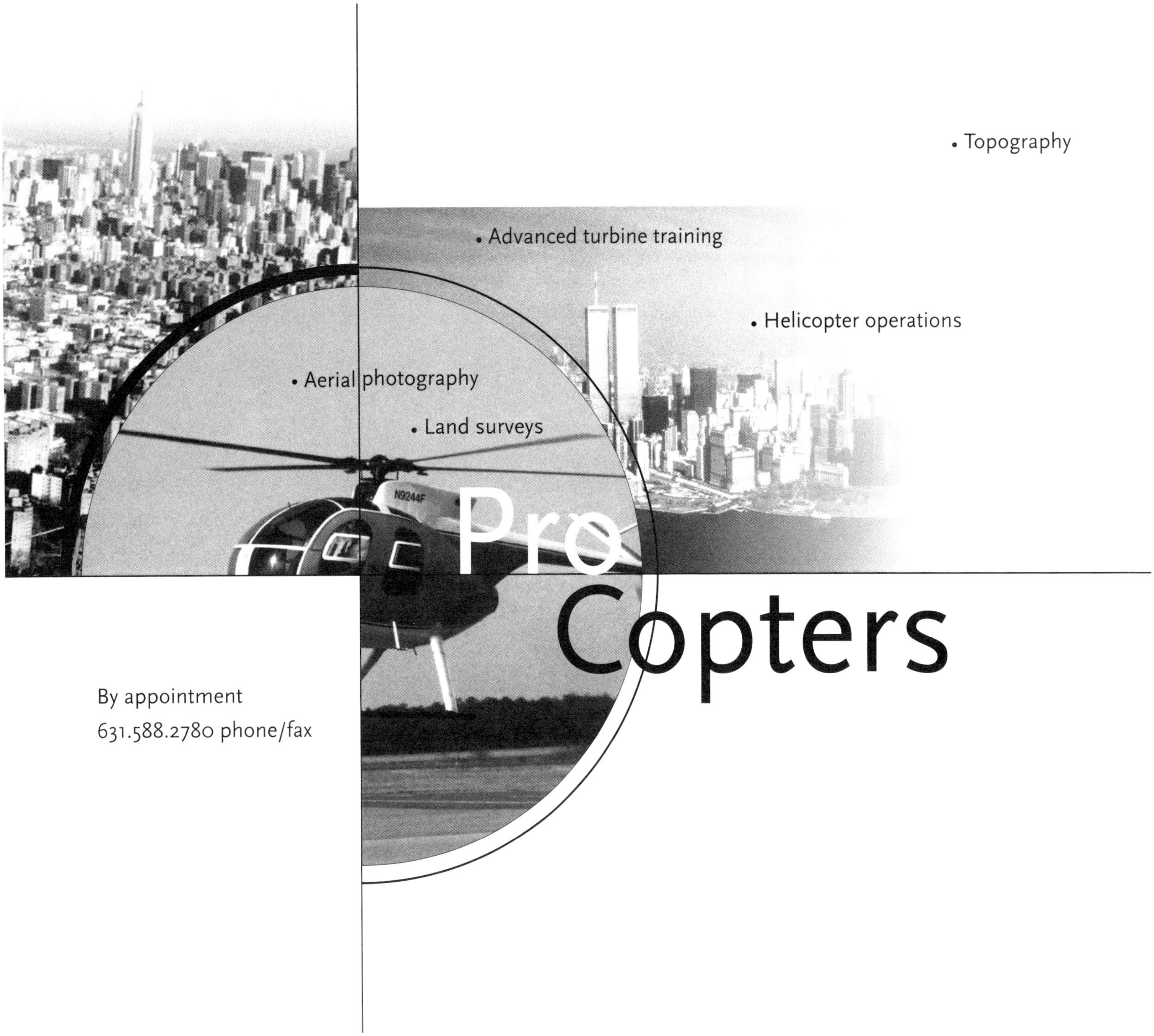

- Charter

- Topography

- Advanced turbine training

- Helicopter operations

- Aerial photography

- Land surveys

Pro
Copters

By appointment
631.588.2780 phone/fax

CHADSWORTH'S 1.800.COLUMNS®
www.columns.com

WOOD • POLYSTONE™ • FIBERGLASS

𝒜 variety of sizes and styles from classic to contemporary, for interior and exterior. Competitive prices. Job-site delivery. Inquire about our award-winning Idea Book, $20 soft cover, $30 hard cover. Includes Columns Product Portfolio.

Columns Product Portfolio $5. Free flier.

Exclusively specified by WILLIAM E. POOLE DESIGNS

1.800.486.2118

277 North Front Street • Wilmington, NC 28401 • Telephone 1.910.763.7600 • Telefax 1.910.763.3191
Atlanta Private Consultation 1.404.876.5410 • London European Headquarters 01.287.8718

ANDREW SKURMAN, ARCHITECT

3654 SACRAMENTO STREET, SAN FRANCISCO, CALIFORNIA 94118, 415/440-4480

John B. Murray Architect, llc

36 WEST 25TH STREET, 9TH FLOOR, NEW YORK CITY
212-242-8600

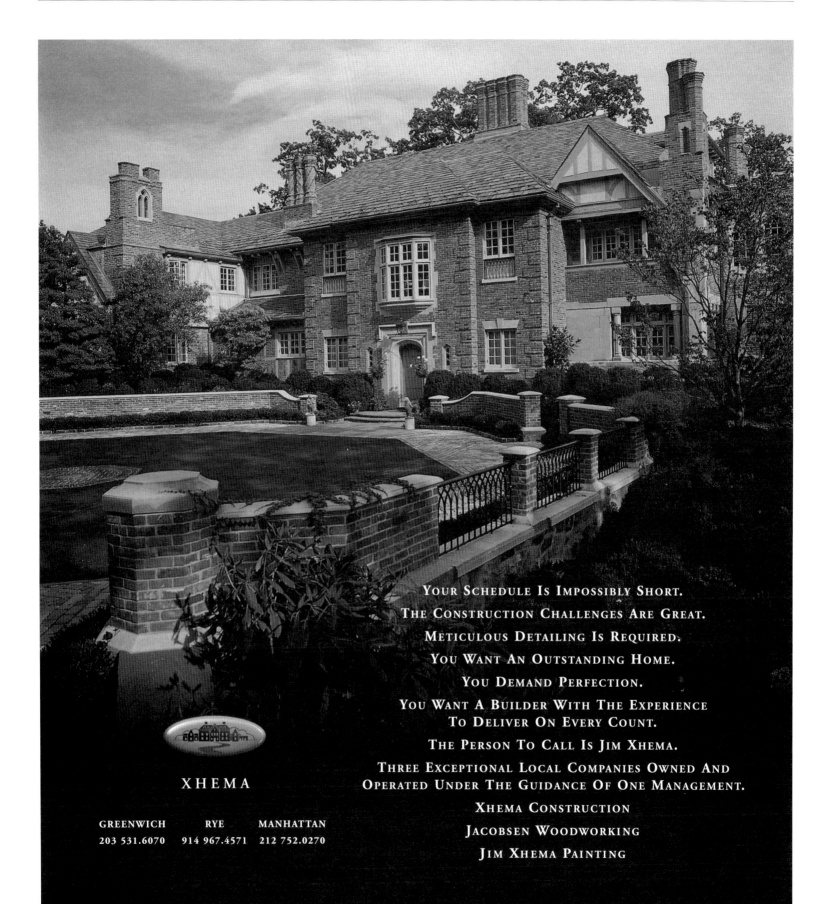

PETER PENNOYER ARCHITECTS P.C.

NEW YORK CITY • 212 779 9765

STUDY FOR A PAVILION, 1999

WATERCOLOR: ANTON GLIKIN

TRAVERS
FINE FABRICS AND WALLPAPERS

SCOTT FRANCES

HILTON · VANDER HORN
ARCHITECTS

31 EAST ELM STREET · GREENWICH, CT 06830
203 · 862 · 9011

NASSER NAKIB ARCHITECT
ARCHITECTURE AND INTERIOR DESIGN
306 East 61st Street, Fifth Floor, New York, N. Y. 10021-8752   Tel (212) 759-1515   Fax (212) 759-1612

Anchises, 1996, sepia watercolor and pencil on paper, 9 3/4 x 6 1/2 inches.

LEONARD PORTER

151 WEST 19TH STREET, #601, NEW YORK, NY 10011

(212) 741-7951 · FAX: (212) 741-7053

THOMAS GORDON SMITH
ARCHITECTS

2025 Edison Road · South Bend, Indiana 46637

Tel: 219.287.1487 · Fax: 219.287.0821 · Email: archtgs@aol.com

Photo by Durston Saylor

FAIRFAX & SAMMONS ARCHITECTS P.C.

67 Gansevoort Street • New York, NY 10014 • T: 212.255.0704 • F: 212.229.9517

Email: Fairfaxarc@aol.com • Website: FairfaxandSammons.com

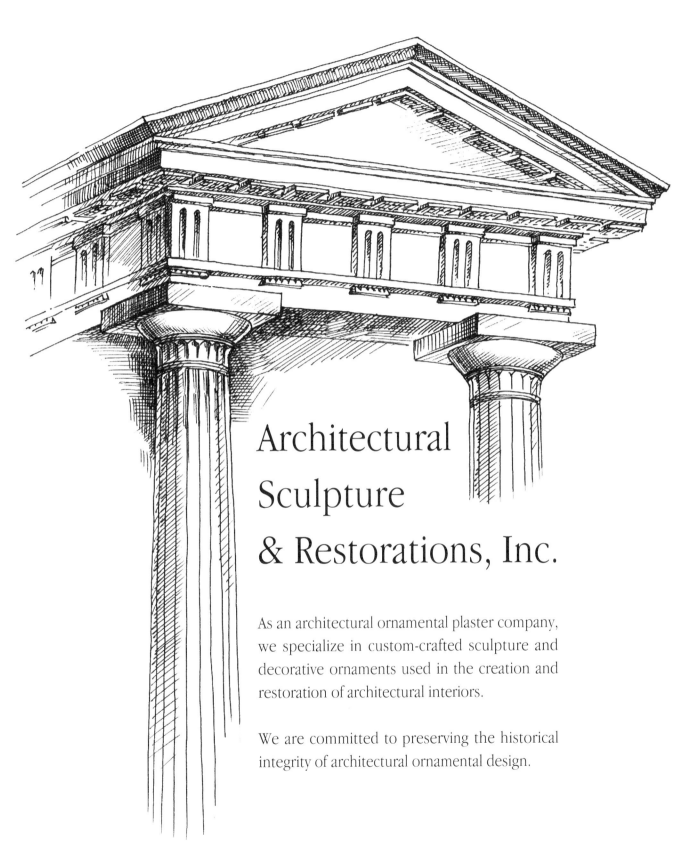

Architectural Sculpture & Restorations, Inc.

As an architectural ornamental plaster company, we specialize in custom-crafted sculpture and decorative ornaments used in the creation and restoration of architectural interiors.

We are committed to preserving the historical integrity of architectural ornamental design.

242 Lafayette St, New York NY 10012 (212) 431-5873

Custom bronze casements.
Classical. Rich. Elegant. Lasting.

Shown: Custom window for a private New York residence

LMC CORP.
Les Métalliers Champenois, USA

77 Second Avenue, Paterson, NJ 07514 | Tel: 973-279-3573; Fax: 973-881-0235 | http://www.l-m-c.com | E-mail: bronze@l-m-c.com

INVENTING BATH STYLE

WATERWORKS®

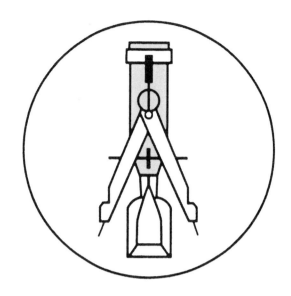

MICHAEL REILLY
DESIGN

THE FINEST CUSTOM WINDOWS AND DOORS

Michael Reilly Design specializes in the fabrication of custom wood windows and doors for large-scale residential, commercial and institutional projects.

Established in 1979, Michael Reilly Design is known among leading architectural firms for its strong sense of service, its unusual attention to detail, and its ability to meet mutually established deadlines.

4062-701 Grumman Boulevard   Calverton, NY 11933
Tel. 631.208.0710   Fax. 631.208.0711

"Incoronato" Silk Screen, 33" x 27"- $1,800

CARLO MARIA | MARIANI

Available through
Lincoln Center/List Collection

Thomas W. Lollar, Director
Tel: (212) 875-5018 Fax: (212) 875-5584
email: tlollar@lincolncenter.org

❧ ARCHIVIA ❧

THE DECORATIVE ARTS BOOK SHOP

❧

DECORATIVE ARTS
ARCHITECTURE
LANDSCAPE AND GARDENS
INTERIOR DESIGN

❧

944 Madison Avenue, New York, New York 10021
Tel [212] 439-9194
Fax [212] 744-1626

MADISON COX DESIGN INCORPORATED

LANDSCAPE ARCHITECTS

220 WEST 19TH STREET 9TH FLOOR NEW YORK NY 10011

TELEPHONE 212 242-4631 FACSMILILE 212 807-8081

COLOPHON

This journal was composed on QuarkXPress 4.11

Equipment used in the production of this journal included:
Macintosh G3/System 8.6
Apple ColorSync 20 monitor
Apple LaserWriter 8500 printer for trial proofs

Text: Finch Opaque 80LB Smooth
Cover: Navajo 100LB Smooth
Photographs: 200 line screen halftones
Printing: offset lithography
Binding: perfectbound
Edition: 1200

Typefaces:
TRAJAN: (logo, cover text, and department heads)
is based on the inscription carved on
the pedestal of Trajan's column in Rome, 113 a.d.

Bauer Bodoni: (headlines) is derived from the designs of
Giambattista Bodoni (1740-1813). This interpretation was
cut in 1924 by Louis Hoell.

Bembo: (text face) is a twentieth century revival of a typeface
cut by Francesco Griffo (c.1450–1518) at the Venetian
printing house of Aldus Manutius.